THE CLAUGHTON & PATRIOT 4-6-0s

by G. Toms and R. J. Essery

with contributions from F. James

WILD SWAN PUBLICATIONS

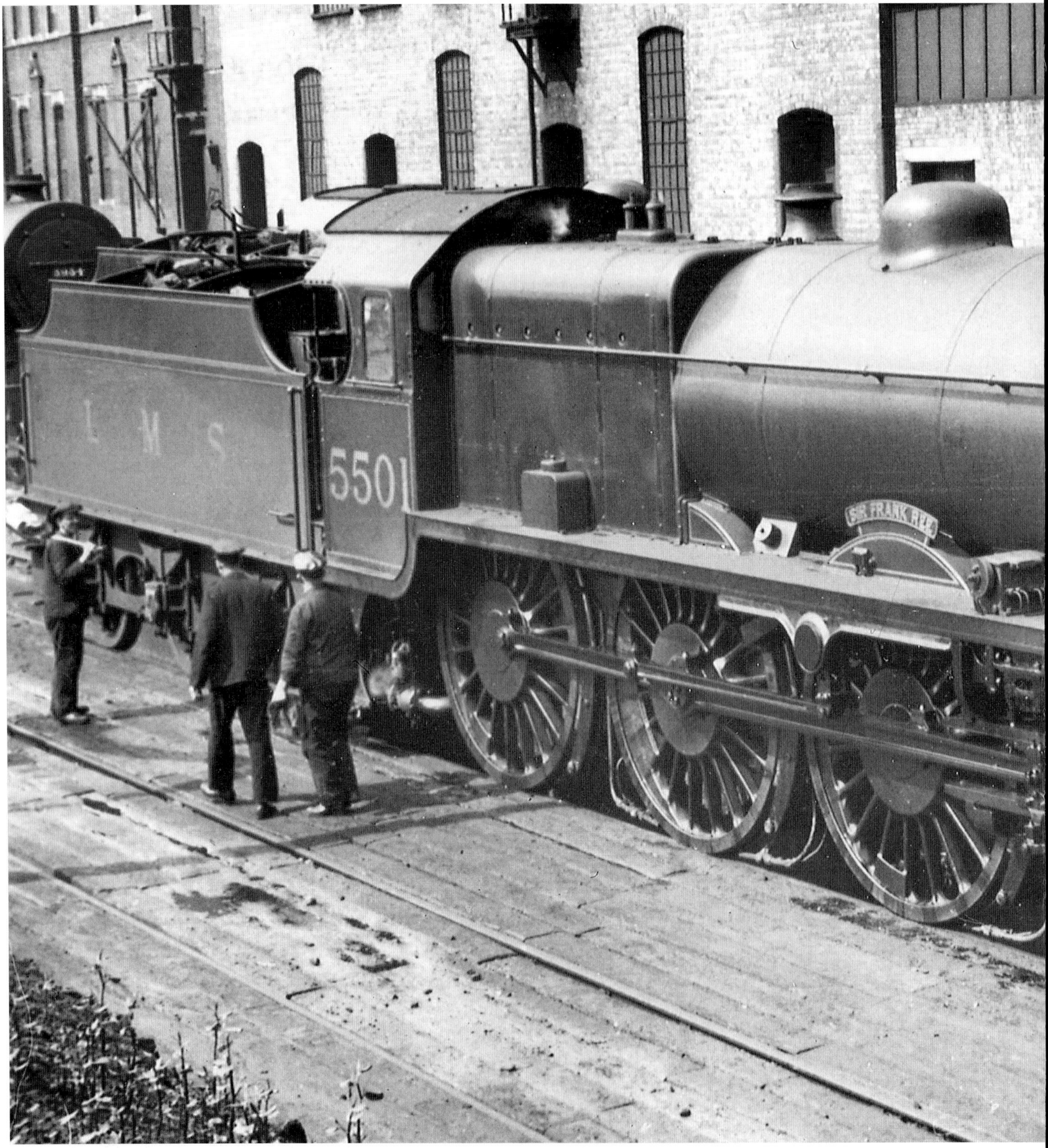
L M S
5501

CONTENTS

Preface	1
Part One THE L&NWR CLAUGHTONS	3
Part Two THE LMS PATRIOTS	59
Tables 1–17	95-105
Appendix 1 LIVERY – THE CLAUGHTON CLASS	107
Appendix 2 LMS LIVERY – THE PATRIOT CLASS	111
Appendix 3 ROD TENDERS	115
Appendix 4 BOWEN COOKE TENDERS	115
Appendix 5 TENDERS COUPLED TO PATRIOTS	118
Appendix 6 BR LIVERIES – THE PATRIOTS	119

© Wild Swan Publications Ltd. and
G. Toms and R. J. Essery 2006
ISBN 1 905184 19 0

Designed by Paul Karau
Printed by Amadeus Press, Cleckheaton

Published by
WILD SWAN PUBLICATIONS LTD.
1-3 Hagbourne Road, Didcot, Oxon, OX11 8DP

The driver of No. 5536 had a good reason to be pleased; the locomotive was named after him. A Patriot carrying the same number as the Claughton it replaced was built in May 1933, which also retained the name Private W. Wood V.C. *Originally No. 6018, it was renumbered as seen here in April 1934. An article by Geoff Holt in* LMS Journal No. 13 *tells the story of the Claughtons that were named after L&NWR employees who won the Victoria Cross in the Great War. Suffice to say that Private Wood, who had been a cleaner at Stockport shed prior to joining the army, won the VC for outstanding bravery in action on the Western Front. Although we cannot date this picture, it was taken during the Second World War, the cabside window was blacked out and note that the numerals had been retouched. In 1948 this locomotive was one of the eighteen Patriots rebuilt with a taper boiler and remained in service until the week ending 29th December 1962 when it was withdrawn from service.*

AUTHORS' COLLECTION

With certain trains, the Caledonian section of the LMS Northern Division used route indicators to assist signalmen to identify the route they were to follow. The more usual arrangement on the LMS was to advise the signalman in advance by the bell code of the class of train and routeing, but since route indicators were used in Scotland, we felt that we should include a picture to show what they were like. Note the two arms in a horizontal position at the top of the smokebox. The locomotive in this undated picture was No. 5548 Lytham St. Annes, a Newton Heath engine from August 1934 until 1943 when it was transferred to Crewe North. The locomotive was named in December 1937, which helps to date this picture of the locomotive working a Glasgow to Liverpool at Galgate. AUTHORS' COLLECTION

PREFACE

It was the LMS Class 8F 2–8–0s which led to the first of our occasional joint efforts describing LMS locomotives. The first joint article appeared in two parts, in the June and July 1983 editions of Steam Railway, dealing with the Class 8Fs at home and abroad. The first result of Bob's keen interest in LMS matters had appeared in print some years previously in what many consider to be the ground-breaking Locomotive Liveries of the LMS, written jointly with the late David Jenkinson, a series that began to be published from 1967 and proved to be a milestone in railway history.

George's interest in LMS matters evolved into researching LMS-designed locomotives in War Department service and after. From a previously published 8F article and Bob's response, the joint effort in Steam Railway emerged. With encouragement from Wild Swan Publications, it developed into another joint effort dealing with the LMS 0–4–4 tank locomotives of 1932; this appeared in the Autumn 1986 edition of British Railway Journal. A further four articles appeared in this journal, dealing with Fowler 3F 0–6–0 tank locomotives, Horwich 2–6–0s, the Class 4F 0–6–0s and Stanier tenders. In the special LMS edition of British Railway Journal, published in 1989, the 8F 2–8–0s were the subject of another article.

The next step was to move from articles to books and a series dealing with specific locomotives was planned. The first was the story of the LMS & LNER Garratts. This was published in 1990, and the series entitled, Historic Locomotive Monographs was born. The second, published in 1994, was about the LMS Jubilees. Curiously, Bob and George never met until the late 1990s when the latter gave a talk on Brush Locomotives at Burton on Trent to the Burton Railway Society and the former was in the audience. If anything, it proved that a writing partnership was possible at long distance in the years before computers and emails.

Although the other titles in the projected Historic Locomotive Monographs series were put on hold, it was always our intention to complete this book about the Claughtons and Patriots. In the interim Bob Essery and Fred James were invited by Dieter Hopkin, at that time Head of Research and Collections at the National Railway Museum, to sort and list the Derby Collection of locomotive drawings and from this work the idea for Midland Engines and LMS Locomotive Profiles, to be published by Wild Swan, was developed. In order to complete these books David Hunt and later John Jennison were invited to join the team of authors and David Hunt became the series editor. In the early stages of the project when, in conjunction with the NRM, the identification of the locomotives classes to be featured was undertaken, the Patriots were considered as being one of the classes to be included within the Profile series. Therefore we have structured this monograph to complement this future title that will deal exclusively with the Patriot class in their original and rebuilt condition.

Now that circumstances have enabled us to complete this title in the Historic Locomotive series we are most grateful to Fred James for his contribution and, subject to reader response, other titles describing LMS classes that cannot, for one reason or another, be included in the Profile series, may appear as Locomotive Monographs.

George Toms, Loughborough 2006
Bob Essery, Rolleston-on-Dove 2006

Left: We thought that we should include some pictures of the various classes of locomotive that were employed on express passenger train working prior to the arrival of the Claughtons, beginning with an Alfred the Great class that had been rebuilt as a Benbow. The story is complex. Suffice to say that this picture shows L&NWR No. 1973 Hood, which was built in July 1903 after rebuilding as a Benbow. In September 1921 it was rebuilt as a Simple Renown and although allocated an LMS stock number, No. 5175, this was not applied and the locomotive was scrapped in July 1926. Right: The Precursor class was built at Crewe between 1904 and 1907 as saturated locomotives although in due course a number of the class were superheated. The class is represented by this picture of No. 1117 Vandal, which was built in November 1904. Becoming LMS No. 5194 in February 1926, it remained in service until withdrawn in November 1931.
AUTHORS' COLLECTION

The superheated version of the Precursor was the George the Fifth class and this shows the first of the class, No. 2663, at Willesden on 3rd June 1922. The LMS stock number 5320 was applied in March 1927 and the cab was altered to suit the Midland Railway standard structure gauge in 1929. As part of the 1934 renumbering scheme, this locomotive should have become No. 25320, but it was not applied and the locomotive was withdrawn in February 1936 without being renumbered. W. POTTER

PART ONE
THE L&NWR CLAUGHTONS

In 1949 three proud old stalwarts built by the London & North Western Railway were lined up at Crewe Works on the former Chester line. This line was utilised as an access to the works, and its sylvan setting, with a backdrop of trees, was also used for photographing new locomotives. On this occasion it was a day that was ideal for photography; the historic event was duly recorded.

The three vintage locomotives were Precursor Class 4–4–0 No. 25297 *Sirocco*, Prince of Wales Class 4–6–0 No. 25752 and Claughton Class No. 6004, formerly *Princess Louise*. All were in LMS livery, albeit faded; all had survived into the British Railways era, but not sufficiently long enough to receive their allotted BR numbers. No. 6004 was still in LMS crimson lake and should have been No. 46004, but there was no point in renumbering the locomotive by adding 40000 to the LMS stock number; her fate was sealed. This engine was the last of the class, surviving the rest by many years, a life prolonged by the war and its aftermath. If a preservation attempt had been made in 1949, what a wonderful collection these locomotives would have made for posterity. In our view it would have been a rather better historical collection than many of the engines that have been preserved and are revered by present-day enthusiasts.

The first of the Claughton class was built in 1913, and the type was to be the last L&NWR passenger class to take to the rails, the logical development of a long Crewe tradition reaching back well into the nineteenth century. John Ramsbottom had become Locomotive Superintendent in 1857 and was succeeded by Francis William Webb in 1871. After thirty-two years in that position and with his health failing, he was replaced by George Whale in 1903. It was not a happy ending for Webb, described by other authors as an autocratic man with definite ideas of how matters should be done. He had many successes and a few failures, but unfortunately he was to be remembered for his persistent and often unrewarding efforts to promote the compounding principle through its application to L&NWR locomotive stock. Some of his successes outlived him by several generations, simple rugged locomotives built to last, seemingly forever. The problem facing the L&NWR at the beginning of the 20th century was common to all the major mainline companies. Improved facilities for passengers meant there was an increase in tare weight per passenger carried, which meant that more powerful locomotives were required to haul the same number of passengers. The six-wheeled coaches of earlier years were being replaced by heavier and more comfortable vestibule bogie stock, in particular, as far as the L&NWR was concerned, on the West Coast Main Line out of Euston, and as a result there was much concern over the amount of double-heading required to cope with the traffic. The locomotives that had worked these services were now too small to pull the heavier trains. New, larger and better designs were required and the L&NWR Board decided that Whale was the man for the job. His mandate was scrap and build.

Away to the breaker's yard went some of the older compounds and the successful Jumbo 2–4–0s were largely relegated to secondary or piloting duties once a 4–4–0 development of them was introduced. During the Edwardian period, forty Alfred the Great Class compound 4–4–0s were modified as '*Benbows*' and this allowed some reduction in the number of trains that required the assistance of a pilot engine. In 1904 the Precursor Class arrived on the scene. These locomotives were primarily intended for use on the Southern Division, working between Euston and Crewe, Liverpool and Manchester. Their success was almost instant and attention turned to the Northern Division, with its gradients and need for something larger to cope with them. Thus came the Experiment Class 4–6–0, which entered service in 1905. Both classes were also used on other parts of the L&NWR, but it was soon demonstrated that there was no need to double-head with trains of less than 270 tons south of Crewe where that limit had previously been in force. The Precursors saw to that and, as a class, eventually totalled 110 locomotives, all built between March 1904 and May 1906.

The L&NWR had a curious loading system, a sort of 'rule of thumb' that was not always accurate in terms of tonnage. To be fair, all the mainline companies used similar systems and an article by Jack Braithwaite in *Midland Record No. 21* goes into the matter in some depth. For example, in his article he refers to the GWR, often different from other British companies, which calculated passenger train weights in 'wheels' although we presume they referred to axles or pairs of wheels. In another letter dated 3rd February 1908, an officer of the London & North Western Railway confirmed that, 'their through Scotch trains are not limited to any dead tonnage weight behind the tender. Our maximum limit for one train according to driver's count is equal to 20½; six-wheelers counting as one, 8-wheelers counting as 1½ and 12 wheelers as 2.' He continued by saying that the 11.50 p.m. ex Euston to Carlisle (exclusive of passengers and luggage) is generally about 376 tons, pointing out that this figure did not include the weight of the engine and tender. The inaccuracy of 'equal to 18' becomes apparent when it could be anywhere between 320 and 350 tons! All in all, things were not equal.

The Precursors could haul 400 tons without any fuss and the Experiments were capable of 'equal to 20' south of Crewe. The latter class ultimately totalled 105 examples, forty-five being built between April 1905 and October 1907 and the remainder in 1909/10. Whale by then had fulfilled his mandate and had provided the L&NWR with a stock of new locomotives, which were cheap to construct, cheap to run and very capable in service. At this time the L&NWR was one of the most prosperous railway companies and good dividends were being declared. The precision and punctuality of the Company's trains were second to none and their coal consumption quite acceptable when related to the standards of the day; the new locomotives were not too hungry on fuel. In many ways, therefore, the L&NWR was at or near its peak.

Whale retired through ill health in June 1909 and Charles John Bowen Cooke, a 100 percent L&NWR man throughout, succeeded him. He was born 1st November 1859 at Orton Longeville, near Peterborough, where his father was rector of the Parish. He was educated at Cheltenham College and King's College London, attended finishing school, as was the custom of those times, at the Technical High School in Neuwied, near Coblenz in Germany. From there he went in 1875, at the age of sixteen, to start his apprenticeship at Crewe Works. Three years later he was to become a private pupil under Webb, finishing his training in 1880. He was posted to Rugby as assistant to A.L. Mumford, the Running Superintendent of the Southern Division. His progress was not what one would describe as swift – he spent twenty-three years at Rugby in this role. Despite this, he was active,

The Experiment class 4–6–0s were introduced in 1905 and did not prove to be as successful as the contemporary 4–4–0s. This picture of No. 1988 Hurricane was taken at Willesden shed in August 1920 and shows an engine which was built in September 1906, became LMS No. 5467 in February 1927 and was withdrawn in September 1928.
J. N. MASKELYNE

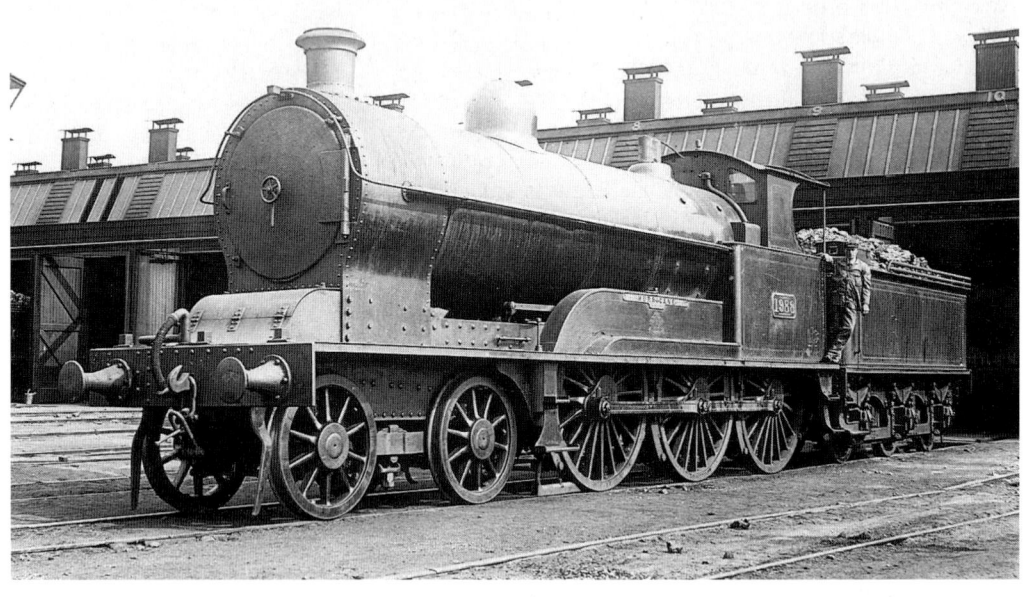

The final class to be featured in this pre-Claughton section is the Prince of Wales class. Just as the George the Fifths were a superheated version of the Precursors, the Prince of Wales were a superheated version of the Experiment class. L&NWR No. 446 Pegasus, seen at Stalybridge when working an express passenger train, was one of twenty locomotives that were built by the North British Locomotive Co. Ltd. in 1915/16. No. 446 was built in 1915 and became LMS 5668 in 1924 and 25668 in 1935. The cab was altered to suit the Midland structure gauge in 1931 and Pegasus was withdrawn in August 1935.
W. H. WHITWORTH

privately pursuing his interests in engineering, in particular that of locomotive design – a sort of shadow CME with some acknowledgement from those senior to him.

In 1899 Mumford retired and George Whale, previously Superintendent of the Northern Division, became superintendent of the whole line with Bowen Cooke as his assistant for the Southern Division but still remaining at Rugby. When Whale became CME, Bowen Cooke moved to Crewe and was promoted to Running Superintendent of the Southern Division. His knowledge of the running side was a solid foundation and thorough, as well it should have been, and it was ably backed up by his active interest in locomotive matters, which included a deep interest in Continental practice. He followed Whale's locomotive policy with keenness and saw the results at first-hand on the Southern Division, the area most affected by it. Whale had an excellent Chief Draughtsman at Crewe, one J.N. Jackson, and an equally proficient Senior Locomotive Design draughtsman, T.E. Sackfield, both of whom were to transfer Whale's ideas onto paper and mould them into reality. Later, when Bowen Cooke was at the helm, Sackfield was to put his ideas into practice.

At fifty years of age, Bowen Cooke was finally appointed CME on 1st March 1909 after a not too straightforward selection, there being several other influential applicants competing for the position. A forty-year-old who also aspired to high position that year was E.C. Trench who became Chief Engineer on 1st October. Despite the seemingly conflicting titles, their jobs were reasonably well defined in practice and did not overlap, Trench being, among other things, responsible for civil engineering works on the line. If there was no overlap there was to be some collision of ideas later when Bowen Cooke presented his Claughton design to Trench for his professional comment and approval for the class to run over the main lines of the Company.

On taking office Bowen Cooke realised that matters were very good indeed, the L&NWR had been well provided with locomotives by Whale, but he was also aware that progress and the march of time do not stand still. Existing equipment does not always keep pace with changing events so he turned his mind to the Company's future requirements and began to plan accordingly. There were certain restrictive elements to contend with in executing his duties as CME, largely inherited from Whale and wholly due to the desire of the Board not to allow an autocratic rule such has had been the case with Webb. It was essential to keep first costs down and make improvements without arousing the wrath of the shareholders. Any increased costs likely to be incurred had to be justified. Because there was no sense of urgency, Bowen Cooke was able to plan for the future on the basis of current practice, not only on the L&NWR but elsewhere. Locomotive exchange trials were arranged with other railways to assess and compare. A large-boilered GNR Atlantic locomotive was compared with a Precursor in 1909 and in the same year one of the massive Caledonian Railway 4–6–0s, No. 903 *Cardean*, was run between Crewe and Carlisle against an Experiment. Perhaps the third exchange was the most informative for the L&NWR.

This involved the loan of an LB&SCR Class I3 4–4–2 tank locomotive, which was put on the 'Sunny South Special' between Willesden and Rugby. The locomotive was superheated and clearly demonstrated some good advantages to be gained from superheating. Due to his long-standing interest with Continental practice and his connections with Germany, Bowen Cooke was sufficiently aware of developments elsewhere in superheating. In particular, Dr. Wilhelm Schmidt had pursued the development of superheating to an advanced stage and Bowen Cooke was eager to apply his methods to L&NWR locomotives. As events emerged, it was to be a limited application coupled with other new applications such as valves of the Schmidt type, which replaced the usual balanced slide valves. The changes were incorporated in one superheated 4–4–0 George the Fifth No. 2663 and ten saturated 4–4–0s with front ends improved on the pattern incorporated in the Precursor 4–4–0s. Both types were built in 1910.

Also in 1910 there was a locomotive exchange with the GWR at the request of the latter. The GWR CME, G.J. Churchward, wanted to resolve an internal doubt in his Company about his own locomotives, so he initiated an exchange to prove the point. The result of the exchange unfairly placed the L&NWR locomotive in an unfavourable light and vindicated the GWR locomotive policy, but it did not influence the course of L&NWR locomotive development. With hindsight (perhaps the rosiest view of all) it could be argued that Bowen Cooke should have paid more attention to the GWR locomotive's performance on the L&NWR and therefore learned something as a result. As it was, Bowen Cooke was pursuing his course towards a higher-powered 4–6–0 for the L&NWR. Meanwhile, the advantage of superheating had been proved to the L&NWR Board and the George the Fifth class 4–4–0s went into production during 1911. Although the design was successful and a large improvement over the previous designs, there were times when the locomotives were working close to their limit over the northern hills. In 1911 Bowen Cooke gained authority to build ten new superheated 4–6–0s of a larger design to work the heavier trains over the West Coast Route, with particular regard to the northern sections of the line.

His knowledge of Continental practice had made him very appreciative of the four-cylinder locomotive having all four cylinders driving the leading coupled wheels. The main advantage to be gained from a non-divided drive was the elimination of hammer blow arising from the less than perfect balancing of the reciprocating and revolving parts. Additionally, he was in favour of a large central boss for the driving wheels, which he believed also helped good balance. The superheater and the Schmid-type piston ring were also to be incorporated into the design. The last named was one single ring and had up to that time shown to be very good in service. With the outline idea decided, Bowen Cooke set

The note on the reverse of this print states 'first view of No. 2222 Sir Gilbert Claughton *April 1913'. We suspect that it was the first time the photographer, whose identity is not known, saw the pioneer locomotive at Crewe, so we felt this justified the inclusion of the picture which is a splendid railway scene of the era. There can be little doubt that the new class would have created considerable interest at the time.*
AUTHORS' COLLECTION

L&NWR No. 2222, Sir Gilbert Claughton *was completed in January 1913 and although we do not have a date for this picture, we believe that it was taken in March of that year. We have included this picture in order to show features mentioned in the text, namely the pair of safety valves, square ends to the buffer plank, which was painted red with a black border, the original L&NWR lamp sockets and four windows in the cab frontplate. The locomotive had been fitted with a shield for the sand pipes in front of the driving wheels, which were the leading coupled wheels and there was also a cover plate on the platform for the reversing gear that is in front of the splasher.*
AUTHORS' COLLECTION

L&NWR No. 1161, later LMS No. 5901, was named Sir Robert Turnbull, *and this picture of the second Claughton to be built was taken at Euston. It has been included to provide another view of the distinctive L&NWR lamp referred to in the text. No. 1161 was built in May 1913.*
W. H. WHITWORTH

THE L&NWR CLAUGHTONS

Sackfield and his team the task of producing a detailed design. This they did and it was submitted to E.C. Trench, the Chief Engineer, who rejected it on the grounds that the axle load was too heavy. The fact that some already-approved designs produced greater stresses on the track from hammer blow did not deter Trench – he was more concerned with pure axle loads. It really is quite astonishing that two departments of a railway such as the L&NWR should have worked in isolation, Bowen Cooke working on an assumption and Trench rejecting a design at the completion stage with no apparent previous intercourse between them. The division between Trench, when he became Chief Engineer of the LMS in 1923, and the Company's CMEs continued, but that is another story.

Quite how strongly Bowen Cooke argued his case is not known, but he returned and gave his draughtsmen new parameters to re-work the design to within the limits acceptable to Trench. To bring the design weight down would take time and the authorised locomotives would be delayed, so Bowen Cooke sought improvement over the Experiment 4–6–0 design of George Whale, and Crewe Works built, in effect, ten 'improved Experiments' instead of the heavier design which he really wanted to build. These locomotives became well-known as the 'Prince of Wales class' and their numbers were increased over the next few years – which speaks well for an interim design that had not previously been considered. The draughtsmen at Crewe were steadily revising the new, if compromising, design to come within the 20 tons static axle load laid down by Trench. The main area of weight reduction was the boiler, perhaps one of the least desirable areas from the point of view of steam-raising capacity. It is also apparent that the revised boiler had much in common with that of the George the Fifth class and component sizes used in the Prince of Wales class. Crewe Works commenced building the first of the new type, the design of which had now met the requirements of Trench, and by the end of 1912 it was nearly completed. It had been decided to name the first locomotive after the current Chairman of the L&NWR, Sir Gilbert Claughton. This was put into effect and the class henceforth became known as the Claughton Class. It was an impressive-sounding title and when No. 2222 emerged from the Erecting Shop on Friday 24th January 1913 it proved to be an impressive-looking locomotive, different to anything Crewe had built before and yet incorporating much that was already familiar. Initially No. 2222 was painted plain workshop grey rather than the standard lined L&NWR black.

Table 2 lists the main data of the Claughtons, but comments here are appropriate. The appearance of *Sir Gilbert Claughton* was of a well-balanced locomotive, with sleek lines and a boiler that looked perhaps slightly small for complete visual balance. This boiler was in true L&NWR style, even if this was one of the first applications of a Belpaire firebox on that railway. On No. 2222 only one set of safety valves was fitted; later the standard for the class was two. The chimney was also a true Crewe product as was the smokebox door, with its central wheel/handle arrangement, four periphery clips and characteristically L&NWR hinge. The smokebox overhung the integral saddle at the front, accentuating the small appearance of the boiler when viewed from certain angles. The cab was commodious and much in the style set by the L&NWR decades previously, complete with its large integrated rear wheel splasher/side panels. The cab of No. 2222 was unique for several years, having two windows above the firebox. The combined long splasher style set by the Experiment 4–6–0s was continued and sat upon a raised platform which itself reached forward from above the rear coupled wheel to the front end ahead of the outside cylinders. The platform took the form of an elongated connecting and coupling rod splasher combined and a neatly designed valance that hid the Walschaerts valve gear from view. Three almost rectangular access holes were cut into the valance in line with and above the coupled wheel centres. Two similar,

This close-up view of the valve gear of No. 6017 Breadalbane, old L&NWR number 169, shows the arrangement on a large boiler engine. The valve gear maintenance was compromised by the valance.
AUTHORS' COLLECTION

We have mentioned two types of cut-outs that appeared on the tenders that were coupled to Claughtons. Here we show No. 650 Lord Rathmore *coupled to a tender with what we have described as semi-circular shape cut-outs. The lozenge-shape cut-outs are illustrated on page 114. No. 650 and No. 163 were built with 15 inch cylinders in an attempt to improve the steaming and in due course No. 650 became LMS No. 5905. The cab was altered to suit the Northern Division structure gauge in April 1930.* W. H. WHITWORTH

but smaller, holes gave access to the otherwise obscured valve gear. Access plates could be removed from the front end for maintaining the inside cylinders, the retaining clips being visible when viewed at certain angles.

The Claughton, like several outside-cylinder locomotives of the late nineteenth and early twentieth centuries, had the coupling rods with a smaller throw than the piston stroke, in this case 26 inches and the coupling rod 24½ inches throw. Concern over the centrifugal force in the coupling rods was the reason for this, and another well-known locomotive type which had this feature was the Great Northern Railway Atlantic.

The buffer plank was not initially trimmed on the lower corners, but soon had to be (at 40 degrees) to avoid fouling the edges of curved platforms. The buffers were in the traditional L&NWR style and presented faces somewhat small in proportion to the size of the locomotive and, more important, its overall length and potential throw-over on sharp curves. Standard L&NWR lamp sockets were fitted to No. 2222 and the other nine locomotives of the first batch, but these were removed almost immediately from the former and by 1915 from the latter. In their place were fitted lamp irons, which were to become standard for the whole class. Footsteps were provided at the rear of the cylinders, perhaps not the best-inspired place because they probably hindered maintenance of the connecting rod and valve gear. Rear footsteps for access to the cab were the unmistakeable Crewe design whereby the bottom part was distinctively raked back, another drawing office tradition perpetuated. The cylinder layout was good and reasonably accessible. The four connecting rods were all the same length and therefore gave a good distribution of steam. It could be said that equal piston stroke meant equal flow in sequence and gave equal distribution. Bowen Cooke eliminated the traditional Crewe use of centre bearings on coupled wheel axles and ensured that what bearing surfaces remained were of a generous size, a most important feature of any good steam locomotive. The nature of the coupled wheels has been discussed previously, and Bowen Cooke made a good job in providing a well-balanced design with no balance weights of any sort (other than lead inserts in pockets) and the crank pins were incorporated in the centre bosses. The boiler was fitted with an 84-element Schmidt type superheater, which raised steam temperatures to 650°F. The firebox was simply shaped and the grate departed from Crewe practice by having a level part to the rear and a downward-sloping portion from above the trailing wheel axle forward. The use of leaf springs was limited to the rear coupled wheels and, for the remaining coupled wheels, coil springs were used, both types being underslung. The frames were 1⅛ inch thick, an improvement on previous L&NWR locomotives, which had proved troublesome in that area.

The tender coupled to the Claughtons was the Bowen Cooke version of a general style that had been developed from the earliest years of the L&NWR locomotives. The outline was familiar, being generally of rectangular appearance (matching the square splasher/cab side sheets) with rounded vertical corners to the water tank. The frames were of steel, following Whale practice. It is of interest to note that wooden tender frames had been abandoned only ten years previously on the L&NWR. Water capacity was 3000 gallons, adequate because L&NWR water troughs were spaced at a distance of approximately thirty miles apart on the main lines. Coal capacity was six tons. The frames had semi-circular cutouts but some later tenders had lozenge-shaped cutouts. Footsteps were provided only at the front end and these followed a long-established Crewe tradition of being swept backwards at the base to link up with the leading axle box.

Combined with the traditional swept-back nature of the adjacent locomotive footsteps, a very neat and harmonious effect of speed was implied.

Sir Gilbert Claughton left the works and, after preliminary runs and adjustments, was soon earmarked for testing with the aid of the new L&NWR dynamometer car. The first test run was on Sunday 9th February from Crewe to Rugby and back, with a load of 400 to 420 tons (equal to 20 on the L&NWR loading scale). It is assumed that the locomotive performed satisfactorily on this run, despite nothing having been made public. It is convenient to add at this point that the criteria for a successful locomotive were somewhat different to that expected in later years when economic pressures were brought to bear. What was reckoned to be good in 1913 was less than indifferent by 1930. Of course different railways had different ideas of what was 'good', even in 1913, but the emphasis on the L&NWR appears to have been a desire to keep initial costs down. Maintenance costs appear to be of less concern at the time. Labour was relatively cheap in those days and not such an important factor as it was to become later. After a few years in service and with worsening conditions, the inherent problems with the Claughtons became more prominent and, as we will see, in some instances rather serious.

No. 2222 returned to Crewe to be prepared for its official photographs, being painted grey with white lining for this purpose. The photographs were taken on 27th February 1913. There are grounds for believing that the photograph depicting the side view of No. 2222 was later altered in the studios to appear as No. 163 *Holland Hibbert* – the nameplate appears reasonable, but the cab side number plate is somewhat crudely portrayed and bears no small details of date and place of construction. It may well be that this procedure was repeated on other Claughtons in 1913, in order that the personalities after whom the locomotives were named might have a personal photograph of their locomotive. No. 2222 then returned to Crewe paint shop to be repainted in the standard L&NWR livery of the period. This livery is detailed in Appendix 1. Soon afterwards, the locomotive went to Crewe North shed and was put to work on the Down Corridor express on a regular basis, leaving Crewe at 5.19 p.m., bound for Carlisle, with a return working on the 1.00 a.m. Up sleeper; the timing meant that neither working was likely to attract much public attention. Publicity of a limited nature was soon to come when the locomotive worked an all-first class special from Euston to Aintree for the Grand National on 4th April 1913. *The Illustrated London News*, complete with an official photograph of No. 2222, duly recorded the event. This was soon followed by another special occasion on 21st April when the Royal Visit to Crewe Works took place. The King and Queen toured the works and saw *Sir Gilbert Claughton*, which was on display.

Although there were teething troubles with No. 2222, the locomotive quickly settled into service and was soon followed by the rest of the batch, bringing the number in the class to ten. Details of these locomotives appear in *Table 1*.

The numbers were scattered throughout the locomotive list, taking up spaces that were vacant, a long (and confusing to the outsider) tradition of the L&NWR and indeed other railway companies. The names chosen were those of L&NWR people of high status; Nos. 1161, 1191 and 1319 were named after General Managers and the remaining six were named after Directors. These nine locomotives had lamp sockets fitted from new (although by 1914 some were reported to be dual-fitted with the lamp sockets and lamp holders, or lamp irons, both descriptions being used at the time) and were equipped with four safety valves (two pairs) rather than the one pair fitted to No. 2222. In 1915/6 on No. 21, Ross Pop replaced the Ramsbottom valves. Unlike No. 2222, which had only one, the others had two front windows on each side of the cab. Windshields were fitted to the leading pair of sand pipes, and were directed ahead of the wheels, but not all the locomotives were fitted with these at the same time and those so fitted varied during the ensuing years. In some cases additional shields were fitted to pipes ahead of the centre driving wheels.

Nos. 1161 and 1191 went to Camden shed and worked on the two prestige runs from London to Crewe and back; these were the 2.0 p.m. Corridor and the 2.10 p.m. Euston to Liverpool and Manchester. No. 1327, being named after a Liverpool member of the L&NWR Board, appropriately went to Edge Hill shed and worked a particularly arduous return working of 386 miles each day. The remaining six locomotives joined *Sir Gilbert Claughton* at Crewe North shed and this locomotive continued to regularly work the 400-ton Corridor, the famous 2.0 p.m. from Euston to Glasgow, between Crewe and Carlisle for many weeks. With ten locomotives in service, valuable experience data was being accrued by the L&NWR on the Claughtons. There were some initial troubles of poor steaming and to some extent this was due to firemen still trying to master the technique of firing a locomotive with a grate that had a sloping section. Attempts to overcome the poor steaming were made by varying the cylinder diameters of individual locomotives of this first batch. *Sir Gilbert Claughton* had entered service with 16 in. diameter cylinders, but Nos. 163 and 650 had 15 in. diameter cylinders. Further changes were made in 1914 on a later batch when 15in, 15½in, 15¾in and 16in cylinders were fitted to some individual locomotives before being standardised at 15¾in but despite these alterations it does appear that finding the correct firing technique was the main answer to the problem, at least with a locomotive in good condition and with selected coal. There is little doubt that the then new locomotives of 1913 were in good condition; it would be surprising if they were otherwise.

Trouble was also experienced with the carbonisation of lubricating oil in the piston valve 'Trick' ports (so-named after their German inventor). This was not confined to the Claughtons and was a result of the higher steam temperatures generated by the use of superheating. Another fact of life concerned with superheating was that due to higher temperatures there was a reduction in its lubricating qualities.

This picture of L&NWR No. 1319 Sir Frederick Harrison was taken near Stafford c.1924 and shows the locomotive at the head of a train made up of six vehicles running under express passenger train headlamps. Built in July 1913, this locomotive was the fourth Claughton to enter service and became LMS No. 5907, the number being applied in June 1926. It was also converted to burn oil fuel the same year.
AUTHORS' COLLECTION

LNWR No. 21 Duke of Sutherland was another of the first batch of Claughtons to be built, in this instance in July 1913. Although we cannot date this picture, it was taken before the original L&NWR lamp sockets were replaced and, since we believe this modification was made by the end of 1915, it would suggest that No. 21 was about two years old.
W. H. WHITWORTH

THE L&NWR CLAUGHTONS

According to the caption in the September 1941 Railway Magazine, *this picture shows an up Liverpool express passenger train shortly after the formation of the LMS, hauled by 2–4–0 No. 824* Adelaide *and Claughton class No. 650* Lord Rathmore. *The picture was taken as the train passed over the water troughs and readers will note that only the train engine was taking water. The arrangements for picking up water with double-headed trains would be agreed between the drivers of the train and pilot engines. It was all down to teamwork and experience.*
H. GORDON TIDY

The carbonisation would build up over a period of time and, as a consequence, performance would deteriorate. Some problems were also experienced with superheaters burning at the return bends. Fitting shorter elements eventually reduced this problem. Despite the foregoing, in 1913 the first Claughtons proved that in good trim they were very capable machines and an asset to the L&NWR, particularly over the northern sections where they did some impressive work. The design appeared to be good, despite the reduction in weight as a result of the rejection of the original design by E.C. Trench. Proof of what the Claughtons were capable of came on 2nd November 1913 when No. 1159 *Sir Ralph Brocklebank* worked a special train of 435 tons, including the L&NWR dynamometer car, from Euston to Crewe, covering the 158 miles in 159 minutes with a very good start when lifting the load out of Euston. This was even more remarkable when one considers that there was a permanent-way slack at Tring and Milford and a dead stand at Crewe. The train was made up of sleeping cars and dining cars, and the 435 tons weight was considered to be 'equal to 22' on the L&NWR loading scale. There was no doubt in the eyes of those L&NWR officers who were responsible for passenger traffic that the Claughtons were a vast improvement over what had previously been available; indeed they had created something of a record for sustained power output over a long distance. Everyone concerned with the building and running of these locomotives had every reason to be proud.

A further run on 4th November with a regular express train of 360 tons (the tare weight was given as 343 tons including dynamometer car) from Crewe to Carlisle produced more confirmation of the prowess of the Claughtons. The same locomotive turned a seven minutes late start into a run 10 minutes ahead of time with speeds well into the seventies. 141 miles were achieved in 142½ minutes, passing Preston (50.9 miles) in 49¼ minutes from Crewe. At Shap summit the train had travelled 109.6 miles in 110¼ minutes, despite a signal check to 18 mph at Mossdale Hall. The tests were a measure of power output and coal consumption. Economy was not one of the most important concerns and no coal consumption figures were released, but it is thought that coal consumption was fairly high! In October 1913 the 'equal to' vehicle loading scale was abandoned and a more accurate tonnage system introduced in its place.

The construction of a further ten Claughtons was authorised and these started to appear in August of the fateful year 1914. These are detailed in *Table 1*. That same month saw the outbreak of the Great War, and as with every other facet of life that the conflict changed forever, the L&NWR went into the unknown. The company was well placed to play its part in the conflict, but it is doubtful if anyone could have conceived that it would have dragged on for over four years and claim millions of lives in the process. Nor would it have been conceivable that nations would be dragged into virtual collapse and that it would develop into a deadly struggle of attrition between not only the opposing armed forces, but also their supporting industries. In particular, the success of Crewe Works made it a prime industrial tool for the war effort, to the detriment of the railway itself. The armed forces formed a drain on the manpower of the company as volunteers joined the colours. All this was to affect the Claughtons in many ways. The first sign of change concerned livery. The last fully-lined Claughton turned out of Crewe was No. 250 *J.A. Bright*, the first of the 1914 batch. The next locomotive, No. 260 *W.E. Dorrington*, was finished in plain black without coat-of-arms or lining, and set the pattern for the next few years. We believe that varnishing was also abandoned for the duration of the war. This policy reduced the time locomotives were to spend in the works; for example, several days were required while the varnish hardened. With the exception of No. 2401, which was patriotically named in honour of Lord Kitchener, the remainder of this batch of ten locomotives were named after L&NWR Directors. As previously stated, these Claughtons had the cylinder diameter reduced to 15in. as standard and received shorter superheater elements.

For some time, traffic requirements remained unchanged except for the introduction and subsequent increase of additional trains in connection with wartime needs. The Claughtons were still expected to keep the pre-war schedules, loaded up to 420 tons, between London, Crewe, Liverpool, Manchester and, when the occasion arose, Holyhead. North of Crewe they had been used to haul 14-coach loads of 420 tons, usually without assistance up the northern hills. The events of late 1914 proved to be of no short duration as the campaign in France settled into the senseless trench warfare and stalemate from the English Channel to the Swiss border. All this demanded men, munitions and war material, and Crewe Works became more involved in producing material for the war effort. Bowen Cooke, likewise, found himself more involved in the war effort to the detriment of managing the locomotive work of the company. Materials to build locomotives became scarce and this had an effect upon the ability of the works as far as new construction was concerned.

To organise the railways so they might cope with a total war footing, the Railway Executive Committee was formed. The year 1915 saw the Claughtons perform some excellent work with unchanged passenger services and additional troop trains, and in many ways this was to be their finest hour with services still resembling peacetime practice. Piloting was still almost unknown, but during 1916 the workload on the L&NWR increased enormously. To exacerbate the situation, Crewe was unable to build its regularly scheduled seventy or so new locomotives per year, only managing to build thirty in 1915. As a result, orders were placed with outside builders to help alleviate the problem. Of the proposed seventy new locomotives for 1916, ten were to be Claughtons. In addition to this, older locomotives were retained in traffic and, generally because they required longer time in the works for repairs, added to the problems facing the Company.

The ten Claughtons on order were built at Crewe over the period from July to September 1916 and proved to be a most welcome addition to stock. All were named, the first three perpetuating the L&NWR Directors theme and three carried the names of the new General Manager, Company Secretary and Chief Engineer. The last-named of course was E.C. Trench, the man who had rejected the first Claughton proposal; quite a paradox. Obviously there were no hard feelings. The naming policy of the L&NWR was being stretched somewhat at this time, with very few traditional or L&NWR personality-inspired names available, so resort was made to naming locomotives after personalities of other railways. The last four of the 1916 batch were named after the General Managers of the L&SWR, SE&CR, GNR and the L&YR. Most had connections in some way or another with the L&NWR. The modified Bowen Cooke tender was introduced with this batch of Claughtons. All of these locomotives were invaluable in working the overstretched Anglo-Scottish services.

The Railway Executive controlled railway services by various means including the selection of certain routes for selected services in order to avoid duplication and aid concentration of traffic. That passengers from London to Edinburgh were allowed to travel only on the East Coast Route was one example of control exercised, but one of the most drastic changes that affected the West Coast Route was the deceleration and reduction of services, which came into effect on 1st January 1917. Perhaps this may have affected the traveller adversely, but for Bowen Cooke it was very much a relief because it afforded help in reducing coal consumption and locomotive repairs. Conversely, heavier trains resulted in higher coal consumption, but this was to be expected to some extent. One result of deceleration was the pooling of work among the Claughton, George the Fifth and Prince of Wales classes on the basis of the first engine available for traffic was the first out of the shed. Bowen Cooke is quoted as writing the following in February 1917:

> 'The Ministry of Munitions has found it necessary to restrict the appointment of material required for locomotive and general work on British railways; this again will eventually seriously affect the question of Engine Renewals, and consequently there will, in the future, be fewer new engines for traffic. The reduction in regular Passenger Train mileage, commencing on 1st January this year, and the deceleration of Express Passenger trains, will no doubt become a helpful factor in the matter of Engine Repairs and Coal consumption, but already there are indications that reduced mileage means heavier trains, and, therefore, the Coal consumption, although reduced in aggregate, may prove somewhat disappointing when applied to the mileage unit.'

The result of the above was that the decelerated timings south of Preston could be worked by 'George the Fifth', 'Prince of Wales' or 'Claughton' locomotives on the basis of whichever was the first available. This made any sort of pre-diagramming unnecessary and greatly helped the running department. Loads over Shap were reduced generally when ticket restrictions and government controls dictated that London–Edinburgh travellers use the line from King's Cross and the a.m. London–Glasgow use St. Pancras.

More Claughtons were ordered for delivery in 1917 and Crewe was exceedingly quick off the mark, with the first of thirty appearing in the February. *Table I* details the numbers and delivery progress, it being sufficient here to state that deliveries extended until October. Only the first three were

THE L&NWR CLAUGHTONS

We have included this close-up view of part of No. 154 Captain Fryatt *in order to show the arrangement of the L&NWR style of name and number plate and the austere look of those locomotives that were painted black without any lining. No. 154 was built in March 1917 and this picture was taken prior to the locomotive entering service. In 1923 LMS stock number 5931 was allocated and this was applied in April 1926, the same year in which it ran as an oil burner as a result of the coal strike.* AUTHORS' COLLECTION

named when new; *G.R. Jebb* was an L&NWR Director and *Captain Fryatt* was the skipper of the Great Eastern Railway steamship 'Brussels' who had heroically defended his vessel in a confrontation with a German U-boat on the high seas. *I.T. Williams* was the Chief Goods Manager of the L&NWR, who at that time was Acting General Manager for most of the Great War. This was to be the last Claughton naming until January 1920 and was in order to avoid the unnecessary use of brass, which was urgently required elsewhere and in short supply. The arrival of these locomotives enabled the shed allocation of the class to be widened. Sheds that had not previously had Claughtons now received them, in particular Rugby and Preston, Rugby being intermediate between Euston and Crewe, and Preston between Crewe and Carlisle. This ensured there was a good distribution of the class along the West Coast Route.

Another feature of 1917 was the famous (or notorious, depending upon viewpoint) Naval Special, which ran daily from Euston to Thurso as from 15th February of that year. This was one of those trains that reached immortality and had a later successor during the Second World War, both serving the manpower requirements of the Royal Navy at Scapa Flow. The journey took 21 hours, so sleeping cars were included in the fourteen-coach formation and sometimes it was necessary for a pilot to be required over Shap. By the autumn of 1917 there were sixty Claughtons in service, distributed to the sheds as follows: Camden 9, Rugby 8, Crewe 33, Edge Hill 5, Preston 2 and Carlisle 3. All were kept in good running order despite war conditions, and when Nos. 986 and 1103 were allocated to Edge Hill they enabled regular working as far as Leeds on the Liverpool to Newcastle expresses. The Rugby allocation enabled selected heavy secondary expresses to be Claughton-hauled. For the time being, the requirement for the powerful 4-6-0 was satisfied.

By 1918, in order to reduce track maintenance around the system, the maximum speed limit was 60mph, but the Claughtons were still doing good work despite this. With the entry of the United States into the war during 1917 hopes were raised for a swift and positive conclusion of hostilities and thoughts started to turn towards the postwar requirements, but the optimism was dashed in 1918 by the German successes on the Western Front as a result of the release of troops from the Eastern Front. The Allied reversals proved to be short-lived, though traumatic, and in mid-1918 Bowen Cooke was looking forward to returning to his beloved locomotive work. Due to the war effort much had been neglected and, although he was aware of problems concerned with the Claughtons, there was little practical remedy that could be done at this stage. He would attend to them as soon as hostilities ceased. 11th November 1918 is indelibly etched in the minds of most people as Armistice Day, the day the fighting stopped. Although the end was officially in 1919, when the Treaty of Versailles was signed, it was clear during the intervening period that Germany was indeed defeated, so the British war machine was run down and industry began to be geared for peaceful needs.

The various items that required addressing by the time peace arrived, had been borne out during the war years as the older locomotives accumulated mileage under less than ideal conditions. Not all were apparent. Using a smaller boiler has already been mentioned, but the fire grate area was generally very deep with the rear one-third of it level. However, one part of the ashpan was very shallow where, by necessity,

Although we cannot date this picture, we believe it was taken c.1920 and shows L&NWR No. 1103, later LMS No. 5955, with a freight train at Manchester London Road. The final years of the last Claughton were spent on freight train work, but from this picture it is clear they were used for this class of work before the Grouping. No doubt when this picture was taken, No. 1103 was not in the best condition and it was rostered on local trip workings.
COLLECTION R. S. CARPENTER

From 1923 Ross Pop safety valves began to replace the original Ramsbottom type and this picture of No. 1429 Colonel Lockwood, which was built in September 1914, shows a locomotive fitted with the new valves. We believe that by the end of 1925 all the original safety valves on the Claughtons had been replaced but No. 1429 did not become LMS No. 5913 until June 1927. This picture is rather interesting. The train appears to have been a Down Euston to Holyhead service photographed in the London area. The clue is the leading vehicle loaded with the distinctive containers used on the Holyhead to Dublin ferry service and the electrified lines. This picture also displays what could be seen in the early years of the grouping, the locomotive and a number of carriages in the old L&NWR livery, but other coaches, in this case the second, third, fifth and sixth, were in the new LMS livery.
AUTHORS' COLLECTION

it had to be arched to clear the trailing coupled axle. This limited airflow to the grate and sometimes led to erratic steaming. As the firebox was very low over the trailing axleboxes, this led to very poor lubrication, despite the axleboxes themselves being of ample proportions and thus caused overheating problems. The locomotive frames were very shallow, being only 18 inches deep over the horn gaps, giving rise to occasional cracking. Perhaps less apparent were the single, wide piston valve rings wearing and allowing steam leakage past. This was eventually dealt with during the LMS period. The coupled wheel coil springs were weak and breakages were common. More superficial were the incidences of cabs and splashers working loose, although, if not dealt with, they led to pipe fractures and vacuum brake failures. The Claughton smokebox door was flat and secured by four so-called 'dogs' around the perimeter. It warped in service and admitted air, compromising steaming. The basic good design of the Claughton gave good reason and encouragement to alleviate the above problems. The rigid four-cylinder arrangement, the virtually perfect reciprocating balance of the driving wheels and the aforementioned earlier successful modifications, which had been by necessity small in number, were positive features and formed a good basis worthy of supplementary remedial work on the locomotive. The L&NWR had to make good the ravages of war and return the system to a peacetime footing. The war had taken its toll and the L&NWR was no exception; certainly it took its toll on Bowen Cooke and some of his contemporaries.

The time for the withdrawal of older locomotives and their replacement was long overdue, so orders for sixty-five more Prince of Wales 4–6–0s and seventy more Claughtons were placed and Vickers Ltd of Barrow in Furness were entrusted to build the seventy boilers for them. To some extent, their building would absorb staff at Crewe formerly engaged on war work. The sense of urgency, combined with the little time available to Bowen Cooke to realise his ambition to fully attend to the needs of improving the Claughton design, led to few modifications being actually incorporated into the latest locomotives. Even so, he realised from experience that an improvement in steaming could be obtained by alleviating the problems of the firemen, caused by the partly sloping grate. A continuous slope was substituted and was eventually applied to the older locomotives as they went through the shops. To reduce carbonisation, changes in the cylinder and valve lubrication were made by having the oil pass through atomisers to the steam pipes, rather than passing direct. The traditional Ramsbottom type safety valve was replaced by the Ross Pop type, which, unlike the Ramsbottom valve, did not lift gently, but blew off suddenly with little or no warning and was rather noisy. From 1923 Ross Pop safety valves became a standard fitting and all the locomotives in the class were fitted with them by the end of 1925.

The first of the new series of seventy locomotives emerged from Crewe Works in January 1920 and building continued, as described in *Table 1*, until June 1921. This first locomotive became the Company's war memorial; it was a splendid idea to honour those employees who gave their lives during the war. The name 'Patriot' was selected and appropriately the locomotive was numbered 1914. Specially prepared nameplates were fitted, as described in *Appendix 1*, and the locomotive became perhaps one of the best-known Claughtons. Its livery was plain and unlined black, without a coat of arms, but it is believed that all the remaining sixty-nine carried the L&NWR coat of arms when new. In all probability there was insufficient space left below the non-standard nameplate. No. 1914 *Patriot* was put to work on the 1.15 p.m. Down Corridor on a daily basis. In addition, No. 1914 was the first of the class to be fitted with the horizontal handrail to the cab sides.

Bowen Cooke was eager to know how his modified fireboxes were faring in service and had one of his Crewe pupils investigate this on his behalf. Successful must have been the verdict because they were later fitted to earlier Claughtons. During 1920 *Sir Gilbert Claughton* was experimentally fitted for oil firing to investigate an alternative fuel to coal due to the high postwar price of the latter. The system examined was the 'Scarab' system, developed in Mesopotamia during the war when the military were having problems with obtaining coal for locomotives in that region. The L&NWR not only fitted a Claughton with it, but also a George the Fifth and a Precursor. The system was not extended to any other locomotives, but its examination and the knowledge gained was put to useful purposes during the coal strike of 1926 when a number of locomotives were altered to burn oil rather than coal.

By July 1920 Bowen Cooke had problems with deteriorating health, brought on by his exertions during the war. On 20th July he travelled from Crewe to Euston in his private saloon drawn by the famous old single *Cornwall*, to visit a Harley Street heart specialist for an examination. As a result, he was ordered to rest for six months and promptly travelled to Falmouth the following day. *Cornwall* was sent back to Crewe on the 20th as pilot to *Patriot* at the head of the 1.15 p.m. Corridor – a fitting tribute as it transpired. Sadly, Bowen Cooke died on 18th October, aged 62, and he was buried on the 22nd; so ended a fine career and the L&NWR suffered a great loss. Fortunately, the railway had a suitable replacement in the man who had been Deputy CME since 1919, Captain H.P.M. Beames. Beames was a Crewe man through and through, but his period of office was short-lived. When the L&YR and L&NWR amalgamated in 1922 he was passed over in favour of George Hughes of the Lancashire & Yorkshire Railway, who was the senior man and seniority was the determining factor when there was one post to fill but more than one contender.

1921 saw the government control of the railways end and the services began to improve, but this state of affairs was short-lived due to a prolonged and disastrous coal strike that devastated the railway services. The coal that was imported for railway use was often poor in quality and not really suitable for use in locomotive fireboxes. As a result, the quality of running and steaming suffered accordingly. Some improve-

As a result of the 1926 coalminers strike, a number of Claughtons were altered to burn oil but in the case of this locomotive, No. 5900 Sir Gilbert Claughton, it had also been equipped for oil burning in 1920. This picture was taken at Oxenholme in 1926, when, as far as we can see, only the last carriage was still in L&NWR livery.
AUTHORS' COLLECTION

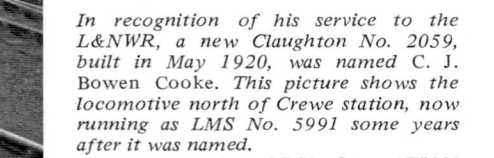

In recognition of his service to the L&NWR, a new Claughton No. 2059, built in May 1920, was named C. J. Bowen Cooke. This picture shows the locomotive north of Crewe station, now running as LMS No. 5991 some years after it was named.
AUTHORS' COLLECTION

THE L&NWR CLAUGHTONS

Following the amalgamation of the L&NW and L&Y Railways, some L&Y 4–6–0s, commonly known as Dreadnoughts, were tested on the old L&NW, and later, after bridge strengthening had taken place, were allowed to run between London Euston and Carlisle. This picture shows No. 1674 in the London area with an express passenger train.
AUTHORS' COLLECTION

ments came following the introduction of the summer timetable and at this time the latest Claughtons came into service. The old traditions were returning, but matters were never to be the same again – too much had changed and times were very different in the post-war era. Attitudes had also changed.

The grouping of the railways of Britain by amalgamation into four large companies was very much a live issue and the necessary legislation was passed for this to take effect from 1st January 1923. Exactly one year before this happened, the L&NWR and the L&YR undertook their own amalgamation. There were many sound reasons for this, but unfortunately for the L&NWR, the company was in a less strong position due to the after effects of the war and the loss of some of its strongest personalities. Furthermore, in anticipation of the 1923 grouping, or as it was called at the time, the Great Amalgamation, Arthur Watson, (General Manager of the L&YR) had succeeded Sir Thomas Williams, when he retired from the position of L&NWR General Manager at the end of 1920. With Watson holding both positions concurrently and with amalgamation on the not too distant horizon, matters were not to fare too well for some of the senior L&NWR personnel who were junior to their L&YR counterparts in seniority. As we have said, seniority was the key when there was more than one applicant but only one post to be filled. The seniority rule applied at all levels and one of us can recall that when he was at Saltley MPD his driver lost a particular job because another driver, whose own job had been cancelled, but who was senior to him, claimed it.

Before the end of 1921 matters began to improve. A Minute of the Locomotive and Engineering Committee dated 20th October resolved, 'a resumption of lining, varnishing and naming of locomotives'. Prior to this, only two Claughtons had been named since the end of the war, the aforementioned 'Patriot' and one other. This other was a special tribute to the much-revered Bowen Cooke. No. 2059, completed in May 1920, was named *C. J. Bowen Cooke* and the date on the nameplates was altered to read 'October 1920', the month of his death. Some of the latest Claughtons managed to receive lined L&NWR black before the Grouping of 1923, as did earlier examples. In early LMS days about one quarter of the class was so treated. In 1922 a few hitherto unnamed Claughtons received names, but application was desultory, probably due to the background of changes that were taking place. Most notable of these were the three locomotives named after L&NWR employees who had won the Victoria Cross during the war. An article by Geoff Holt in *LMS Journal No. 13* explores the story behind the men and their exploits. Before 1921 was out, tests were undertaken with various locomotives. These involved an L&YR Dreadnought 4–6–0 on both L&NWR and L&YR lines and a Prince of Wales 4–6–0 and Claughton No. 192 on L&NWR lines. These tests were of a limited nature and to some extent foreshadowed what would occur on several occasions during the next few years. It was also another example of how the two companies were beginning to draw closer together.

After the 1922 amalgamation of the L&NWR and L&YR, a policy of integration was pursued, but not as one would expect with outward visible signs such as livery changes and renumbering. No doubt the impending larger amalgamation was in the forefront of the minds of those charged with management and through a combination of seniority and the reluctance of some in their final years of service to move house, it was L&YR men that became senior managers. We must not overlook the question of human nature. Old allegiances were strong, which is not surprising because the old companies were run in such a way that everyone instinctively knew where they stood, so when amalgamation came, the old order was supported and often the alien ideas were rejected without being given the consideration they merited. What is clear is that despite L&YR men in management, the number of L&NWR Directors outnumbered those of the L&Y.

The position of CME was resolved quickly when George Hughes was appointed as Chief Mechanical and Electrical Engineer; Hughes was by far the senior man. He had held the post on the L&YR before Bowen Cooke's time as CME on the L&NWR. It was a natural choice, but the way in which Beames was treated could be considered as being somewhat callous; he was not even made Deputy or Assistant CME; instead he became Divisional Mechanical Engineer Crewe with G.N. Shawcross Divisional Mechanical Engineer Horwich. Following the Grouping in 1923, Beames, together with Shawcross, were joined by Hookham at Stoke on Trent and Pickersgill at St Rollox, their titles being Mechanical Engineer Crewe, Horwich, etc. Hughes continued to operate from the L&YR headquarters at Horwich Works. The final orders for L&NWR locomotives were completed and it could be said that in one blow the lineage of Crewe locomotive development stopped dead, with the Claughtons representing the ultimate in purely L&NWR passenger locomotive design. From this time on, the influence of Crewe in terms of design was considered less, and the influence of first Horwich and then Derby (from 1923) increased, although as the locomotive works were reorganised by the LMS this was to change.

Hughes decided to collect as much data as possible on various locomotive types and much of 1922 was taken up with such activity. The Claughtons were compared with their L&YR counterparts, the Hughes 4-cylinder Class '8' 4-6-0s, commonly described as the 'Dreadnoughts.' These locomotives were an up-to-date superheated design based upon a recent rebuild, whereas the Claughton design was still basically that of 1913, but with minimal improvement. The Class '8' was a rebuild and development of a saturated 4-6-0 design of 1908, which had never been successful. The redesign dated from 1920 and new locomotives appeared from August 1921 onwards. Furthermore, they were regarded as being more powerful than the Claughtons. Naturally, Hughes, as the designer, wished to see their use extended beyond the L&YR lines onto the old L&NWR territory. He was also keen to learn more of the Claughtons. Thus emerged the first threat to the latter as the first-line locomotive class on the West Coast Route.

Dynamometer trials were organised to take place in 1922, utilising the L&YR dynamometer car, but little of consequence was ever released. A useful pointer will be found in the LNWR Rolling Stock Committee minute 67 dated 27th July 1922. G.R.T. Taylor, a member of the committee, asked whether the 20 engines, which were being built on the revenue account would be of sufficient power to draw the maximum load without the necessity of double-heading, and the General Manager stated that he had been very much impressed with the desirability of abolishing double-heading, but the difficulty which had been encountered so far was the fact that some of the Company's bridges were not sufficiently strong to take engines of the necessary power. He went on to compare Great Western practice, which had the advantage of a loading gauge originally used for broad-gauge and the fact that many Great Western engines would not pass over most lines of other companies. He also said that experiments had been made recently with engines built at Horwich which were now taking trains of over 400 tons weight between Crewe and Carlisle without difficulty, but until a bridge at Wolverton was strengthened, which he expected would be within a week or two, it was not possible to bring these engines into Euston. When the bridge strengthening had been completed, these engines would be used for drawing main-line expresses between Euston and Crewe, and Crewe and Holyhead, and he anticipated they would be a complete success.

The final paragraph of the minute is rather revealing and is quoted in full. 'So far as limiting the weight of engines was concerned; the General Manager explained that when the 'Claughton' type was first projected, it was thought they would haul, without difficulty, trains up to 440 tons and the traffic plans were based accordingly. Unfortunately these anticipations were never realised and the matter was one which was giving them serious thought with a view to getting such a type of engine as would avoid the necessity, under any ordinary circumstances, of double-heading.' As we will see later, the Claughtons did not come up to expectations and the comments from contemporary observers and others probably stem from the fact that a Claughton in poor condition was 'not up to the job'. Therefore it is possible that the additional piloting that took place was all about the use of engines on a 'common user basis' and ensuring that the weight of trains and condition of the locomotives used to haul them did not lead to loss of time.

THE POST 1923 PERIOD

The first L&NWR passenger engine to be repainted red was No. 2511 Croxteth, *which emerged from the paint shop as LMS No. 5971 in July 1923. This work was carried out before the adoption of the LMS emblem that was applied to the cabside during the period when the only number visible from the outside of a locomotive was the plate on the smokebox door, although this was not always fitted to ex-L&NWR locomotives.*
AUTHORS' COLLECTION

In 1923 there was a very strong Midland influence that nearly made the LMS into a 'Greater Midland Railway'. Words similar to these (and what the Scottish constituents made of all this in their remote world is left to the imagination) have appeared in the past. It seems to us that we should begin the story of the Claughtons under LMS ownership by correcting a few false impressions, beginning with Scotland. North of the border there was a Local Scottish Committee that was appointed to administer the (LMS) railways in Scotland. The committee enjoyed freedom of action and permission to spend up to £500 on capital projects, without reference to the Board in London, who were the ultimate authority. From an operating standpoint, the LMS was divided into four geographical divisions. The Northern Division was Scotland and, as we have said, in many matters had a degree of independence from the various committees in London that made overall decisions. Western Division B was the old Lancashire & Yorkshire Railway but in due course it became the major part of the Central Division, and when this change was made, the former L&NWR lines, referred to as Western Division A from 1923, became simply Western Division. The Midland Division covered the former MR area but during the first years of the company some divisional boundaries were adjusted; for example, the Midland Railway lines in South Wales became part of the Western Division. All the minor constituent and subsidiary companies were included in one of the four divisions.

The Chairman and one of the two Deputy Chairmen were amongst the twelve directors appointed by the London and North Western Railway, which also included those ex Lancashire and Yorkshire directors who were on the enlarged L&NWR Board from 1st January 1922. The Midland Railway appointed eight directors, one being the other Deputy Chairman. In January the arrangements in respect of the Caledonian Railway had not been made, but directors, one from each company, had been appointed representing the North Staffordshire, Furness, Glasgow and South Western and Highland Railways. The Chief Officers were: Arthur Watson General Manager (ex L&NWR, previously L&Y); Principal Assistant to the General Manager, H.G. Burgess (ex L&NWR); Chief General Superintendent, J.H. Follows (ex Midland); Superintendent of Motive Power, J.E. Anderson (ex Midland). In view of what has been written by other authors, it seems to us that two other posts seem to be significant: Assistant to the Chief General Superintendent (Passenger Services) H.E. Home (ex L&NWR) and Assistant to the Chief General Superintendent (Train Diagrams, Engine Workings, etc) W. Sargent. Unfortunately, we have not been able to trace the pregroup company that employed this officer prior to 1923.

This was the background to the scene that the Claughtons now entered as the Western Division's premier express passenger locomotives. Although the story of the Claughtons spans two railway amalgamations, most readers would probably only consider the 'Great Amalgamation' of 1923, which we will in future refer to as 'The Grouping'. If the amalgamation of 1922 was distressing for certain elements of the L&NWR, then the Grouping of 1923 was to prove to be more so. That the newly created LMS was divided from the start and remained so for most of its early years has been described by many previous authors, although we are inclined to think that this was at lower levels of management and has perhaps been rather overstated. With regard to locomotive policy, there were three major works in England, those at Crewe, Horwich and Derby. Previous writers have said there was little love lost between Crewe and Derby at the best of times and after 1923 the former Midland Railway faction fought to gain the upper hand. Much has been made of the suggestion that Horwich, under the newly appointed LMS CME George Hughes, was struggling to maintain authority as Derby undermined it. Perhaps it would be more accurate to say that with Hughes' tenure as CME not likely to be overlong and his refusal to move from Horwich unhelpful, a power struggle began to develop, with those at Derby seeing an opportunity for either personal or their preferred policy's advancement. There is nothing unusual in this at all; mergers and amalgamations of large companies, and the LMS was a very large company in global terms, would see this happen. While this was taking place, Crewe Works came a poor third in locomotive matters. Furthermore, it has been suggested that the influences at Derby were from the Motive Power Department more than anywhere else, which we believe is true. In 1923, LMS motive power matters had been separated from the CME's department and the Motive Power Department was officially responsible to both the CME and the Chief Operating Officer.

We are unsure how many L&YR Class '8', the official name for the 'Dreadnoughts', were used on the Western 'A' Division. We know that No. 1519 went to this Division in October 1921 and in 1922 No. 1511 (with an 8-wheel tender) together with Nos. 1657 and 1658, were transferred from 'B' Division for Crewe–Carlisle workings, but their use on the old L&NWR main line predated the formation of the LMS and expanded thereafter. An article in *LMS Journal No. 1*, based upon a circular signed by F.W. Dingley (Superintendent of Motive Power, Crewe) that was sent to the District Locomotive Superintendents and Running Shed Foremen in March 1926, gives the following: Preston 10450–10452, Carlisle 10453–10474. Writing in *Locomotive Panorama*, E S Cox stated that the L&NWR men were generally hostile to what they called the 'Lanky Claughtons'. Their main drawbacks were high coal consumption and bearing troubles, the latter being due to the fact that they were more at home on the runs on the old L&YR lines with fairly intermittent stops rather than the long and sustained runs of the West Coast Route.

The L&Y Class '8' locomotives that were built 1908/9 and were rebuilt from 1920 onwards, together with the new construction that entered service between 1921–1925, did not reach the expectations described earlier; in fact they had many shortcomings. A memorandum from E.S. Cox to S.J. Symes, who was based at Euston as Locomotive Assistant to the CME, gives what we believe is an accurate summary of these locomotives. The unabridged report will be found in *LMS Journal No. 11*, so we will not repeat everything that was written, but will give a brief summary. Cox went on to become Assistant Mechanical Engineer British Railways and started his railway career on the L&Y, so his findings are factual. The opening words of the report are rather telling. The fact that Horwich Class 8 Engines stood lowest in miles run per hot-box amongst principal passenger classes in 1930, suggested some investigation at the sheds. At the same time, opportunity was taken to enquire into any other defects, which were general to this class. In his report he highlighted the poor axlebox arrangements. He itemised other problems but in the final summary he said that 'the engines give good results and are especially suitable for heavily graded sections. Steaming is good and a trip made on No. 10462, showed that they have good riding qualities'. No mention was made about coal or water consumption.

The Claughtons were also showing some signs of wear and tear. Coal consumption was rising, particularly when the locomotives were some time ex-works, and troubles with the trailing coupled wheel bearings were evident. On the first count no one really knew what was the cause, and on the second the problem lay in lateral movement of worn bearing components shearing lubrication delivery pipes. Later we will set out a report that was made in 1931 which exposes the problems of the Claughtons in full, but what appears to be clear at this point in their lifetime is that they were not as good as they could be and they were becoming a major concern to senior management on the operating side of the LMS.

There was much about the Midland Railway that was as good as or better than what existed elsewhere on the newly formed LMS. An example of this was the Midland system of power classification for locomotives, which was also used by British Railways until the end of steam. This system placed the Claughtons into power class 5. Another good feature was the Midland locomotive stock numbering system, which was also introduced. The majority of the former Midland locomotives retained their old numbers within the number block 1 to 4999. This was followed by the L&NWR block 5000 to 9999, which meant that all former L&NWR locomotives had to be renumbered, as did all the rest of the constituent company locomotives. The Midland system was a logical one and it did group locomotives together numerically as classes. These classes were grouped into adjacent classes according to duty and power, and blocks of numbers were left vacant to allow for future construction.

It is often stated that the LMS was overwhelmed and largely taken over by the 'Midland Men' and the adoption of the Midland Railway livery for the Company's locomotives and carriages is used to justify this statement. It may be useful if we give the facts about how and why Crimson Lake was adopted by the LMS. The LMS Board of Directors minute 119, dated 27th April 1923, confirms that the question was to be referred to a committee consisting of the Chairman, the two Deputy Chairmen and the Chairman of the Rolling Stock Committee. Minute 187 dated 1st June confirmed that although some L&NWR features were to be used in future construction of carriages, the practices of the Midland Railway, including the colour would be used. What is interesting is that the prime consideration was not the colour of the locomotives but that used for carriages, and the old Midland colours were selected. Minute 53 of the Rolling Stock Committee dated 31st May 1923 is also rather revealing and states 'and it was necessary to come to some decision in regard to the locomotives. After consideration it was ordered, that in future, the passenger engines be painted in the crimson lake colour, following the decision in respect of the coaching stock, and that the freight engines be painted black without the lining which has hitherto been adopted.' The Chairman of the Rolling Stock Committee was Mr D. Vickers, an ex-Midland Railway director, and there were two other ex-Midland directors on the committee, which was made up of nine. As the other six were ex L&NWR directors, it would seem that the ex-L&NWR directors preferred the old Midland colours, which is a little different to what many writers have said in the past. We should add that the minute also contained technical details about wear and durability, so the choice was not entirely based upon colour.

Shortly after the grouping the renumbering of the new company's locomotive stock was agreed and the Claughtons were to be renumbered 5900–6029. The old Midland Railway system of power classification was adopted and the Claughtons became Class 5. At this date the later 'P' for passenger and 'F' for freight had not been introduced. The shock that must have been experienced by ex-L&NWR men when No. 5971 (formerly 2511) *Croxteth* appeared in crimson lake in 1923 can be imagined. This was (to Crewe men at least) the ultimate desecration. Had not black been *the* livery for all L&NWR locomotives for decades? What would the men who decided upon black in 1873 have said about this? Whatever the men of Crewe thought, it is an inescapable fact that the new LMS livery did suit the Claughtons, as indeed did the old black livery. Many people came to accept it with the passing of time, although much time passed before all members of the class actually received it. Not many of the 130 locomotives that were repainted appear to have received the pre-1928 scheme and many more retained some remnant of L&NWR livery for six years or so after the Grouping. *Table 8* records individual LMS liveries of locomotives, where known to us.

The L&NWR used cast number plates that were attached to cabsides and these had to be removed when the locomotive was renumbered. On tender locomotives, the new LMS stock numbers were applied to the side of the tender and on tank engines the number was on the side of the tank. All locomotives were to carry a cast-iron smokebox door number plate of Midland pattern, but photographic evidence shows that there were many instances when this was not done. At first the numbers were transfers and followed Midland practice, but cases of hand-painted numerals of a slightly different style were commonplace in later years. It would be easy to be diverted into the story of the various LMS livery variations that were applied to ex-L&NWR locomotive stock and we would refer interested readers to *An Illustrated History of LMS Locomotives Vol. 2* by Essery & Jenkinson (OPC 1985). Suffice to say that it took several years for Nos. 5900 to 6029 to receive their allotted numbers and to be repainted Crimson Lake, which replaced the so-called L&NWR 'blackberry' black. LMS livery details appear in *Appendix 2*.

It has been recorded that in 1923 there was a reduction of the maximum load limit for the Claughtons south of Carnforth to 360 tons. As a result, there was a need for additional pilot engines on a grand scale and events on the Western 'A' Division became confusing, to say the least. It has been suggested this move was intended to initiate changes in working the West Coast route, as mentioned above, but we believe that a more likely reason was that it was the result of the shortcomings of the Claughtons becoming apparent to those responsible for day-to-day operation. It has also been said that the ex-L&NWR crews, who knew what the Claughtons in good condition could do, set out to prove that it was not necessary. We can be sure there was an intense pride and sense of rivalry between all grades of men from the various constituent companies. Individual situations produced differing reactions and, in contrast to some indifferent performances, the crews often provided some very lively runs in the traditional manner.

Over the years, numerous writers have suggested that 'The Midland faction sought to reorganise the timetables of the LMS on the Midland pattern, using Midland Compound 4-4-0s on light but frequent trains and sought to prove these locomotives as suitable'. We have examined many of the various committee minutes that are at Kew and can find no evidence to support this statement. What could have happened was that changes in operating express passenger trains were determined at a lower management level and the minutes have not survived. Unfortunately, we have not been able to discover the relevant carriage diagrams and all the working timetables from this period to enable a judgement to be made. There is probably some truth in what has been said, but it has not yet been proved to our satisfaction. What can be said is that the Compounds on the lighter London to Birmingham trains, providing they were driven correctly, were ideal. What is also true is that George Hughes, as CME, sought to select what he considered to be the best motive power from within the constituent companies and this led to the various trials that took place. The first trials were held between Leeds and Carlisle, from 10th December 1923 to 17th January 1924, but did not involve the Claughtons. They involved the Midland Compounds versus various Class 4 locomotives. Rather more revealing were the trials between Carlisle and Leeds in November and December 1924. In an article by William Dunn in *LMS Journal No. 6*, readers will find an unabridged copy of the LMS test report. He also quotes

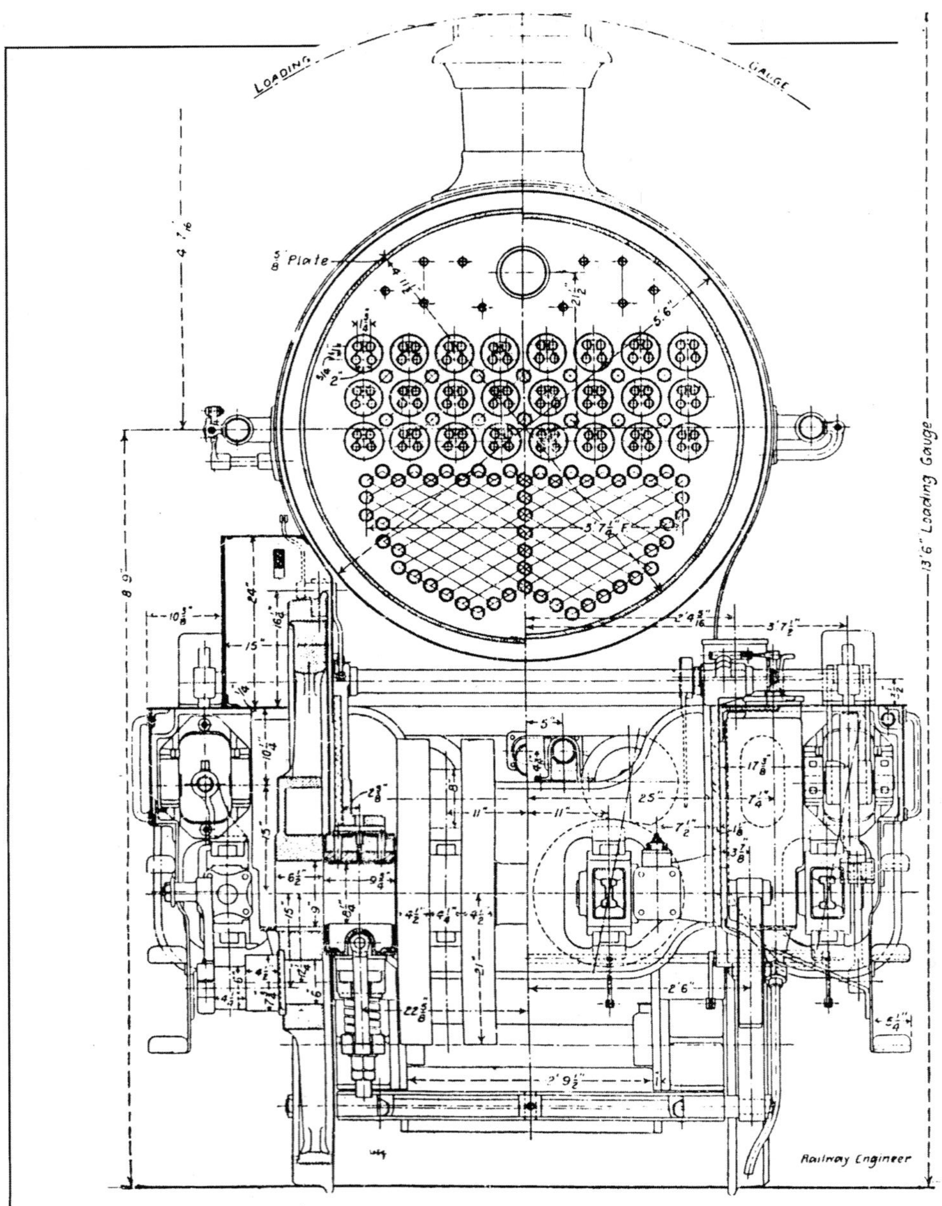

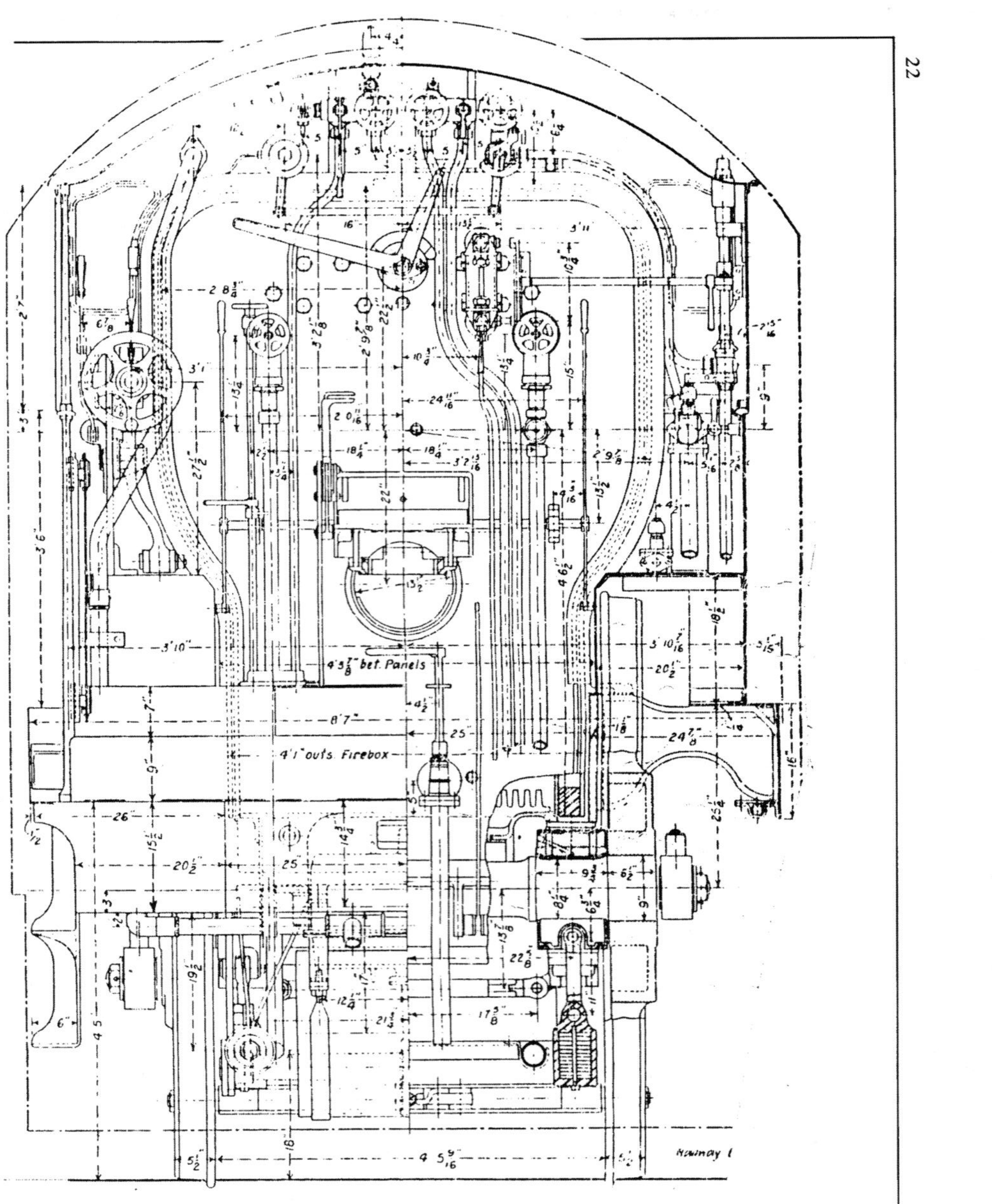

This view shows the arrangement of the cab fittings. At the top of the boiler, just below the cab roof, is the manifold with valves for the injectors, carriage warming and brake valve. Below is the regulator handle which was pulled down to open. To the right is the water level gauge while below are the two injector delivery clack valves with hand wheels for shutting off the valve in case of leakage. The injectors are below the cab floor. The reversing wheel is on the left and on the right of the cab is the carriage warming reducing valve and the vacuum ejector. Either side of the delivery clack valves are the sanding levers and below the firehole door is the handle for the manual blowdown valve.

This drawing shows, to the left, the cross section at the driving wheel and, to the right, the cross section at the reversing shaft. On the left-hand side we can see a section through the boiler showing the arrangement of the superheater and fire tubes. Also visible on the left side are the driving wheels, axlebox and springs and crank axle. On the right-hand side the motion plate, slide bars, section through the connecting rod and vacuum pump are visible together with the profile of the outside motion plate.

implified

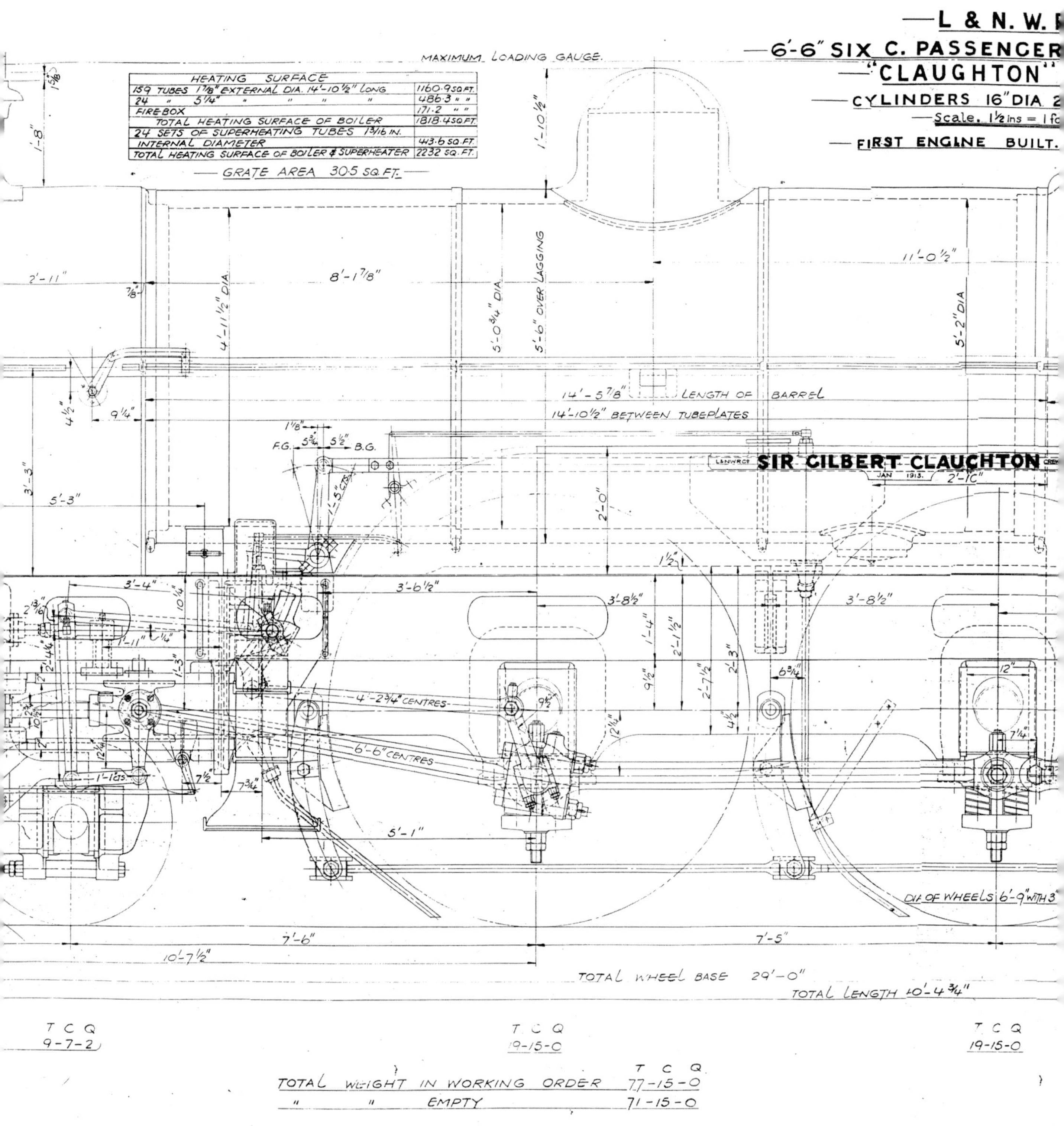

L & N. W.
6'-6" SIX C. PASSENGER
"CLAUGHTON"
CYLINDERS 16" DIA
Scale. 1½ ins = 1 f
FIRST ENGINE BUILT.
MAXIMUM LOADING GAUGE.
HEATING SURFACE
159 TUBES 1⅞" EXTERNAL DIA. 14'-10½" LONG 1160.9 SQ.FT.
24 " 5¼" " " " 486.3 " "
FIREBOX 171.2 " "
TOTAL HEATING SURFACE OF BOILER 1818.4 SQ.FT.
24 SETS OF SUPERHEATING TUBES 13/16 IN. INTERNAL DIAMETER 413.6 SQ.FT.
TOTAL HEATING SURFACE OF BOILER & SUPERHEATER 2232 SQ.FT.
GRATE AREA 30.5 SQ.FT.
5'-0¾" DIA
5'-6" OVER LAGGING
4'-11½" DIA
5'-2" DIA
14'-5⅞" LENGTH OF BARREL
14'-10½" BETWEEN TUBEPLATES
SIR GILBERT CLAUGHTON
L&NWRCo
JAN 1913.
4'-2¾" CENTRES
6'-6" CENTRES
DIA OF WHEELS 6'-9" WITH 3"
TOTAL WHEEL BASE 29'-0"
TOTAL LENGTH 40'-4¾"
T C Q
9-7-2
T C Q
19-15-0
T C Q
19-15-0
TOTAL WEIGHT IN WORKING ORDER T C Q 77-15-0
" " EMPTY 71-15-0

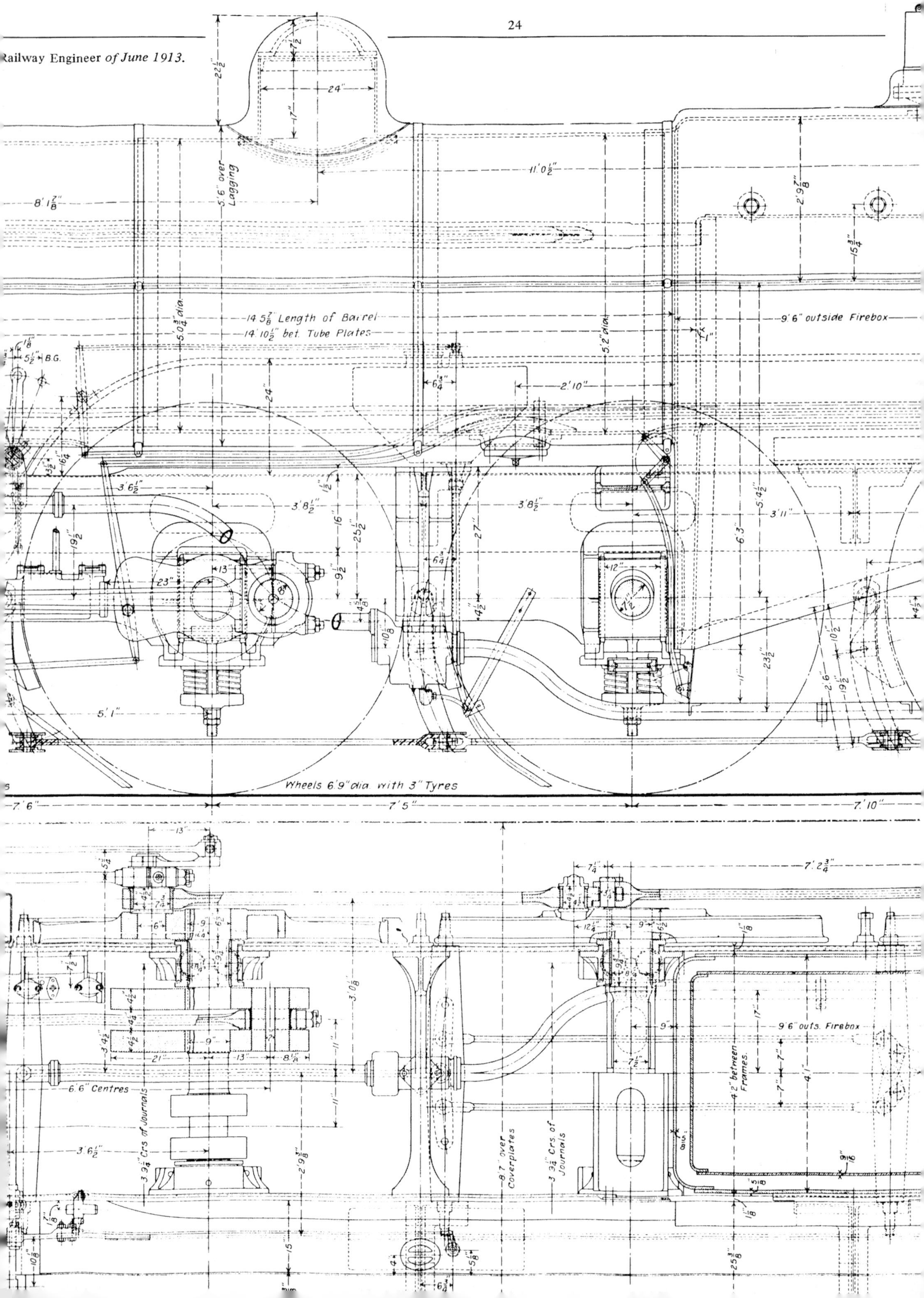

Railway Engineer of June 1913.

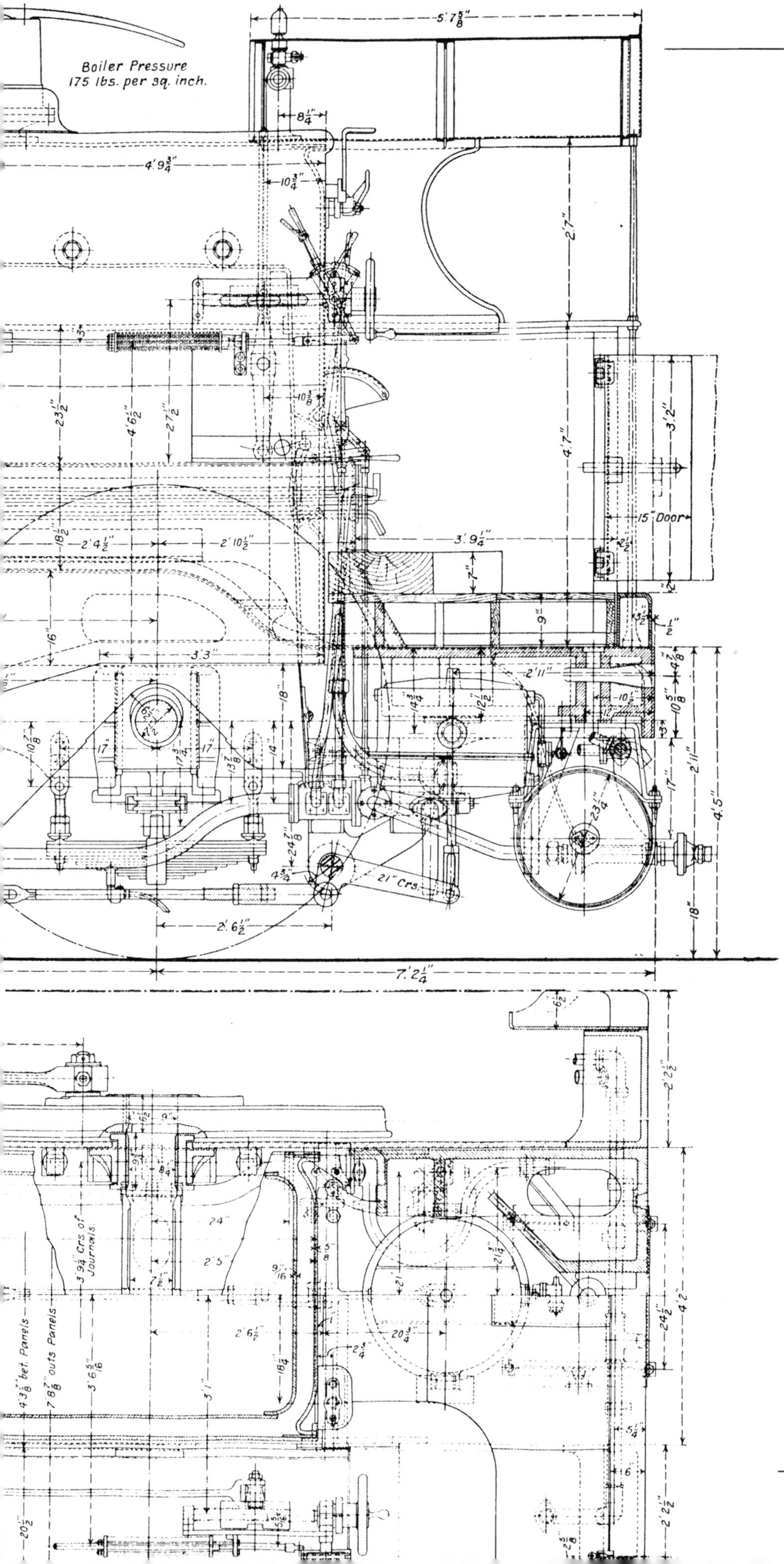

Boiler Pressure 175 lbs. per sq. inch.

This is a Crewe drawing that shows a full side elevation of No. 2222 Sir Gilbert Claughton in the form of a General Arrangement drawing containing most of the dimensions and data required for modelling purposes.

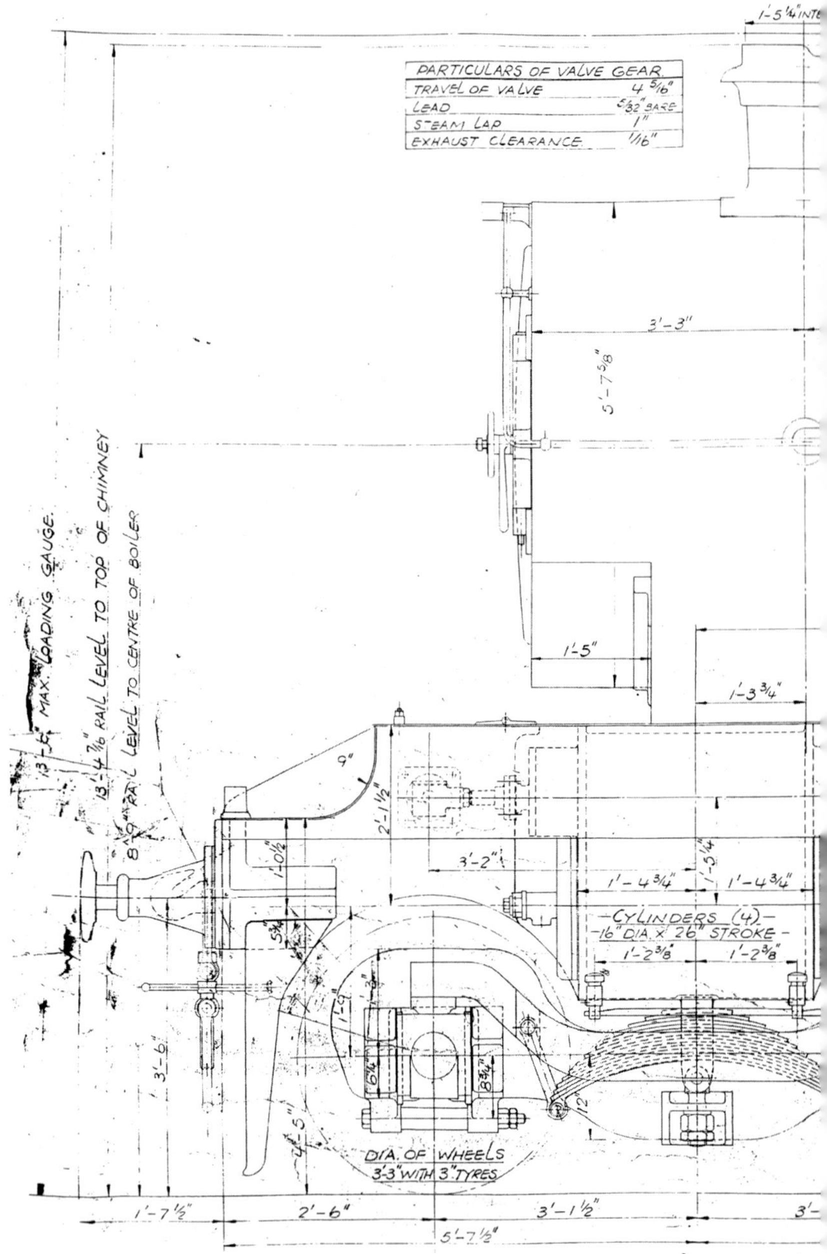

Claughton General Arrangement drawing. The side elevation shows a section on the centre line of the locomotive showing sections through the smokebox, boiler and firebox. Also shown are the cylinders, slidebars and inside valve gear. At the rear end under the cab are the brake cylinder and vacuum reservoir. In the plan view, which is a section from the boiler centre line looking down, it shows the cylinders, motion, coupling rods profile, firebox and frame arrangement.

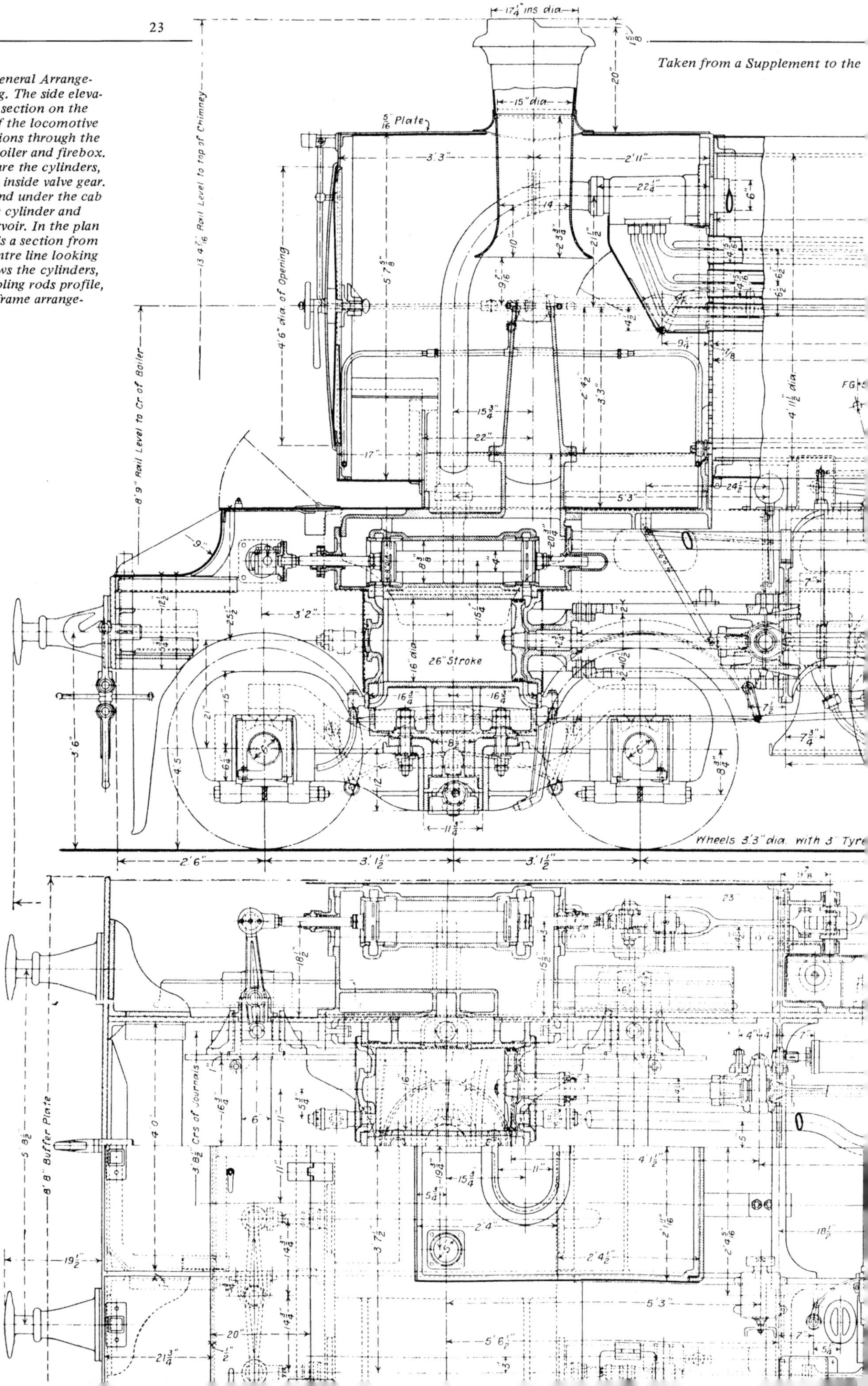

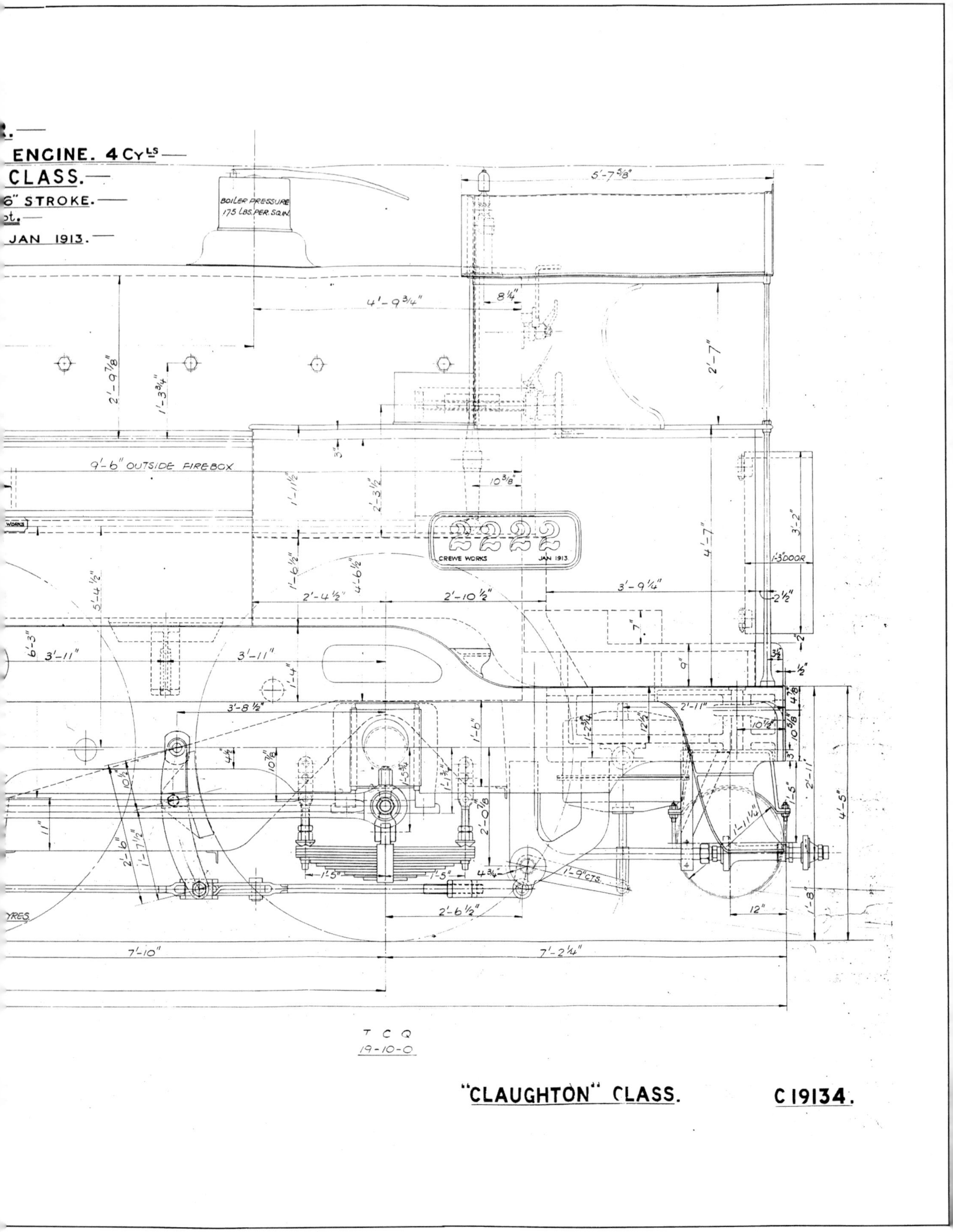
ENGINE. 4 CYLS
CLASS.
6" STROKE.
JAN 1913.
BOILER PRESSURE 175 LBS. PER SQ.IN.
9'-6" OUTSIDE FIREBOX
2222
CREWE WORKS JAN 1913
1'-3" DOOR
T C Q
19-10-0
"CLAUGHTON" CLASS.
C 19134.
5'-7 5/8"
4'-9 3/4"
8 1/4"
2'-7"
2'-9 7/8"
1'-3 3/4"
3"
1'-11 1/2"
2'-3 1/2"
10 3/8"
4'-7"
3'-2"
1'-6 1/2"
4'-6 1/2"
5'-4 1/2"
2'-4 1/2"
2'-10 1/2"
3'-9 1/4"
2 1/2"
7"
2"
6'-3"
3'-11"
3'-11"
1'-4"
9"
3 1/2"
1/2"
3'-8 1/2"
1'-6"
2'-11"
12 1/2"
1'-2 3/4"
10 1/2"
10 5/8"
4 7/8"
3"
4 1/2"
10 7/8"
1'-5 3/4"
1'-1 3/4"
2'-0 7/8"
1'-5"
2'-11"
4'-5"
1'-11 1/4"
11"
2'-6"
1'-7 1/2"
10 1/2"
1'-5"
1'-5"
4 3/4"
1'-9" CTS.
2'-6 1/2"
12"
1'-8"
7'-10"
7'-2 1/4"

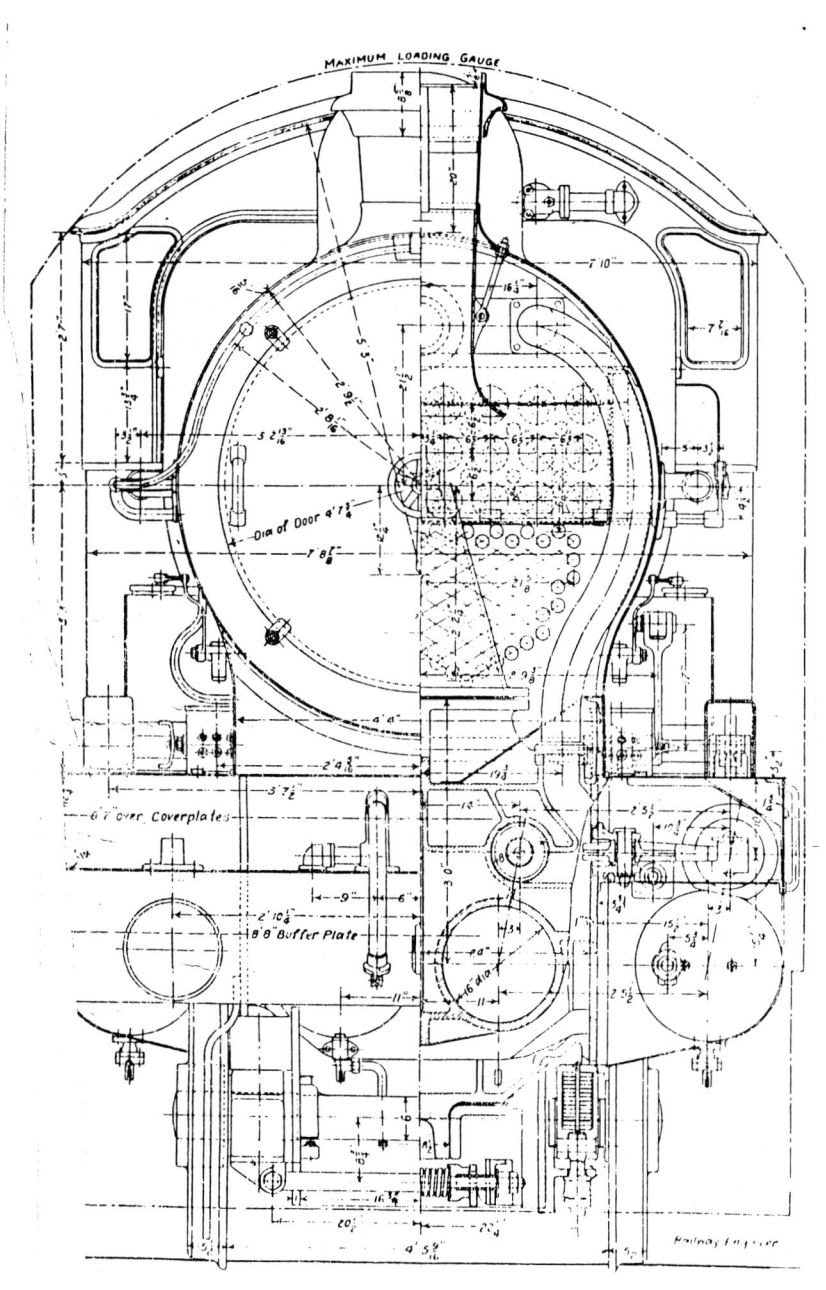

See also page 22.

During the early years of the grouping there was a considerable delay in renumbering many ex-L&NWR locomotives and although the sheds were issued with a document that gave the old and new numbers, the delay was clearly inconvenient. As a result, a number of engines were renumbered by simply removing the old L&NWR number, carried on a cabside numberplate, and replacing it with the new LMS number painted in the style used by the L&NWR for its numbers in what appears to have been white paint. At the same time the new LMS power classification was applied. One example of this approach can be seen in this picture of LMS No. 6019, originally L&NWR No. 180 Llewellyn *which was renumbered in April 1926.*
G. W. SHOTT

O.S. Nock, who refers to these tests in his book, *The Midland Compounds* (David & Charles 1964). From what he said it is clear that Nock was biased in favour of the Claughtons and did not paint an accurate picture. The conclusion of the reports states: 'From the foregoing results, the Compound engine gave the best engine performance generally and for economy in coal and water. The 'Claughton' engine proves itself to be very free running engine, but it has a heavy coal and water consumption and has, also, a very poor steaming boiler'. In truth, a Midland Compound was not big enough for the heaviest trains. The Claughtons, despite being free-running locomotives, were heavy on coal and could be accused of poor steaming, but, had the true cause been known at the time, the class may have taken a different course through history.

The first LMS Locomotive Building Programme was described in Rolling Stock Committee minute 129 dated 29th November 1923 as Winter 1923/24. It was introduced to the meeting by the Chief Mechanical Engineer who said that it had already been submitted to and approved by the Traffic Committee. The main emphasis was on a new design of 2–8–0 freight locomotive, which in the event did not materialise. A total of 150 locomotives was to be built, but the only passenger locomotives were 20 4–4–0 Superheated Passenger Compounds. The Rolling Stock Committee was restructured in 1924 and became the Locomotive and Electrical Committee and on the 30th April George Hughes, the Chief Mechanical and Electrical Engineer, reported how, following the amalgamation of the L&NWR and L&YR, he appointed a committee with a view to standardising and co-ordinating the design of locomotive and workshop practice.

He continued by saying that a new committee consisting of the Mechanical Engineers of the group, with Sir Henry Fowler as Chairman, had been formed on the completion of the larger amalgamation. It would appear they had looked at a number of issues including standard parts and their first recommendation was the use of limit gauges to be adopted by all the Locomotive Shops in the group in order to ensure that parts made in one could be correctly assembled in another. The 2–8–0s proposed at this time were not built because the Chief Engineer would not accept the design, but the Committee minutes make it clear that all new construction was proposed and approved at each level of management before construction took place.

In the meantime, for mainline express passenger work, Hughes was planning his 4–6–2 locomotive and the LMS continued to build Compounds for general use throughout the system. Crewe Works was somewhat busy with its ongoing modernisation and re-organisation, so for this reason many ex-L&NWR locomotives were not being renumbered or repainted into LMS livery quite as fast as they should have been. During 1923 and 1924 reasonable progress had been made, once the initial policy decisions had been taken, but from 1925 the scheme tailed off and later provoked an almost impromptu renumbering at sheds and elsewhere by removing plates and stencilling the new numbers in their place. The Claughtons tended to receive LMS markings on black livery without much resort to the stencil. One notable exception was red-painted No. 5900, which took part in the Stockton & Darlington Railway Centenary celebrations in 1925. On 20th April 1925 George Hughes submitted his resignation with effect from 15th November, by which time he would have had 43 years service. On 27th July Sir Henry Fowler was appointed to succeed him at £4,500 per annum. This marked the beginning of the decline of importance of Horwich and the LMS minutes make it clear that the rationalisation and standardisation that was underway would see Crewe and Derby as the major locomotive works in England with Crewe the most important.

Although the surviving records are not complete, it is clear that Derby was involved with improving the Claughtons. Dated 21st December 1925, Order No. 6581 was headed 'Tests on a Claughton Engine'. Sheet 1 of this order referred to work to be done in connection with the modifications to the ashpan, firebar arrangement and brick arch arrangement of a Claughton engine for test purposes. The order continued by saying that a Claughton engine would be brought to Derby shortly and that full particulars of the alterations would be issued in due course. We have not been able to find a copy of sheet 2, but sheet 3, dated 29th July 1926, refers to tests on 'Claughton' engine No. 1093 and begins: 'Further to Sheet No. 2 of this order dated 30th March, please put your work in hand in connection with taking the boiler out of the above engine and fitting new tubes plates with the tubes as shown on RS–587 (this is the number of the drawing to be used). 125 steel boiler tubes 15ft 2⅞ inch × 2⅛ inch × 1⅞ inch have been specially ordered, and a new steel smokebox, a new copper firebox tube plate with copper ends have been obtained from Crewe for this work. These are now in the stores and should be requisitioned when required'. Although these Derby orders throw some light on efforts being made to improve the Claughtons, we have not been able to find any Crewe records.

Further trials took place. Claughton No. 30 *Thalaba*, a Dreadnought 4–6–0, a Prince of Wales 4–6–0 and a standard Compound 4–4–0 were compared between Preston and Carlisle in May 1925. This time the Claughton was in good condition. The two Class 5 4–6–0s ran comparable tests, as did the two Class 4 locomotives. The Claughton was driven with skill and common sense and as a result bettered the Compound on coal consumption in relation to work done. The Dreadnought was driven enthusiastically, much to the detriment of its coal consumption, but the moment of triumph for the Compounds came during the ascent of Grayrigg Bank when No. 1065 put up such a good performance over the best L&NWR 4–6–0 timings.

Derby must have been pleased that the Compound had done so well – it fitted in with their operating policy of small but frequent trains – but it appeared that with the Claughton in good condition, the LMS had a very good locomotive which was not so excessive on coal consumption and which had a greater power output than a Compound. The sad fact was that on everyday running, the Claughtons were generally not showing such good performances, which appeared to be due to indifferent detail design. Costs were rising and economies were needed. After Sir Josiah Stamp took office as President of the Executive in January 1926, he began an exercise of examining the costs at all levels of running the LMS. He was an economist and overall policy decisions moved towards first establishing the costs and then seeing what could be done about reducing them. One of us remembers that as a young railwayman c1948, the name Stamp was associated with cost savings, or, as it was described, 'cutting out jobs'. Unfortunately, in many areas the LMS was not as efficient as it could be and 1929 was to be the Company's peak year for generating income until the Second World War distorted the figures. One of the projects Stamp instigated was to evaluate locomotive costs and the Engine History Cards were the result. Although the first cost evaluation of the locomotive stock does not appear to have survived, later comparisons have and some information has been published in *LMS Journal*.

The true message appears to have been lost on the LMS at the time – that it was neither Compound 4–4–0s nor Claughton 4–6–0s that were now needed, but modern and efficient Pacifics. We think that we can summarise the position by quoting from page 387, 'British Locomotive Practice and Performance' in the November 1926 edition of the *Railway Magazine*. This was a regular monthly feature, which debated and recorded current locomotive practice. Although Cecil J. Allen did not give the name of the correspondent, the tone suggested that he was a railwayman with considerable experience of the subject. This is what Allen said:

> 'First of all, in regard to the general LMS locomotive question, he says it has never been the ultimate intention to replace either the 'Claughtons' or the Class 8 Horwich 4–6–0 engines with 4–4–0 Midland Compounds. The position simply is that large numbers of 4–2–2 [we think this should be 4–4–0 and that it was an error in the article] and 2–4–0 engines have been scrapped all over the system. New express engines have been built, and tests have proved that the compounds are *by far* the most economical passenger engines on the system, and that there is very little difference between their maximum efforts and those of the 4–6–0 'Claughtons' and 'Princes,' when all three types are capably handled. Therefore there was every justification for building large numbers of standard compounds, *provided* that the problem of building a really adequate 'big' engine was tackled at the same time. This is where the LMS failed. The compound programme has been wholly commendable, but these engines have been prejudiced because they have been tacitly regarded as the *whole* solution of the problem.'

Unfortunately, we do not know who the railway officer was who wrote this letter, but Allen goes on to say that he has logs of runs to prove what the LMS Standard Compound could do and refers to the method of driving. In his regular series he had frequently compared driving methods and the skill of the men involved. Of ex-L&NWR men, after describing a particularly good run, Allen said, 'Such work as this few of the L&NWR drivers seem to get out of their engines', but elsewhere he is complimentary and the November 1926 edition of his regular feature, 'British Locomotive Practice and Performance', contains a summary of his discussions with ex-L&NWR drivers which sets out his views rather well. He said 'I think the position is now rapidly changing, and I have been told by L&NWR enginemen that the 'Crimson Ramblers' [the nickname for the Compounds at this time], though still unpopular with those drivers who are too conservatively-

4-6-0-TYPE LOCOMOTIVE WITH BEARDMORE-CAPROTTI VALVE GEAR; L.M.S. RAILWAY.

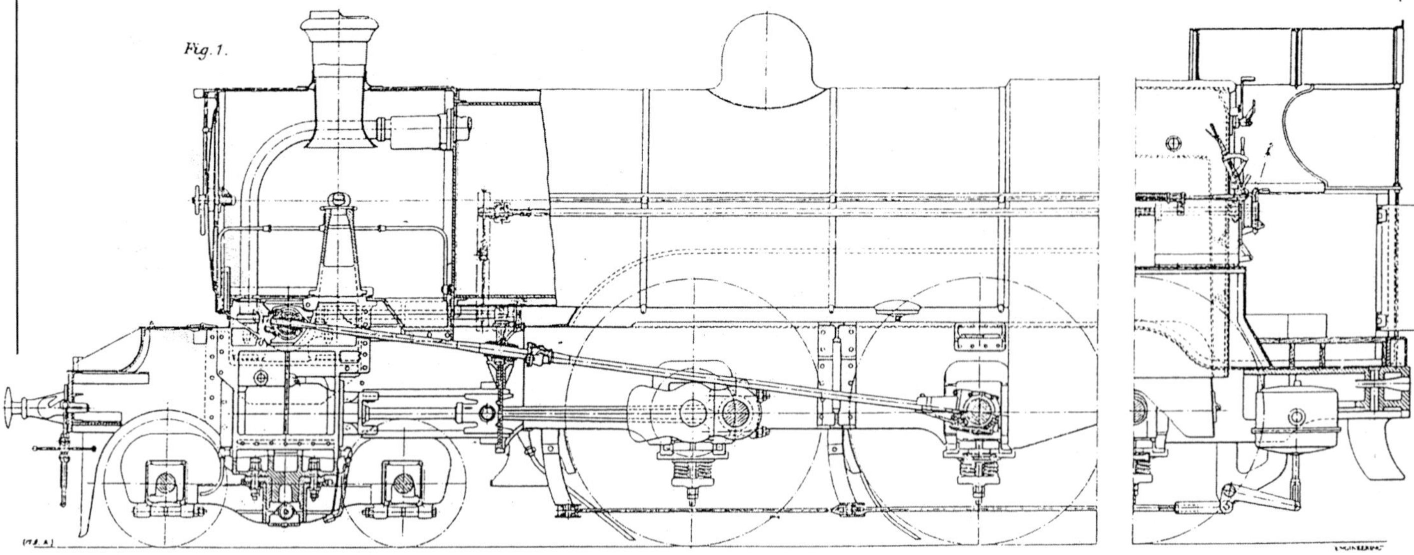

Fig. 1.

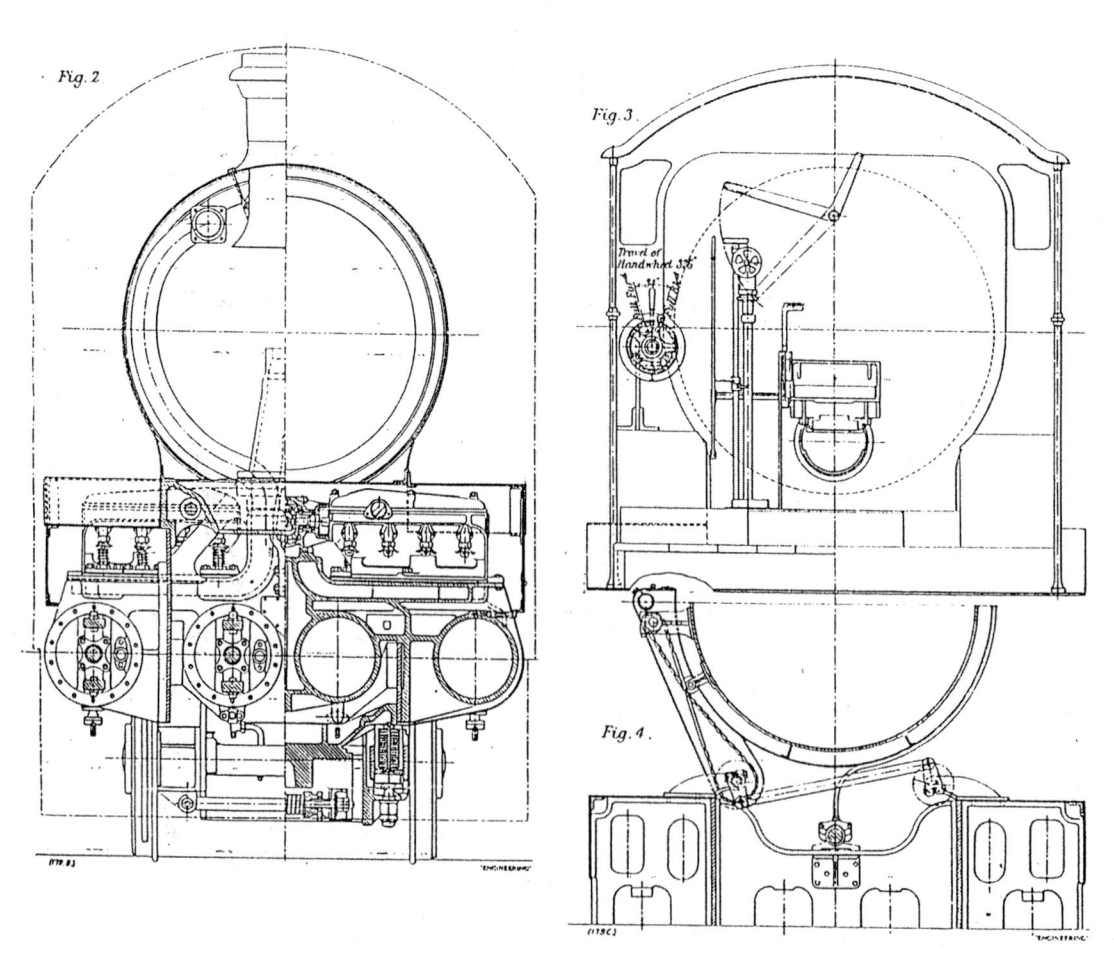

Fig. 2.

Fig. 3.

Fig. 4.

The drawings and notes on this page are taken from the 2nd September 1927 edition of Engineering, which summarised the principal features of the Beardmore Caprotti valve gear as follows: 'The valves are of the double-beat, double-admission poppet type, and four of them are fitted to each cylinder. These four valves are operated by three cams, two of which control the opening and closing of the two steam valves, and the third the opening and closing of the exhaust valves. The camshaft itself is driven from the driving axle and at the same speed. The timing of the valve, relative to the crank position, is varied through the medium of a quick pitch screw cut on the camshaft. This screw engages with scrolls, the endwise motion of which are derived from the reversing shaft or control lever, thus changing the angular position of the cams. This enables the cut-off to be varied through wide limits, without at the same time sacrificing the advantages of constant admission and constant lead. In fact, down to 25 per cent cut-off the steam valves are fully open, a condition which is, obviously, very different from those obtaining when the usual link gear, operating D or piston-slide valves, is employed. Moreover, the compression and exhaust phases are constant on all notches, making it possible to bring the end compression very near to the admission pressure at all speeds.'

THE L&NWR CLAUGHTONS

minded to adapt themselves to the new type, are undoubtedly the fastest engines ever known on L&NWR metals.'

Many trains on the West Coast route were double-headed and there was a locomotive shortage, albeit unnecessary, as a result. There is some evidence to show that competition for Anglo–Scottish business was growing and, with increasing numbers of Gresley Pacifics becoming available, the train services on the East Coast route were improving slightly. Henry Fowler realised the need for a bigger locomotive – he had designed a 4–6–0 compound locomotive, but even this perished in the 'small locomotive policy'. It was also a time of deteriorating economic conditions nationally and internationally as the post-war boom came to an end and the world started to slide into depression. Economy became a key word everywhere and no longer could the old economic tolerances be continued – what was good in 1913 or even 1920 was no longer so. Classes such as the Claughtons and Dreadnoughts started to show in unfavourable lights, particularly when they had accrued some mileage. 1926 was a very troubled year, and not only for the LMS – there was a general strike, which was followed by a coal strike that continued into the winter of 1926/7. The repercussions of the general strike resulted in the removal of the temporary maximum loads hauled and the coal strike led to imported coal of dubious quality and the limited introduction of oil firing. It also meant that the revenue, which would have accrued from the transport of coal, was not earned and the overall LMS revenues suffered. Before the General Strike the Claughtons could be seen piloted by Dreadnoughts, Compounds and other L&NWR classes, but, after the load limit was waived, it became like old times with a reversion to the L&NWR order Claughtons hauling heavy trains single-handed. Some of the Dreadnoughts and Claughtons had special care and attention to keep services running and were marked with an 'S' on the cabsides, indicating 'special' condition. The term 'special' really meant 'good' because an ex-works locomotive really would be in good condition. As a locomotive's mileage increased, it would lose the 'S' until it went into the works again and re-emerged in good condition again.

Several changes occurred with the Claughtons in 1926. The first, which we will discuss, was the fitting of Caprotti valve gear. Beames had remained at Crewe and was responsible for the works. He had not been idle and had shown interest and concern about possible improvements to the Claughtons, particularly with regard to their high coal consumption when some time out of the works. Arturo Caprotti, an Italian engineer, had presented a paper on his valve gear in 1924 that caught the attention of engineers, including Beames. It would probably be convenient to tell the story of what happened by quoting the appropriate minute. Set out below is Locomotive and Electrical Committee Minute 222, dated 27th January 1926.

Fitting of Claughton engine with Caprotti Valve gear for trial purposes
The Chief Mechanical Engineer reported that Messrs. Sir William Beardmore & Co. Ltd. had called attention to the advantages of the Caprotti Valve Gear which was being extensively used in Italy, the arrangement being one in which "Poppet" valves are operated by means of a cam allowing the valves to open and close rapidly at varying cut-offs and at exhaust, and Mr. Beames, who had visited Italy, was satisfied not only with the working of the valve, but also with the question of the durability and wear of the mechanism. He stated that Messrs. Beardmore & Co. guaranteed a 10% saving in coal consumption as compared with engines working with the Walschaert gear, and in the event of such economy not materialising the firm would, if required, take back the gear, and reimburse the Company with the cost of the same and all costs incurred in fitting the gear.

He therefore recommended that the new gear be fitted for trial purposes to one of the Company's Claughton engines at a total cost of approximately £1,200 including fitting but exclusive of freight, insurance and customs charges, which cost, however, in this instance was in excess of what would be incurred if the valve gear were supplied to a new class of engine, owing to it including certain alterations to the cylinders, etc. Mr. Beames stated that he had received every facility for inspecting the new gear, not only in the workshops where they were manufactured, but also in actual use on the Italian State Railways. He had been informed that the gears were most satisfactory over a period of three years, and he had inspected the engine and gear after practical running tests, and he anticipated that inasmuch as the use of the gears would eliminate a large amount of shed repair work, there would be an additional saving under this head equal to the savings in fuel. He understood that the Italian State Railways were at the present time fitting an additional 20 engines with the gear, and were also making financial arrangements for the supply of a further 70.

So far as the arrangements with this Company were concerned: it was proposed that the firm should supply the boxes containing the gear and that the Company themselves should make at Crewe the whole of the drive and cylinder, the gear boxes being supplied to the Company at a cost of £350, plus customs, insurance and freight, and the pattern at £200. The royalty would be £150 per set for a four-cylinder engine and £100 per set for a two-cylinder engine, but arrangements had been made for the royalty on the first set for a "Claughton" engine and on the first set for a two-cylinder engine to be waived, and one-half royalty only charged on the first ten gears supplied.

Sir Henry Fowler explained that on the last occasion that Messrs. Beardmore & Co. tendered for engines they had included an amount of £350 as an extra for the Caprotti Gear, so that if the Company decided to adopt this device to any extent, he thought the price would be materially less than that which had been quoted for a small supply for experimental purposes.

Approved, and Ordered, that the Board be recommended to sanction an expenditure of approximately £1,200.

Although not really part of the story of what happened, we should record a further Minute No. 691 that was dated 24th October 1928, which authorised the fitting of five Claughtons with Lentz Poppet Valve Gear. The Chief Mechanical Engineer reported that 'in view of the fuel economy which had been obtained with the Caprotti Valve Gear fitted to the Claughton engines, he considered that experience should also be gained with the Lentz Valve Gear, which was marketed by Lentz Patents Limited, and for which a saving in fuel of 10% was claimed. He, therefore, recommended that five Claughton engines be fitted with the gear at a total estimated cost of £5,696, three of the engines being provided with Lentz rotary cam poppet valve gear and two with Lentz gear worked by the existing valve motion. Approved in view of the fuel economy obtained with the Caprotti valve gear fitted to the Claughton engine.' However, this minute was cancelled on 29th October 1930 and finally the Lentz trial was made using Horwich moguls.

Although we have included a picture of No. 5908 when rebuilt with Caprotti valve gear below, we felt that we should also include this picture of the locomotive when it was undergoing tests. This picture was taken at Crewe station when the engine was fitted with an indicator shelter. At the time the picture was taken, the locomotive was setting back towards the platform, no doubt prior to working a train. G. W. SHOTT

As we explain in the text, the Caprotti valve gear was fitted to No. 5908, old L&NWR No. 1327 Alfred Fletcher when the locomotive was carrying its original boiler. At the time of the conversion, the engine was painted black and carried the LMS emblem on the cabside. The only evidence of a stock number is the cast-iron smokebox numberplate. This picture clearly shows the altered appearance of a Caprotti valve gear engine at the front end of the locomotive. AUTHORS' COLLECTION

THE L&NWR CLAUGHTONS

The Caprotti system consisted of two cam boxes, one each side of the locomotive, driven by bevel gears off the centre coupled axle by a single shaft. Each cam box drove eight valves associated with the inside and outside cylinders of the respective sides. After adjustment and limited running associated with ironing out any problems, No. 5908 went into traffic between Euston and Carlisle. In January and February 1927 a series of comprehensive comparison trials took place, involving several Claughtons and a Compound 4–4–0. The Claughtons were No. 5908 in its modified condition, one standard engine (fitted with new standard cylinders with Schmidt rings) and one that had been modified with multiple ring pistons and several detail boiler modifications.

The coal consumption of the Caprotti Claughton was the lowest and the standard Claughton some 15% more. The modified locomotive was a considerable improvement on the standard in performance and coal consumption, but the Caprotti had the extra attraction of reduced maintenance costs, despite high first costs of installation. Beames was very impressed by the Caprotti performance and he managed to gain authority to convert a further nine examples while continuing to compare No. 5908 with standard Claughtons. Those so fitted are listed in *Table 3* and we also include them here: Nos. 5908, 5927, 5946, 5948, 5957, 5962, 5975, 6013, 6023 and 6029.

Before moving on, we should record another development in 1926 that concerned the Claughtons; some of them were converted to oil firing. They were not the only class so treated at the time, but it was necessary to keep the services going during the period of the coal miners' strike. *Table 4* lists the locomotives that were converted. This conversion was due to the prolonged coal strike when the imported coal (at best of indifferent quality) caused problems. To alleviate the situation therefore, some conversion to oil-firing was made necessary. The experiment of 1920 was recalled and the conversion to the same Scarab system swung into action for the duration of the strike.

The third event of 1926 that was to affect the future of the Claughtons was the loan of a GWR Castle Class 4–6–0 to the LMS. This came about as a result of the realisation that the present motive power simply would not suffice for the Anglo-Scottish services. It would appear that the arrangement had the backing of J.H. Follows, who was a Vice President of the LMS. We have not been able to find any documentary evidence to support the story that, as a result of the impression *Launceston Castle* made on the LMS authorities during its loan in September, soon afterwards the LMS wished to have fifty locomotives built to the GWR design. Sir Henry Fowler was instructed to make the necessary approach to see if a complete set of Castle drawings could be borrowed by the LMS. If this is correct, we cannot find anything in the Company's minutes. Furthermore, the introduction of these locomotives would have been contrary to the LMS standardisation policy. It would be acceptable to introduce a new class using as many standard parts as possible but it would be an entirely different matter to build what could be considered an alien design. In the absence of firm evidence we are inclined to think this is a 'tall story'.

The story continues with the LMS approaching the Southern Railway to assist by supplying drawings of their own Lord Nelson class 4–6–0 (again we can offer nothing to support this, but it is more believable) and that the drawings were loaned to help with the design of the new 4–6–0, which became known as the Royal Scots. That advantageous detail features could be incorporated into a new LMS design was not a new idea, but expedient at the time.

What is recorded in the LMS Traffic Committee minute 1171 dated 15th December 1926 is reproduced in full.

> 50 Improved 4–6–0 passenger tender locomotives. A limited number of an improved and more powerful engine than the 4–6–0 "Claughton" Locomotive is required for certain main line passenger services, and, as a result of experiments and tests made with a "Castle" class engine loaned by the Great Western Railway, it has been ascertained exactly what is required. It is therefore proposed that 50 locomotives to satisfy these requirements be provided, and that these be purchased from the North British Locomotive Company who promise to commence delivery in 25 weeks, and to complete the order in 35 weeks.

Delivery of the Royal Scots commenced in 1927, a little late, but the result was a fine feat of engineering manufacturing and expertise. Therefore, in 1926 the Claughtons had little over a year left as the front line locomotive type on the West Coast route, and Fowler's proposed 4–6–2 was dropped. Although not entirely pertinent to this part of the story, it is worth pointing out that the appointment of Josiah Stamp as President of the Executive in 1926, was a major step in the unification of all aspects of the LMS. He was an economist and soon the results of his thinking became apparent in various areas. As far as locomotives were concerned, as we have already mentioned, he became well known for his scheme to identify individual locomotive costing, and it could be said that the appointment of William Stanier as CME in 1932 was part of its fulfilment. We are, again, several years ahead of events, but it is necessary to provide a little background in advance, so to speak.

In 1926 many of the Claughtons were still in black livery, bearing various identities and livery combinations. There were crimson lake Claughtons, black Claughtons with red tenders and some with LMS markings hurriedly applied in order to avoid an overlong delay in applying proper transfers following repainting. By December 1926 No. 1914 *Patriot* had been renumbered and became No. 5964, but this locomotive was still painted black, and yet in one way it was appropriate – it was the war memorial locomotive. As a result of some relaxation for axle loading requirements, Beames was able to gain acceptance for his suggestion that a larger boiler might be tried on the Claughtons. This meant that the original idea of Bowen Cooke, way back in 1911, was at last being implemented. Beames was allowed to pursue his ideas and quite how much of detail (if any) of the original boiler was resurrected is not known. Although the Royal Scot order eliminated any great urgency for the project, Beames quietly continued with his ideas. The new boiler was officially designated Class G9S, a Derby classification, but it had been referred to

Here we show another example of temporary renumbering. In this picture, taken at Birmingham New Street during 1927, we see old L&NWR No. 2122 after it had been renumbered by the LMS as No. 5956. The cabside number plate had been removed and the new LMS number painted where the cast numberplate had been. No. 5956 was built in September 1917 and probably never ran in lined L&NWR livery; in this picture it was painted black with L&NWR coat of arms on the splasher. The tender, however, had L&NWR lining.
L. W. PERKINS

A number of the small-boiler Claughtons were coupled to ex-ROD tenders for use on the Midland Division where the greater water capacity of the ROD tender helped to compensate for the longer distance between the water troughs on this Division. In order to work over the Midland Division, the original cab had to be modified, or 'cut down' to use the common term for this work. This picture shows No. 6001, old L&NWR number 23, with its altered cab. The work is recorded as being carried out in April 1928, which was probably the date the locomotive was coupled to the ROD tender. No. 6001 was one of four Claughtons, two with their original boilers and two with large boilers that were fitted with Kylala blast pipes for steaming and coal consumption tests. Photographed at Crewe in 1931.
AUTHORS' COLLECTION

As a result of the good impression gained from the tests with Caprotti engines, approval to convert additional engines was given and No. 5975, old L&NWR No. 12 Talisman, *was one of them. Built in April 1920, it was rebuilt with a large boiler, cab altered to the Midland structure gauge, and Caprotti valve gear in June 1928.*
AUTHORS' COLLECTION

at Crewe as the 'Scheme 3 Claughton' boiler. It proved to be a highly successful design and with it the boiler pressure was raised from the 175 lb. inch. to 200 lb. inch. It was pitched higher than previously to allow more room for better access to the rear coupled wheel axle boxes and a better ash pan. It also had larger firetubes which were well spaced and this gave improved steaming capabilities. The chimney and dome were of somewhat squat appearance when compared with the original, but was necessary to avoid fouling the loading gauge. The man who drew up Beames's G9S boiler scheme at Crewe was Jack Francis. Later he was transferred to Derby and drew up some of the Derby proposals to further improve the Claughton design. Most favoured was the G9S boiler mounted on the original frame (suitably modified), with three cylinders and divided drive. There was to be a new cab and raised platform, but the original Claughton wheels were to be retained. Interestingly, there was much Royal Scot influence to be found, as the new design was formulated during 1929/30, including the motion.

The first locomotive to appear in the new guise was No. 5999 *Vindictive* in April 1928, quickly followed by another nineteen in the same year, as detailed in *Table 3*. Curiously, some of these emerged from Crewe still retaining the black livery. All ten Caprotti Claughtons received the new boilers, some concurrently with the new valve gear, so there was scope for comparison between the two types of valve gear. The comparison was soon made; all were the subject of much scrutiny and observation from 1928 onwards by inspectors representing the CME's Department. Observation finally ceased in 1931. Additionally, two of the rebuilds (5980 and 5975) and two of the original Claughtons (5912 and 6001) were fitted experimentally with Kylala blast pipes, but comparison tests between each type and also 6001, fitted with and without it, proved that steaming was better but at the price of increased coal consumption. There the matter rested.

The new boilers were an undoubted success and the rebuilt locomotives retaining Walschaerts valve gear were allocated to Preston shed for working the Scottish expresses from Liverpool and Manchester, replacing some of the Dreadnought 4-6-0s, whereas those with Caprotti valve gear went to Longsight and Holyhead for working the Euston to Manchester and 'Irish Mail' expresses respectively. They were treated like well-groomed horses by all three sheds and were kept in top condition. The LMS decided to classify these locomotives 5X, being between 5 and 6 on the power classification scale.

During 1927, as the Royal Scots were being built, preparations were made to publicise a new phase in the West Coast services. The 10 a.m. departure from Euston for Glasgow had for over seventy years never boasted an official name, but that was now to change. The train was to be named 'The Royal Scot' as from the start of the summer timetable of 1927. The first locomotive due from the North British Locomotive Company was due to be named *Royal Scot* and from it the official class name was born. Like the LNER with its *Flying Scotsman* locomotive and train, the LMS was able to reply. The publicity value was considerable and it was hoped that the first few locomotives would be delivered in time, but alas, there was some delay. The inaugural run of the named train was on 11th July 1927. Claughton No. 5934 worked this train, but normal power for the 'Royal Scot' train during that summer was a Claughton piloted by a George the Fifth or a superheated Precursor, on the nonstop run from Euston to Carnforth. Thereon a pair of Compounds would take over. At 417 tons with the prevailing schedules, double heading was almost ridiculous; in years gone by the L&NWR would have had a single Claughton in good condition on a better and quicker schedule. Furthermore, the L&NWR would not have allowed the Claughton haulage to stop at Carnforth, but clearly there was a reason. Unfortunately, we have not found any documents to explain why!

Although we have used two other pictures of No. 5908, we include this one in order to make the point about locomotive identity. The number should have been on the tender, but it was not; so the question arises, had the tender been changed? From the view at page 34 we know there was a smokebox door numberplate, but it cannot be seen on this broadside view. This helps to explain why, under the old Midland system whereby the tender carried the same number as the locomotive, when both units were in the works, the tender was set aside to wait for the locomotive. Usually the locomotive took longer to go through the shops than the tender. However, on the old L&NWR the practice was to use the first suitable tender available when the locomotive left the works. This helps to explain why there was a need to purchase surplus ROD tenders during the mid-1920s, a subject that we explore in greater detail in the text. Finally, note the large 'S' at the top of the cab side. This was used to identify locomotives that were in good condition and to be used on the most demanding jobs.
AUTHORS' COLLECTION

When this picture of Patriot was taken, the 'War Memorial' engine No. 1914 had been repainted and was now in LMS crimson lake, carrying its allocated stock number 5964. In 1930 the cab was altered to conform to the Midland structure gauge and the original L&NWR tender replaced by a ROD tender as seen here.
P. RANSOME-WALLIS

THE L&NWR CLAUGHTONS

In view of our references to the new Royal Scot class of 4–6–0, we felt that we must include a picture of a 'replacement for the Claughton class'. There can be little doubt that the Royal Scots were magnificent-looking locomotives that were improved when they received 4000 gallon Stanier tenders, but although they were better from an operating standpoint when they were equipped with smoke deflectors, we feel they lost something in appearance. This picture was taken at Oxenholme in May 1928 and shows No. 6103 Royal Scots Fusilier *on an Up Aberdeen to London Euston express.*
AUTHORS' COLLECTION

Regardless of which boiler was carried, very few Claughtons were painted in the post-1927 livery style with 10in numbers. Writing in An Illustrated Livery of LMS Locomotives Vol. 2, *the authors draw attention to this picture of 5999 but were unable to confirm if it ran in traffic with this livery, but were able to confirm that it did receive 14in numbers when painted crimson lake. We now think that it did carry 10in numbers when it ran in revenue service and have included this works grey picture because it does provide a very good example of the lining style applied to a large boiler Claughton when it was painted red.*

The first new locomotive, No. 6100 *Royal Scot* was despatched from the North British Queen's Park Works on 14th July 1927, followed by 6101/2 on 11th August. On 11th August also, Hyde Park Works despatched its first pair of locomotives, Nos. 6125/6. Both works continued deliveries until mid-November when the order for fifty locomotives was completed. The first Royal Scot locomotive to haul the Royal Scot train is believed to have been No. 6127, just ex-works, in late August. On 26th September, amid the glare of publicity, No. 6100 *Royal Scot* led the new regular 4–6–0 service and enabled the train to be run non-stop from Euston as far north as Carlisle, from that day onward. The immediate effect of fifty Royal Scots suddenly appearing on the scene was to relegate the Claughtons to second-line duties, but that is not to suggest that all the class disappeared from main-line duties. The improvement in loadings now available was worth some comparison. A Royal Scot was allowed to haul 450 tons unassisted from Euston to Carnforth, whereas for a Claughton it was 390 tons. Between Carnforth and Carlisle it was 420 tons and 320 tons respectively; and north of Carlisle 330 and 290 tons, not that many Claughtons had worked that far north. In terms of additional carriages in a train a corridor coach was around 30 tons tare weight so the increase was generally between two and three coaches.

On the West Coast route, the Claughtons were allocated in selected batches to those duties for which Royal Scots

The last survivor of the Claughton class was No. 6004, the locomotive spending its final years working freight trains. This undated picture was taken when it was still employed on top-link passenger work and is seen here at the head of an express passenger train carrying a 2C Northampton shed plate.
AUTHORS' COLLECTION

As we have said, the final years of the last survivor, No. 6004, were spent generally working freight trains and this undated picture shows the locomotive carrying a 1A Willesden shed plate, with a 'Maltese Cross' express freight train. Commonly referred to as 'Maltese', this class of train should have had the four wagons fitted with automatic vacuum brakes coupled to the engine. This additional braking power enabled the train to be booked to run at a higher speed than other non-fitted freight trains.
AUTHORS' COLLECTION

THE L&NWR CLAUGHTONS

were not usually available. These were the Euston–Liverpool and Euston–Manchester trains plus the Irish mail trains from Euston to Holyhead and return. Also included was the 'Midday Scot', as the much improved and publicised 'Corridor' had officially become, from Euston to Glasgow. The term 'Corridor' had been fondly bestowed upon the train decades earlier when corridor stock had been introduced. Inevitably some Claughtons moved away from the Western Division and it was to the Midland Division that they went. One of the first to go was No. 6025. Leeds (Holbeck) shed was its destination, where it was joined by 5971/77/78/84/6001/5, a total of seven locomotives. Ex-Midland Carlisle (Durranhill) shed received six; Nos. 5900/23/32/44/49/60 and two others (5973/4) also went to the Midland Division, we believe to Kentish Town, London. Before they were transferred, they had their cabs cut down to conform to the Midland loading gauge, and some, if not all, were coupled to ex-ROD, GCR Robinson-design six-wheeled tenders of six-tons/3800 gallons capacity (originally 4000 gallons).

These tenders, fifty-five in number (of which twenty-two were allocated to the Claughtons), were purchased from the Government by the LMS as war surplus stock during 1927.

A number of Claughtons were transferred to the Midland Division and we have included four pictures of these engines at work, Nos. 5900, 5923, 5932 and 6009. In order to work on this division, it was necessary for the cab profile to be altered so that the locomotive would pass under the Midland structure gauge and generally they were coupled to ROD tenders, which carried more water than the original L&NWR tender. No. 5900 Sir Gilbert Claughton was photographed at No. 2 platform Leicester on 4th August 1934 when working the Thames Clyde express. At the time, the locomotive was stationed at Durran Hill.
AUTHORS' COLLECTION

This picture of No. 5923 Sir Guy Calthrop was taken at Nottingham on 1st September 1934. The locomotive is seen here with express passenger headlamps but, from what can be seen of the train, it was not standing at a platform. We believe that the locomotive would replace the engine of an incoming train and that the carriages were 'strengtheners' or 'through coaches'.
G. BARLOW

Old L&NWR No. 155 now running as LMS No. 5932 Sir Thomas Williams photographed at Steeton & Silsden at the head of an express passenger train.
AUTHORS' COLLECTION

This rear three-quarters view of No. 6009 provides a good view of the large ROD tender that was an essential requirement to enable the Claughtons to work on the Midland Division. This picture was taken at Kentish Town on 18th May 1932. These pictures all show Claughtons at work on the main line from London to Carlisle, but at page 56 we also show a picture of No. 5984 at Saltley, which suggests that Claughtons did work on the West line from Derby to Bristol.
H. C. CASSERLEY

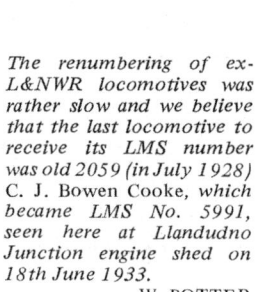

THE L&NWR CLAUGHTONS

The renumbering of ex-L&NWR locomotives was rather slow and we believe that the last locomotive to receive its LMS number was old 2059 (in July 1928) C. J. Bowen Cooke, which became LMS No. 5991, seen here at Llandudno Junction engine shed on 18th June 1933.
W. POTTER

Traffic Committee minute dated 23rd February 1927 authorised the purchase of 75 Government locomotives. It appears there was a severe shortage of tenders on the Western 'A' Division and at £340 for each 2–8–0 locomotive and tender, it made sense to purchase 75 locomotives. At the time the minute was written, it was intended to repair and use 20 locomotives, which would mean there would be 55 tenders available for use with ex-L&NWR locomotives and the Government locomotives could be sold for scrap after the serviceable parts had been recovered. The estimated cost of making the tender suitable for use on the LMS was £400 per tender, so it was an advantageous deal. Another useful factor was the larger water capacity when compared with the normal Claughton tenders. The L&NWR was well-equipped with water troughs, spaced at closer intervals than those on the Midland, so the extra 800 gallons water capacity was a sensible arrangement and avoided the need for extra stops to take on water when working express passenger trains. All the Claughtons transferred to the Midland Division were generally used between Carlisle and London St. Pancras, displacing Compounds and virtually eliminating double-heading on the Settle and Carlisle route. It appears that because of weight restrictions, the Claughtons did not work on the old Midland route through the Peak District. Notes on the Government engines, often described as 'MM' but generally referred to today as 'ROD' tenders, are to be found in *Table 9* and *Appendix 3*.

Previous mention of Sir Josiah Stamp has been made. As an economist, he was soon investigating costs and set about reducing them wherever possible within the LMS against a backdrop of an ever-worsening international financial scene. In the mid-1920s the LMS was spending £3 million annually on locomotive repairs, and following his appointment he wanted to know how it was being spent. His system of individual locomotive costing was extremely penetrating and unearthed many facts which had previously been accepted as normal in better economic climates. In particular, it logged coal and oil consumption, detailed repair costs, mileages and thus provided a reasonably accurate picture of the situation generally. This analysis was both by class and individual locomotive. It soon became clear that it made economic sense to scrap and replace old pregroup designs even if they may not have reached the end of their economic life. For example, if a small class of locomotives could not be fitted with an existing boiler then it was better to withdraw them from service than build more non-standard boilers.

Conversely, newer locomotives must be investigated further if necessary, in order to improve them. What was unacceptable was the rapidly growing appetite of the Royal Scots for coal. When new, a Royal Scot could run from Euston to Carlisle consuming five tons of coal, but after two or so years in service it rose to about nine tons, an increase of 80%. Clearly this could not be allowed. Investigations ensued and by early 1930 the main culprit was identified as steam by-passing the Schmidt-type single-ring piston valves. These wore in service, but were not sufficiently flexible to re-profile and maintain a seal. The problem with the Schmidt type had been realised elsewhere by 1927, but reservations regarding application of replacement types deferred progress.

E.S. Cox was very active in witnessing changes at the time and considered it significant that a breakthrough was made in investigating valves and curing their problems. Although they involved superficially minor changes from short to long lap and from single 'or at most double stiff' wide rings to more numerous flexible narrow rings, arguably they were regarded to be 'amongst the really profound influences which changed steam locomotive performance and efficiency out of all recognition'. The former 'promoted more expansive use of steam, with enhanced freedom of exhaust, while the latter ensured minimum internal steam leakage from steam to

No. 5908 was the locomotive involved in trials to compare Caprotti valve gear with Schmidt type rings. This c.1931 view shows Alfred Fletcher when fitted with straight smoke deflector plates and carrying a 26 Edgehill shed plate.
AUTHORS' COLLECTION

exhaust areas, and sustained this property without marked deterioration for periods of 30 to 40,000 miles between examinations'. The economies gained by using the long-lap valves produced a general saving of 25% in coal per drawbar horsepower hour, 'a good deal more than was claimed by the French engineers for compounding'. Before improvements were made to the Royal Scots in particular, a new locomotive would undertake the 300 miles through run from Euston to Carlisle on five tons of coal but, as we have said, two years later, despite having good valve events, nine tons was common.

The foregoing accelerated remedial work and resulted in No. 6158 being fitted with valve heads each having six plain narrow rings ¼in width, and further testing proved that 30,000 miles could be run before examination, with a reduced deterioration of only 8% instead of the previous 80%. In Cox's own words, 'Not only was this arrangement adopted as standard for future construction, but it was eventually applied retrospectively to almost all of the 'standard' types having a high life expectancy. It was also applied to some of the last of the Claughtons and Hughes' rebuilt 4–6–0s, so that their final days, as they were being taken off the more important services, they both displayed the efficiency of which they were intrinsically capable – but too late to re-establish their true worth. It was rather sad!' In the light of the Stamp-induced economies of the LMS, this was a damning situation, but the LMS tackled the problem sensibly and undoubtedly a watershed had been reached.

After so many years of high coal consumption on other classes fitted with the Schmidt valve, it may be pertinent to wonder why it had lain undiscovered, but it must be realised that the problem could not be recognised easily from the exterior, the valves and cylinders had always appeared to be a tight fit. The cure came in the form of a solid head piston, with six narrow rings on each head of the Ramsbottom type. The effect was an immediate and spectacular success, and in due course thoughts turned to other classes fitted with the Schmidt valve, in particular the ex-L&Y Dreadnoughts and the Claughtons. No. 6001, a standard Claughton, was fitted with the new valves and tested. It was found to have almost identical coal and water consumption figures as those shown on No. 5908, the first Caprotti Claughton. The expenditure on modifications was considerably less than fitting Caprotti valve gear, although maintenance costs were higher. Additionally, it was also discovered that the low position of the firebox foundation ring restricted the air supply into the firebox. E.S.Cox reveals the result of fitting narrow rings for piston valves in a memorandum to S.J. Symes. Dated 7th April 1931, it begins by reviewing the present position and stating 'All new engines are now beginning to be fitted with narrow rings on the piston valves in place of the wide Schmidt type of ring, to reduce the amount of steam which leaks past the valve.' The report continues by noting 'that the saving on the Claughton class by the adoption of the narrow rings in conjunction with the suppression of the Trick port (which derived its name from the German engineer Trick who invented it) and the use of hollow type of valve has given coal savings of up to 30%.'

By 1928 the LMS had decided that a change of livery was desirable. By reducing the number of classes eligible for wearing crimson lake livery, savings could be made and placing the locomotive number on the cabside instead of on the tender, gave greater flexibility if tenders had to be exchanged. This also enabled a distinctive number series for tenders to be introduced at the same time. The ex-L&NWR tenders retained their old company tender numbers – the

The first Claughton to be withdrawn was No. 5971. This was the result of damage sustained in an accident that took place on 12th February 1929 as described in the text. This undated picture shows No. 5971 Croxteth *piloted by another Claughton, which we believe was either No. 5936 or 5956, with a thirteen-coach Down express leaving Rugby.* H. GORDON TIDY

L&NWR numbered their tenders separately from locomotives, but the Midland did not. As a result, the ex-Midland tenders, together with any other unnumbered tenders that became LMS stock at the Grouping and hitherto unnumbered standard LMS tenders, were incorporated into the new scheme, and given what were referred to as Distinctive Tender Numbers. The Claughtons were to retain their crimson lake livery under the revised scheme, although in practice there were still examples running in black livery. Some of these, bearing L&NWR lined black livery (albeit faded), received the revised insignia of cabside numbers and 'LMS' on the tender! The situation was to change within a short space of time and the class took on a reasonably uniform appearance in crimson lake, now that the reorganisation of Crewe Works was completed and painting of locomotives had recommenced. The last Claughton to receive its LMS number was No. 5991 in July 1928, 4½ years after the Grouping.

As a result of accident damage sustained at about midnight on 12th February 1929, the first Claughton to be withdrawn from service was No. 5971. This locomotive was one of those allocated to the Midland Division. It was hauling the 9.30 p.m. sleeping-car express from St. Pancras to Glasgow and running under clear signals, when it collided head on with a Class 4F 0–6–0 No. 4491 at Doe Hill, near Chesterfield. No. 4491 was on a Sheffield to Birmingham freight train,

As we describe in the text, very little of the original engine was used when the first Patriot was built. This picture of No. 5971, in unnamed condition, was taken at Leeds in April 1931, a few months after it emerged from Derby Works coupled to what later became known as an 'old standard 2500 gallon tender'.
AUTHORS' COLLECTION

which had wrongly started from Morton Sidings signal box on the Down line instead of the Up line. As a result of the accident, No. 5971 was found to be beyond economic repair and was withdrawn. As the new decade dawned, the future of the Claughtons still appeared good. From 1927 onwards, the drawing office at Crewe had considered various schemes to improve the Claughtons in detail, some of which did come to fruition. It was ongoing and a train of thought started to become reality after the two Claughtons were involved in accidents; the locomotives concerned were Nos. 5902 and 5971.

Although the Claughtons were ex-L&NWR locomotives mostly working on the Western Division, it would appear that the plans for a 3-cylinder engine came from Derby. The first of two orders was dated 11th October 1928 and referred to the driver's brake valve. The instruction read 'In addition to modifying Claughton piston valves and liners it has been decided to fit improved type of drivers brake valves on two Claughton engines'. The second was dated 6th December 1929; Order No. 7560 was issued by the CME Dept and signed by the Works Superintendent, H. Ivatt. This wording has been reproduced in full and makes interesting reading:

'Two "Claughton" engines to be re-built as a three Cylinder Type (N.W.O. 1813). Two existing "Claughton" engines are to be rebuilt as a three-cylinder type. Particulars of the alterations will be issued from the Drawing Office in due course, but it should be noted that two boilers of the modified type with a working pressure of 200 lbs per square inch will be supplied from Crewe.

'Please put your work in hand as the drawings are issued. These engines will not be included in the new work programme but will go through as repaired engines. The two engines to be rebuilt will be called in when all the material is ready. This work will be dealt with by the Central Order Office and all charges are to be made against this order No.'

Therefore it would appear that the rebuilding was planned during 1929 and the order to proceed issued accordingly. Clearly some time elapsed before all the material was ready and then the unfortunate accidents to Nos. 5971 and 5902 presented the opportunity for the work to take place. Leeds Claughton No. 5902 was involved in a head-on collision on 6th March 1930 at Culgaith, in Westmorland. Again a Class 4F 0–6–0 was involved, this time No. 4009, which had been shunted onto the Down line, in the path of No. 5902. The repair became a rebuild, if that is the correct term. Very little of the original locomotive was to remain as a basis of the rebuild. The wheels, bogie, axleboxes and brake gear were retained, together with a few fittings and it has been stated on several occasions that the frames of 5971 and 5902 were the original Claughton frames modified with a new front section. This is incorrect because the Claughton frames were nine inches shallower and would require a piece of plate about thirty feet long to be welded on to the existing frame. We do not think that frame-welding techniques were advanced as they later became. According to Eric Langridge, in an article in the June 1997 issue of *Steam World*, when the works saw the amount of welding and alterations to be carried out, they did not approve, so new frame plates were made. The original axle box guides were re-used, however. This view was supported and confirmed by the late David Tee, in conversation with one of the authors. On one of his visits to the Locomotive Drawing Office, he was shown the drawing of the new frames. According to John Hooper, the tender first coupled to No. 5971 was 6309, an ROD tender which Claughton 5971 ran with. The Baby Scot ran with this tender for about six weeks.

The driving wheel sets required considerable alteration. The wheels were pressed off the axles and refitted with the cranks set to 120° for the three-cylinder arrangement. The leading and intermediate wheels changed places. The leading set had the crank axle replaced by a plain axle and became the new driving wheels. This was because the bore of the crank pins varied; it was 6 inches in the leading pair and only 5 inches in the other pairs. An eccentric throw driving crank pin with a four-stud fixing for the return crank replaced the original one. This pattern crank pin was used on the remaining Claughtons when requiring new driving crank pins. The intermediate wheels were pressed on to a new crank axle and became the leading wheels. The crank pins were replaced by the flush washer pattern to increase clearance behind the slidebars.

Essentially it was a rebuild that was presented in a way that was most acceptable to the LMS accountants. No.5971 emerged from the works in December 1930 looking every inch the descriptive name, which it and its successors were unofficially bestowed, namely 'Baby Scots'. It was an affectionate title which it appears that LMS authorities sought to discourage, but, like it or not, it was very apt. We will use it in this book.

No.5902 was similarly treated and with 5971 would form the basis of a new class, that officially became known as the 'Patriots', which were later developed as the taper-boiler Jubilees, a class we have described in *Historical Monograph No. 2*. It is worth noting that the boilers dated from 1929, being part of a batch of five built in anticipation of further Claughton re-boilering.

On 7th April, E.S. Cox wrote to S.J. Symes in respect of the use of narrow rings for piston valves. Although this report covered a range of locomotives and therefore much is not relevant to this work, the Claughtons are mentioned and this is what he had to say. 'With the Claughton class the adoption of the narrow ring in conjunction with the suppression of the 'Trick' port and the use of a hollow type of valve has given coal savings of up to 30%'. With the successful rebuilding with the larger boiler and the discovery of the steam leakage problem, one could be forgiven for thinking that the future of the Claughtons as a mainline express locomotive was good, but with the increased cost-consciousness that was being implemented and with many of the Claughtons falling due for new boilers and cylinders, those responsible started to examine the class in detail. The result of these further investigations can be seen from the report dated 17th April 1931, which we have set out below. It has not been edited in any way and makes fascinating reading.

Chief Mechanical Engineer's Office,
Euston Station.
17th April, 1931.

Memorandum to S.J. Symes Esq.

"Claughton" Engines.

I attach herewith a statement giving the results of investigations at sheds into what are the outstanding troubles with these engines. There are three possible lines of action in regard to the remaining unrebuilt engines:-

(1) To retain the engines in their present condition but to deal with each of the defects outlined in the statement on the lines suggested. Whilst no estimate can be given without further investigation as to the cost of this, owing to the number of items involved, it would inevitably be fairly high and when done would not necessarily ensure a trouble-free engine, because the general design is unsatisfactory in a number of ways. For example, the light construction of frames, footplates, cabs and splashers would always cause trouble owing to undue vibration, and the lack of clearance between foundation ring and trailing axleboxes would make it difficult to ensure cool running by any means.

(2) To rebuild the existing engines similar to the 5X class, embodying the recommendations contained in this report. This would undoubtedly result in a more trouble-free engine, but by the time all was done might be nearly as expensive as building a new engine, without having the same expectation of life which a new engine would have.

(3) Scrap the existing engines and replace them by new engines embodying every modern improvement which experience has indicated as being desirable, on the lines of the two 3-cylinder engines Nos. 5902 and 5971.

Summary of present position of unrebuilt engines

The principal faults with the normal "Claughton" engine have been high coal consumption, poor steaming and high maintenance.

The first two items have been greatly improved by the introduction of the hollow piston valve with narrow rings, savings in coal up to 30% having been obtained. All engines are being so fitted as they pass through the shops at a cost of £4,509.

As regards high maintenance, enquiry at the sheds has shewn the following sources of trouble:

Trailing Coupled Boxes
In the last six months of 1930, there were ten times as many cases of hot trailing axles on the "Claughtons" as on the "Royal Scots" for an equal number of engines. The design is such that there is insufficient clearance between the axlebox top and the foundation ring of the firebox, and this factor is a handicap to every proposal for improvement.

Alternative suggestions are:
(1) To improve the present oil pipe by enlarging the hole on the top of the axlebox and by cutting away the splasher where the oil pipe passes over the top of the frame. This is being done experimentally on five engines.

(2) To fit mechanical lubrication.

As there were 60 cases of trailing hot boxes on the "Claughton" engines in the last six months of 1930, it will be seen that this is an expensive item of maintenance, and a really satisfactory improvement can only be obtained by the radical alteration of raising the centre line of the boiler.

Connecting Rods
The outside connecting rods of the marine type with solid bushes frequently run hot due to rubbing of the old type of return crank boss. The maintenance cost per engine per annum of "Claughton" connecting rods is £5 16. 0. as against 12/6d on the "Royal Scots".

A new return crank of the 4-stud type is being fitted as new crankpins are required and 17 engines have been so far fitted. When all the "Claughtons" are fitted, there will be a net yearly saving of £95, allowing for the cost of the conversion.

Two engines have also been fitted with solid ended connecting rods, and similar rods for 8 more engines are in the Crewe stores for engines requiring renewals. While these new rods cut down the cost of maintenance, from the point of view of running hot they save no appreciable time in dismantling for periodical examinations, and in view of their first cost of £91 10.0. per engine, they are not justifiable economically otherwise than as a renewal.

It is proposed that the 4-stud return crank be fitted to all engines as they pass through the shops.

This picture of the L&NWR war memorial engine, whose original number was 1914, was taken at Northampton on 3rd April 1934 by which time the locomotive had been renumbered by the LMS, becoming 5964. Note the cab roof, which was altered in 1930 to enable the locomotive to run under the Midland structure gauge.
L. HANSON

This rather evocative view of the 'running shed yard' has been included to show a typical early 1930s LMS scene with both the old and new order on view. To the right we can see new Patriot No. 5936, which was built in August 1932 and became No. 5507 Royal Tank Corps later. The Claughton to the left had been renumbered but its stock number cannot be seen beneath the grime and dirt.
AUTHORS' COLLECTION

THE L&NWR CLAUGHTONS

Brakes
With the old Crewe type of vacuum brake there is a large amount of iron piping, and owing to vibration, leakage at the joints is continuous. The vacuum pump gland is also a source of trouble. The maintenance cost in wages of the brake gear on a standard "Claughton" is £13 6.0. per engine per annum, as against £5 17.0. in the case of the 5X "Claughtons" having the "Midland" type of ejector on the side of the boiler.

It is suggested that the "Midland" type ejector and drivers valve be fitted to all engines, and that the design of the vacuum pump be examined to reduce the trouble with the gland.

Sanding Gear
The hand sanding gear is a continuous source of trouble, the sand becoming damp and refusing to run, and the sandpipes becoming loose. Maintenance cost in wages at the sheds is £13 6.0. per engine per annum, as against £5 17.0. in the case of 5X "Claughton" fitted with steam sanding. Whilst improvements of a detail nature can be made, conversion of the hand to steam sanding is recommended.

Smokebox Door
Is of weak construction. It warps and draws air in service. A door similar to that on the standard engines with angle ring and dogs is required. Authority has been given for this as new smokebox fronts are required, but very few engines have been dealt with as yet.

Valve Spindles
The present screwed connection between valve spindle and crosshead is unsatisfactory. A scheme has been prepared to replace this by a cottered connection at a total cost of £1,515, or £350 if only done as the old parts wear out and require renewal, but sanction has not yet been obtained.

Cabs and Splashers
Are continually working loose due to inadequate bolting on to frame and platform. This is largely a matter of poor design in the first place, the construction not being robust enough to stand up to the vibration in running. In any scheme for rebuilding the engines, the splashers should be done away with and a new cab fitted.

Engines riding roughly
Is one of the most constantly recurring items reported by the drivers. The springs seem to be weak and allow the engines to get down in the horns at the back end. These springs are of the double coil type and breakages are frequent. It is interesting to note that the trailing axles had collars and laminated bearing springs in the original design in 1913, but both were abandoned within the next two years due to trouble experienced.

Buffers
The Crewe type of buffer is weak in the body casting, and breakages are frequent. The substitution of standard buffers is desirable.

E.S.Cox.

Before considering the Claughtons further, we think that another report, written by E.S. Cox on 1st December 1932, albeit in advance of where we are with our story, puts the subject of locomotive costs and operating problems into perspective. The searching inquiries, largely originated by Stamp, following his appointment, can be shown by a letter written on 28th June 1932 by Sir Harold Hartley which referred to the fact that the Executive Committee had agreed that the cause of locomotive failures should be analysed to establish the reason. Certain criteria were laid down and in this instance the examination was to be based upon speed and weight of the locomotives to see whether they occur in particular localities or to particular types of engines. In the analysis, slightly over half of the casualties came under 12 of the 41 possible headings and the highest proportion occurred on the Western Division. 25% more of these casualties occurred on passenger than on freight locomotives and this was considered to be due to an element of speed. 28% of the casualties were due to negligence of footplate or shed staff. No definite proportion could be ascribed to different classes of locomotives, but generally earlier and non-standard classes were the most troublesome. The incidence of casualties was not dependant on either the size or weight of locomotives, but principally on their design and the standard of maintenance to which they were subject. Although this was written after the future of the Claughtons had been decided, it is one of the best examples we have to show the Company was questioning all aspects of its locomotive policy during the late 1920s onwards. However, to return to 1931, the following official summary makes interesting reading:

CHIEF MECHANICAL ENGINEER'S DEPARTMENT,
EUSTON.
13th August, 1931.

To. E.J.H.Lemon, Esq.

"CLAUGHTON" ENGINES.

The attached statement gives a summary of repair and fuel costs of the different forms of the above engines at present running. The following notes amplify the figures given:-

(1) Ordinary Claughton
The high repair costs with this class have been found from enquiry at the sheds to be due to the following causes

Hot Boxes
During 1930, 121 hot boxes occurred, and the total cost of these to the Company is estimated at £2,530.

Connecting Rods
These run hot and knock. Maintenance cost in Sheds is over £5 per engine per annum greater than for rods on Royal Scot engines.

Brakes
Leakage at numerous joints in brake piping requires continual attention at Sheds. Cost of this averages £7.10.0. per engine per annum more than similar engines fitted with Standard type brake ejector.

Other causes of high maintenance costs are —
Sanding Gear, Springs frequently breaking, Smokebox, and Cabs and Splashers coming loose.

(2) 5X Walschaerts
It will be seen that apart from the boiler, which is not comparable, the repair costs in shops are less than for the above. Shed running repairs are, however, about the same, and although the smokebox, sanding and brake have been improved, the other sources of trouble remain the same as on the ordinary "Claughton".

The figures for coal consumption are an average of 9 engines over 182,840 miles since they have been fitted with narrow ring piston valves. It will be noticed that the figure almost equals that obtained with the Caprotti engines, thus bearing out the results of the recent Dynamometer Tests.

(3) 5X Caprotti
The shop repair costs per mile are 42% less than with the 5X Walschaert type, but the miles run per annum and between general repairs are both 32% higher in the case of the Caprotti engines.

COMPARISON OF COSTS. CLAUGHTON ENGINES. ORDINARY. 5X CAPROTTI. WALSCHAERT AND 3-CYLINDER.

NOTE.— For the purposes of this comparison, as there is insufficient information available regarding the 3-cylinder rebuilds, the figures for the first 10 "Royal Scots" averaged over 1929 and 1930 have been taken as regards the chassis, and the same figures as the Caprotti engines assumed for the boiler.

Shop Repairs. Heavy and Light.	(1) ORDINARY	(2) 5X WALSCHAERT	(3) 5X CAPROTTI	(4) 5X 3-CYLINDER	NOTES.
Boiler	Figures not available split up under different headings.	2.244	1.258	1.258	(1) Ordinary Claughton (all engines) Repairs - 3 years 1927, 1928, 1929. Coal - 120 weeks to 18th April, 1931.
Superheater		.039	.037	.030	
Frames		.459	.288	.261	
Wheels		.777	.522	.322	(2) 5X Walschaert Repairs - 2 years 1929, 1930. Coal - Average since fitting with narrow ring piston valves.
Motion		1.003	.517	.611
Cylinders		.270	.088	.125
Brakes		.155	.097	.085
Pipework		.096	.067	.060	(3) 5X Caprotti Repairs - 2 years 1929, 1930. Coal - 120 weeks to 18th April, 1931.
Paint		.115	.077	.063
Miscellaneous		.208	.123	.147
TOTAL	5.04	5.366	3.074 X	2.933	(4) 5X 3-cylinder Shop Repairs - Chassis - based on first 10 Scots over 2 years 1929, 1930. Boiler - Assumed same as Caprotti, 2 years 1929, 1930.
Total less Boiler	4.11	3.122	1.816	1.675
24 weeks to 13th June, 1931 Shed Running Repairs	1.90 2.00	1.71 2.035	1.67 2.085	1.22 (actual) 1.793
TOTAL REPAIRS. pence per mile	7.04	7.401	5.159 X	4.726	Shed Repairs - Assumed same as first 10 Scots over 2 years, 1929, 1930. Coal - Actual figures for two engines 5902 and 5971. Mileage - Assumed same as first 10 Scots.
Saving per engine per annum (40,000 miles) compared with ordinary Claughton.	—	No saving.	£313	£386
COAL. 24 weeks to 13th June Lbs. per mile pence per mile	54.39 55.2 4.14	50.99 50.58 4.33	49.49 50.03 4.29	44.27 47.54 4.07	X These figures are very largely influenced by the fact that the Caprotti engines have averaged 32% greater mileage per annum and between general repairs than the 5X Walschaert.
Saving per engine per annum (40,000 miles) compared with ordinary Claughton.		£68	£75	£112
Total saving per engine per annum		£ 68	£ 388	£ 498
Total saving for 20 engines		1,360	7,760	9,960
Average Annual Mileage	37,219	40,729	53,677	54,629
Average Miles between General Repairs.	49,324	48,681	64,659	60,574

Figures shown in red are latest available for 24 weeks up to 13th June, 1931.

This is the statement that formed part of the report dated 13th August 1931 by E. S. Cox, which is reproduced in full on pages 49/51.

THE L&NWR CLAUGHTONS

There seems to be no intrinsic reason connected with the design of the engine why this difference in mileage should obtain, and enquiries at sheds have not brought to light any explanation. It seems to arise mainly from the work on which the engines are employed, the Walschaert engines generally not working such important trains as those handled by the Caprotti.

It will be noted that Shed running repair costs and coal consumption differ very slightly from the Walschaert engines.

(4) 3-Cylinder Rebuilds

Only two of these engines are running and direct comparative figures with the above are not obtainable.

As the chassis part of these engines is almost identical with the "Royal Scots" the repair cost figures for the "Scot" other than the boiler have been taken as representative of what may be expected with these engines. It will be seen that this shows a saving over the Caprotti both in Shop and Shed repairs.

The coal consumption is that actually shown in the Accountant's returns for the two 3-cylinder engines, but over a large class with engines in differing states of repair it is possible this figure might more nearly equal the Caprotti figure.

NOTE

The existing "Claughton" tenders have only got 3,000 gallons capacity and are therefore not suitable for working on the Midland and Northern Divisions where the troughs are spaced more widely apart.

It is therefore desirable that the new engines as rebuilt should have the standard 3,500 gallon tender, and the matter is being looked into as to how far the displaced tenders can be used to make up the present shortage of 3,000 gallon tenders on other types of Crewe engines, particularly the 0–8–0 class.

E.S. Cox.

This report led to the proposal to rebuild the class and again we have reproduced the relevant section of the report by E.S. Cox in full.

Chief Mechanical Engineer's Office,
Euston.
12th October 1931

Memorandum to E.J.H.Lemon, Esq.

Proposed Rebuilding of "Claughton" Engines

In 1929 it was decided to rebuild certain Claughton engines with larger boilers, and that no more boilers of the old type should be built. Twenty engines were dealt with, ten being fitted with new boilers only retaining the old cylinders and motion, and ten with new boilers, new cylinders and Caprotti valve motion.

The cost of maintenance, particularly in the sheds, of the original Claughton engines is very high, and while some improvement has been obtained with the rebuilt engines considerable trouble is still experienced with axleboxes and various other details. Later on two were converted from four to three cylinders and fitted with modern Walschaert valve gear, improvements in brake gear, spring gear and oiling arrangements for the axleboxes, etc.

An investigation, as shown in the attached report, has now been made into the advisability of rebuilding and improving further Claughton engines as they become due for new boilers and cylinders.

The following proposals have been examined:-
(1) Rebuilding with 3 cylinders and Walschaerts Valve gear.
(2) Rebuilding with 3 cylinders and Caprotti Valve gear.
(3) Rebuilding with 4 cylinders and Caprotti Valve gear.*

* These engines would be similar to the 10 existing Caprotti engines, but with improvements in axleboxes, brake gear, spring gear, etc.

Cost of Rebuilding

Estimates have been got out of the cost of rebuilding under each proposal, including improved axleboxes and various other items, similar to the improvements embodied in the two recently rebuilt three-cylinder improved Claughtons, and these are shown below, together with the figure for the cost of an ordinary Claughton engine undergoing a general repair and requiring new boiler and new cylinders. A number of the existing Claughtons have now reached the stage when both new boilers and cylinders will normally be required. The estimated costs of rebuilding are as follows:-

	£
Estimated cost of rebuilding as a 3-cylinder "Claughton" with Caprotti or Walschaert gear without tender	3,500
Estimated cost of rebuilding as 4-cylinder Claughton	3,590
Cost of general repair with new cylinders and boilers, of original design	1,674

It will be seen from these figures that the difference in cost between carrying out this heavy repair and rebuilding as a 3-cylinder engine with Walschaerts gear would be £1,876 per engine.

Maintenance Cost

The estimated cost of maintenance for shops (not including boiler) and sheds per mile are as follows:

Ordinary Claughton	5.70d
Rebuilt Claughton with old cylinders and motion.	6.28d.
Existing Caprotti Claughton	4.48d
Estimate for the 3-cylinder Claughton with Walschaerts gear*	3.94d

*These figures are the "Royal Scot" costs and it is estimated that the 3-cylinder Claughton costs will be somewhat less.

The cost figures given above are taken over two years, 1929–1930, and while the Caprottis are shown to be lower than the unrebuilt engines, examination of the detail figures indicates that if the engine was generally modernised similar to the three-cylinder Claughtons and the Royal Scots the costs would still be further reduced.

The present position is that the maintenance costs in the shops of cylinders and motion is less for the Caprotti than for the Royal Scots, but this advantage is nullified by the cost of maintaining the other parts of the existing design, which give trouble in service. On the other hand, Caprotti motion has only been in service a short time, and one is not yet in a position to say what important details may require replacement a few years hence.

The two rebuilt Claughtons are designed on approved experience, and the expenditure so far as the motion is concerned cannot vary greatly from the figures shown.

Coal Consumption

So far, the three-cylinder rebuilt Claughtons show the lowest coal consumption, but a great deal depends upon the class of work the various engines are engaged upon and I think it may be said that there can be very little, if any, difference in the coal consumption of a well designed long travel Walschaerts motion compared with the Caprotti valve gear.

Tenders

Either engine can be made to take the old Claughton tender, provided vacuum brake is fitted but owing to the spacing of the troughs on the Midland and Northern Divisions the present tenders are not large enough in capacity for working over these Divisions, and it would seem desirable that these engines should be fitted to work over all Divisions. A separate investigation, which has been made into the spacing of troughs and size of tenders, indicates, I think, that nothing less than a 3,500 gallon tender should be used.

The estimated cost of a new standard tender is £1,000, and if it is agreed to build these the present Claughton tenders by slight alteration could be used on other engines, and thus make up the present deficit.

This rather impressive overhead view of No. 5910 J. A. Bright was taken at Bushey troughs when working an express passenger train but before it was fitted with smoke deflectors. A view of the locomotive with smoke deflectors is on page 54.
AUTHORS' COLLECTION

This three-quarter right-hand side view of No. 6023 Sir Charles Cust shows the handsome proportions of the large boiler Claughton in LMS Crimson Lake livery before they were fitted with deflector plates. This locomotive, originally L&NWR No. 207, was built in May 1921 and rebuilt with Caprotti valve gear and a large boiler in August 1928.
AUTHORS' COLLECTION

THE L&NWR CLAUGHTONS

There can be little doubt that the Patriots without smoke deflectors looked very impressive, and the nickname 'Baby Scot' is understandable. This picture of No. 5902 which, following the 1934 renumbering programme, became No. 5501, was taken at Birmingham New Street.
AUTHORS' COLLECTION

Saving
The annual saving in maintenance cost which it is expected would accrue from conversion to a three cylinder engine, as against the present design of Caprotti, based on the present yearly mileage of the Caprotti engines (48,677 miles) would amount to about £110 per engine per annum and based on present figures a further £90 might be expected due to reduced coal consumption, making a total saving of approximately £200 per engine per annum.

Compared with the original "Claughton", the saving in maintenance and coal costs which may be expected is about £500 per engine per annum.

The Operating Department have reported very favourably on the two rebuilt three-cylinder Walschaert engines and that they fully meet their requirements, except that some improvement in the axleboxes might be made (original axleboxes were used) and the cost of these has been included in the estimate.

Recommendation
A number of the original 'Claughtons will shortly be requiring new cylinders and new boilers and it is recommended that an order be given for rebuilding 20 more of the improved three-cylinder engines with Walschaerts gear; the drawings and patterns being already to hand.

With regard to the Caprotti gear, the Motive Power Superintendent raised objection to the need of having specially trained men on these engines, and it would seem that this is mainly on account of the great difference in the manipulation of the gear compared with the more standard engines. This matter gave considerable and serious trouble when the engines were first introduced, but latterly we have heard very little about it, and it would seem that if any further engines are fitted, some arrangement might be made whereby the manipulation of the gear would conform very closely to that of an ordinary link motion.

There are also various small details which the Motive Power Superintendent has pointed out might be improved in design.

The new design was a success and further 'rebuilds' were authorised. The Claughton wheels were not re-used and Royal Scot driving wheels were substituted together with the axles, axle boxes, springs and brake gear of that type. Only the first ten engines retained the original Claughton bogie; the rest of the class had new bogies. At first a Claughton was withdrawn for every 'Baby Scot' built but this did not apply to the final ten, which were regarded as new engines. The 42 Claughtons that were withdrawn and officially rebuilt as new locomotives are detailed in *Table 10*.

According to E.S. Cox in *Locomotive Panorama Volume 1* pp68/9, the success of the rebuild may be judged by the fact that when the Patriots were compared with the Claughtons, there was found to be a 50% reduction in repair costs on average over an eight-year period. This had been foreshadowed in February 1931 when comparative tests took place between 'Baby Scot' No. 5902, large-boilered Caprotti Claughton No. 5908 and Claughton No. 5910 (also with large boiler, but with the new six-ring piston valves). All three locomotives had run 6,000 to 8,000 miles since new or repair and worked the same trains for a period of three weeks, with results of the tests being monitored by the Horwich dynamometer car No. 2. The Caprotti Claughton had a coal consumption of 11% higher than that of the 'Baby Scot' and 9% by the other Claughton. Water consumption was about equal.

On 31st May 1930 the first of twenty further Royal Scots (built at Derby) went into traffic. Delivery of the batch continued until November and during that period they were drafted to the Western Division, displacing more Claughtons. These displaced locomotives went to the Midland Division, with the usual alterations for loading-gauge purposes, though with additional cut-down features such as chimney and dome to conform to the Northern Division loading gauge. Perhaps someone envisaged them working through to Glasgow. The seven locomotives involved in the 1930 transfer were Nos. 5905/12/33/40/42/68/76. All were overhauled and modified at Crewe Works prior to transfer to Leeds shed, where they replaced more Compounds. Due to subsequent transfers and withdrawal, their life on the Midland Division was comparatively short, but they did some fine work nevertheless. In 1932 the reboilered Claughtons started to receive smoke deflectors of the straight-sided pattern, flanking the smokebox in the same manner as those fitted to the Royal

As a result of the good impression gained from the tests with Caprotti engines, approval to convert additional engines was given and No. 5975, old L&NWR No. 12 Talisman, was one of them. Built in April 1920, it was rebuilt with a large boiler, cab altered to the Midland structure gauge, and Caprotti valve gear in June 1928.
AUTHORS' COLLECTION

Comparative tests were undertaken between a 'Baby Scot', a large-boiler Claughton fitted with Caprotti valve gear and No. 5910, a large-boiler Claughton fitted with six-ring piston valves. At the time this picture was taken, No. 5910 was stationed at shed 27 Preston.
NATIONAL RAILWAY MUSEUM

THE L&NWR CLAUGHTONS

Scots. They were attached to the platform above the cylinders, but were soon replaced by a similar type with an inward angled top portion to give a better air flow. The smaller chimneys of these boilers probably had been collecting smoke around their bases and obscuring forward vision of the crews. We have reproduced the minute from the Mechanical and Electrical Engineering Committee in full.

> 27 January 1932
> 6. Fitting of smoke deflectors to 70 "Royal Scot" and 22 "Claughton" engines. N.W.O. 2678.
> The Chief Mechanical Engineer reported that to overcome the trouble which had been experienced with exhaust steam from the chimney of "Royal Scot" engines and "Claughton" engines, fitted with large boilers, drifting downwards and obscuring the driver's view of signals, three engines were fitted, as an experiment, with an arrangement of side or deflector plates alongside the smokebox which had the effect of inducing an upward current of air alongside the boiler in front of the cab window. In view of the success of the arrangement and having regard to the importance of taking immediate steps to rectify the trouble, instructions had been given, with the approval of the Vice President, for the sideplates to be fitted to the 70 "Royal Scot" and the 22 "Claughton" engines concerned as they pass through the sheds or the shops, the estimated outlay being £788 (Capital).
> Approved.

During the early 1930s, despite there being Claughtons in service not yet fitted with modified piston rings, much good work was still being done. Sometimes they were loaded over their 380 tons limit on the Western Division and they were doing good work between Leeds and Carlisle, but during 1931 the writing was clearly on the wall when the order for 'Baby Scots' was placed. In the past many authors have attributed the LMS 'Scrap and Build Programme' to the newly appointed Chief Mechanical Engineer William Arthur Stanier, but this is not so. From the time of the amalgamation in 1923 the aim had been to reduce the diverse number of classes in service and to standardise the company's locomotive stock. The entire policy was driven by the need to reduce operating costs. What must be appreciated is that the LMS was a highly structured organisation and the ultimate authority was the Board of Directors. The Board approved or rejected proposals from the various committees and the Company's senior officers served on one or more committee. Therefore the CME did not act in isolation and the decision to scrap and build was a Board decision linked to economic considerations that are really outside the terms of reference that we have drawn for this book.

We have included extracts from a further minute from the Locomotive and Electrical Committee that sets the scene prior to the arrival of William Stanier as CME in the following year.

> With reference to Minute 1185 of 20 May 1931 authorising the conversion of Claughtons. N.W.O. 2664. A further 15 of the remaining 107 original engines require general overhaul and new boilers and it is recommended that they be rebuilt on the lines of the two already converted with further improvements to the axleboxes so as to prevent operating trouble. Having regard to the probability of more intensive use of the improved locomotives, this amount might be further increased.
> It was also recommended that, in order to overcome the restricted use of "Claughton" engines fitted with original tenders, owing to deficient water carrying capacity, and also to obtain an economy on repairs of tenders representing 0.25d. per mile, equal to £114 per tender per annum, 15 new standard tenders be provided at a total cost of £14,805, of which £690 represented the value of improvements.
> The tenders displaced would enable worn out tenders of less capacity on other engines to be withdrawn from traffic and broken up with consequent economies of operation and costs, provision being made for such renewals and displacements in the next Renewal Programme.
> Authority was therefore asked for the conversion of 15 engines at a cost of £58,560 and the provision of 15 new standard tenders at a cost of £14,805, the allocation of the total expenditure of £73,565 to be dealt with subsequently.
> As and when the remainder of the original 92 engines became due for general overhaul, their treatment would be considered having regard to future developments and demands. The matter had been recommended to the Board by the Traffic Committee, subject to reference to this Committee.

In *Chronicles of Steam* at page 32, E.S. Cox states 'Despite good improvements, there remained serious and fundamental faults on the Claughtons which were both costly to improve matters or eliminate. The trailing bearings frequently ran hot and were so situated as to prove to be a nightmare to access or rectify, mainly from the restricted and normally inaccessible area in relation to the close proximity of the firebox and frames. Vibration and oil feed pipe fractures exacerbated matters by denying bearings in an already hot area sufficient oil.' The Claughton brakes system was another problem, not so much with the rigging, but rather with the numerous joints that leaked on the pipework which threaded its way around the locomotive. Cox stated that 'As on all ex-LNW classes the brakework was a nightmare, and it was established that it cost just twice as much to maintain it as was the case with the steam and vacuum combination on the standard engines'.

The arrival of William Stanier in 1932 merely put the seal on their fate as a class. He confirmed the decision (already taken during Lemon's tenure of 1931) to withdraw them, signing a report dated 8th January 1932, which must have been one of the first during his time with the LMS.

1932 saw twenty-four Claughtons of the original design withdrawn and replaced by 'Baby Scots'; the details are listed in *Tables 1 & 10*. Stanier confirmed more replacement 'Baby Scots' because he had not yet worked out any improvements of his own for them. 1933 saw another sixteen replaced, leaving a balance of 87 Claughtons by the end of that year Clearly events were moving on, and one sign of those times was the general acceleration of Anglo-Scottish services from 2nd May 1932. After the 'races to the north' of the late 19th Century, timings had been agreed between the railway companies that provided the east and west coast routes from London to Scotland but that agreement was retained too long. In 1932 there was far better motive power available on both routes and the old timings were an anachronism. The old eight hours agreement from London to Glasgow or Edinburgh was scrapped, with the result that the former was brought down to 6 hours within five years. With the accelerations, came more modern and more powerful locomotives, including Stanier's 4–6–2s, so there was little reason for retaining many Claughtons on first-line duties and even some sec-

With increasing numbers of the more efficient Stanier Class 5 and Class 5X 4–6–0s entering service, it became possible to withdraw the original Claughtons, the last to go being old L&NWR No. 499, which was built in May 1920 and withdrawn in October 1935. This picture was taken inside Saltley shed on 2nd March 1935 and shows the engine coupled to an ROD tender. Although Saltley did have some passenger work, its locomotives mostly worked freight trains, so this picture suggests that the final months of No. 5984 were spent on freight trains.
COLLECTION R. S. CARPENTER

The first of the Claughtons that had been rebuilt with large boilers to be withdrawn was No. 5986. Built as L&NWR No. 1092 in May 1920, it was rebuilt in April 1928 and withdrawn a week before the first original Claughton, No. 5984, in October 1935. This picture was taken at Camden shortly after the locomotive had been rebuilt. AUTHORS' COLLECTION

ondary services. Coal consumption had improved on those Claughtons fitted with the new six-ring piston heads, but even so, compared with the Royal Scots they were considered inefficient. Within themselves some were better than they had ever been, but they were out of context with the times.

By 1934 some of the problems were becoming serious and adversely affecting reliability. In the October of that year Caprotti Claughtons had to be removed from important expresses because they were the cause of 35% of the failures within the Edge Hill allocation of locomotives. Much of this was concerned with leaking smokeboxes and, in particular, one Claughton had failed fifteen times in five months due to this problem. Leaking smoke boxes also afflicted the 'Baby Scots'. By this time there were few of the original Claughtons left. Forty had been withdrawn and replaced by 'Baby Scots' and there had been a further forty-one withdrawn in 1934, leaving just forty-six survivors, of which twenty were the large-boiler type. The withdrawals of 1934 were a consequence of the introduction of Stanier's Jubilee 4-6-0s that year, a trend that continued into 1935. They also led to some of the rebuilt Claughtons being transferred, some going from Preston to Carnforth shed for working the 'Ulster Express' between Morecambe Promenade and Crewe.

With increasing numbers of Stanier' Class 5 and 5XP locomotives, withdrawals of Hughes Dreadnoughts and the original Claughtons continued, and in 1935 the final original Claughtons were withdrawn. Twenty-six were withdrawn from service, the last being No. 5984 (formerly L&NWR No. 499), on 28th October 1935. The previous week saw No. 5986, the first of the rebuilt Claughtons, withdrawn. A total of four of the 5X Claughtons were to go before the end of the year, leaving just sixteen members of the once 130-strong class in service. The addition of a heavier boiler and the increased piston loads had adversely affected the light frames and brought the day of reckoning forward. One of the rebuilt locomotives, No. 6004, *Princess Louise*, had its nameplates removed when the name was transferred to the new Princess Royal class 4-6-2 No. 6204 in 1935.

The last of the Caprotti Claughtons was withdrawn in 1936, indeed six were withdrawn that year, so it was left to ten Walschaerts-fitted Claughtons to carry on. By December 1937 another six had been withdrawn and only four remained in service. One would have expected that all should have been withdrawn that year or 1938 at least, but the quartet remained intact until 1940, when No. 6017 *Breadalbane* was withdrawn. Nos. 5946 *Duke of Connaught* and No. 6023 went during 1941, leaving the sole survivor, No. 6004, to enjoy a lengthy spell in solitary operation. For several years No. 6004 had been a familiar sight hauling fitted freight trains between London and Edge Hill, her crimson lake livery becoming ever more faded and covered with wartime grime, no doubt receiving the occasional patch-painting and touching-up of her livery. Her home shed was Willesden. She survived in service until April 1949, eight years after the last of the others had been taken out of traffic. In order to understand why this happened, it is necessary to examine Traffic Committee minute 5359 dated 27th October 1937. This minute confirmed the proposed construction of ten additional passenger engines and the retention of engines authorised for displacement. The authority quoted in the minute was N.W.O. 4677, which was for the ten Class 7 4-6-2 express passenger engines.

The minute also contained a justification for retaining certain engines, which were scheduled for breaking up on the grounds of difficulties in obtaining materials as well as the anticipated additional traffic, and the key was that this should only be done when there was no need to build new boilers. The minute contained a table showing the classes of engines covered by this proposal, which were all ex-L&NWR and L&YR, and also gave the anticipated number of each class in stock at the end of each calendar year. From a total of 170 shown as at 24th July 1937, the numbers decreased to 137 at 31st December 1937 and to 29 at 31st December 1940. There were four Claughtons shown as being in stock in July 1937 and the four remained as part of the anticipated stock on 31st December 1940. By that date the Second World War had imposed immense demands upon the railway system; therefore it seems that the withdrawal of locomotives was based upon whether or not it was possible or worthwhile to repair locomotives in order to keep them in service. Having survived nationalisation, No. 6004 was allocated the number 46004, but never received it, trundling around in her old familiar guise until being called into Crewe Works for scrapping. Before she was scrapped, someone had the forethought to photograph her with the two other L&NWR locomotives, as described at the beginning of this account – a fitting tribute indeed. By the end of 1949, BR had scrapped her, the boiler passing on for further use on unrebuilt Patriots.

One reflects as to what place did the Claughtons have in railway history. It is fair to say that E.C. Trench and his restrictions compromised the locomotives on paper, but despite this, the design that did emerge into reality was a good one. When new they were admirable for the task allotted and, even when they had run up considerable mileage and coal consumption rose, the L&NWR had the facilities to keep them in service. Excessive coal consumption did not seem to worry that Company unduly when both coal and labour were still cheap, but in the post Great War period conditions changed and it was another matter. Any problems encountered during the first few years were marked down for attention after the Great War. This leads us into another factor, which not only delayed remedial treatment, but also actually extended the problems by the construction of more Claughtons during the Great War. When the war was over, some modifications were put in hand, but first the not unbiased outside influences of Horwich and Derby weighted against them and the old L&NWR system. Steam technology in Britain often lagged behind elsewhere and there was also bigotry to contend with, so it was not until the late 1920s that we find the Claughtons being dealt with in a more serious manner. Thus we see that there had been two periods when the Claughtons had 'marked time' as it were.

Reboilering was a success, as was the fitting of the six-ring piston valve, but times had changed and the Claughtons were late in achieving their vital improvements. It was also true that many of the other items that required attention continued to plague them well into the 1930s, by which time any money available for spending was quite rightly channelled into new construction, and this includes the 'Baby Scots' (otherwise known as the Patriots). History has often been unkind to the Claughtons. It is true that they had their troubles, they were often unreliable in the 1920s and 1930s, but it was not all their own fault. Outside influences and changing attitudes showed them in different lights at different times. As a class they nearly made the grade and individual locomotives put up some astounding performances.

It must not be forgotten that for ten years they were kept in good trim and successfully hauled heavy express trains between Euston and Carlisle, with plenty of power available to do this. They were introduced during the end of an era where attitudes and practices of many years had prevailed; they were proliferated during a national wartime struggle and its aftermath; they were sidestepped during a short-lived merger and replaced by more powerful locomotives by a new order demanding strict economy in all matters. Their failings were remedied too little, too late or not at all. They could not be considered, collectively, as bad locomotives when properly used and maintained – and there lies the answer to the Claughton myth – a near miss.

This official picture of No. 6004 was taken about the time it was taken out of service in April 1949. Built in August 1920, it was named Princess Louise *from February 1922 until June 1935 when the nameplate was removed and the name transferred to one of the new Princess Royal class Pacifics. Rebuilt with the large boiler in April 1928, it was the last member of the class to remain in service and, although allotted British Railways number 46004, it was never renumbered.*   NATIONAL RAILWAY MUSEUM

PART TWO
THE LMS PATRIOTS

The first twelve Baby Scots used the original Claughton bogie but with side bolsters and a central pivot; their post-1934 numbers were 5500-5511. This picture, taken at Tring in 1933, shows one of the first twelve engines, No. 5936, later No. 5507, which was named Royal Tank Corps *in November 1937. This locomotive was completed on 12th August 1932 and was allocated to Crewe until 6th October 1934 when it was transferred to Longsight after being renumbered on 23rd July 1934.*   AUTHORS' COLLECTION

The Patriots began their careers known by various titles, not all of which were official. Originally they were described as 'Three-cylinder Converted Claughtons', not a title likely to gain popular usage. Other titles were 'Rebuilt Claughtons' and 'Converted Claughtons', neither of which were official nor very accurate descriptions. They were likely to allow confusion to arise when compared with the reboilered Claughtons. Unofficial though it may have been, the affectionate title 'Baby Scots' was the best and most accurate one, and for a few years it was the most popular term used by railway enthusiasts, if not by the LMS itself, until the title 'Patriots' was decreed. We will use whatever term that seems to us to be appropriate.

The locomotives were in effect smaller versions of the Royal Scots, both in design concept and appearance, and the major relationship with the Claughtons was the acceptance of the large boiler design used on the rebuilt members plus the very few parts salvaged from withdrawn Claughtons which the locomotives were supposed to replace. The manner by which the building of the new locomotives was financed by the LMS has done much to perpetuate the myth of rebuilding from the Claughtons and has much to do with the question of renewal or capital accounts paying for the work in question. Indeed the entire subject of how the LMS financed the company would make an interesting study, which is outside of our self-drawn terms of reference. The Patriot design combined the aforementioned boiler with the successful Royal Scot chassis and cylinder layout, to produce a second-line express passenger locomotive which was able to travel over lines barred to the Royal Scots due to weight restrictions. Additionally, the locomotives were to provide a suitable back-up for the Royal Scots themselves on a regular basis. It will be seen therefore, that the locomotives were envisaged as a second line of motive power from new – the opposite approach to the traditional methods of cascading older locomotives from top-link duties.

The train of events that led to the first two 'Baby Scots' being built has been described in Part One. In effect their combination of origins of major components paralleled those attempts at Derby to produce an improved 4–6–0. There was one common element, Jack Francis, who was transferred from Crewe to the Derby drawing office. He, with others in the drawing office, was involved with various schemes to develop the more modern and economical 4–6–0. A scheme for a four-cylinder 4–6–0 with rotary Lentz valve gear was drawn up, and followed by a similar scheme with three cylinders. Then came the three-cylinder arrangement combination which resulted in the 'Baby Scot' design. Some utilisation of Claughton parts was resorted to, these, as we have seen, becoming available from the remains of crash victims Nos. 5971 and 5902, the demise of these two locomotives being described in Part One. Unlike the frames, the coupled

Patriot No. 6005 was completed at Crewe 19th August 1932 and became No. 5509 on 10th August 1934. During the LMS period it was not named but in 1951 it was named The Derbyshire Yeomanry and on page 86 we show the locomotive in British Railways ownership carrying this name. This picture of the engine only was taken at Crewe, where it was stationed until November 1933 when it was transferred to Longsight. In December 1932 the locomotive was fitted with a Kyala exhaust and the non-standard flowerpot chimney casing seen here. We believe that it reverted to a normal chimney before it was renumbered.
AUTHORS' COLLECTION

The first type of smoke deflector plate to be fitted to the Patriots was straight and this picture of No. 6010, later No. 5508, was taken when the locomotive was working a Down express from Euston. The engine history card gives the allocation for this locomotive as Crewe North from 9th August 1932 until it was transferred to Manchester Longsight on 21st October 1933 before being transferred to Derby on 1st December 1934. The change of number from 6010 to 5508 was made on 17th April 1934, when it was a Longsight engine. In this picture the shed plate is a Western Division plate code 1 Camden. Was the engine history card in error or was it a loan not recorded on the card?
AUTHORS' COLLECTION

wheels were retained, but the leading set was moved to the centre in modified form to achieve the divided three-cylinder drive. The old L&NWR bogie was retained, as were the L&NWR reversing screw and whistle. The decision to utilise the remains of the two Claughtons was authorised by Fowler with perhaps some discussion beforehand between Symes, Beames and Anderson prior to submission to him. Work was authorised under Order No. 7560 at Derby.

The first twelve 'Baby Scots' (5500–5511) used the original Claughton radial bogie whereas the remainder (5512–5551) used the frames and wheel sets of the original Claughton bogie, but with side bolsters and a central pivot. This bogie, slightly modified, was used on the Crewe-built Jubilees 5552–5556 and 5607–5636. The first twenty 'Baby Scots' were fitted with bye-pass valves below the cylinders, which showed as a casing below each cylinder with the pressure relief valves protruding below.

The outline of these 'Baby Scots' was in the Derby tradition, with a clear relationship to that of the Royal Scots. Gone were the L&NWR platform and covered motion, along with the beloved Crewe cab, with its box-shaped lower side sheets. Of aesthetical interest, the cab side window surrounds were derived from the Royal Scots, which in turn appeared to have inherited them from the Lord Nelson 4-6-0s. This was Southern Railway practice at the time featured on at least the latter class and the Schools 4-4-0s. The smokebox door lost its traditional Crewe hinge and plain appearance, and steam pipes, visible to the outside world, appeared. Paired with the LMS standard 3,500 gallon tender of Fowler design, the new locomotive looked every inch a Baby Scot and represented the latest offering in aesthetics. The resultant locomotives emerged from Derby Works in November/December 1930, complete with improved lubrication, sanding, brake pipe work, axle boxes and big end design, all of which had been problem areas on the Claughtons. Above all, the old Schmidt piston valve rings were discarded in favour of the multi-ring type, proven on the Royal Scots and some Claughtons. The coupled wheel spacing was made the same as that on the Royal Scots, although retention of the L&NWR bogie with 6ft. 3in. between wheel centres introduced some differences with the Royal Scots that had a 6ft. 6in. spacing.

No. 5971 was the first to appear, painted in standard LMS crimson lake livery, happily retaining the name *Croxteth* which

We show two pictures of No. 6012 which became No. 5510 on 25th June 1934. The first picture was taken at the old Midland Railway shed at Leeds Holbeck when the locomotive was fitted with straight smoke deflector plates. The second picture shows the locomotive as No. 5510 at the old Midland Railway station at Sheffield in October 1934. A number of Patriots were never named, this locomotive being one of them. AUTHORS' COLLECTION

THE LMS PATRIOTS

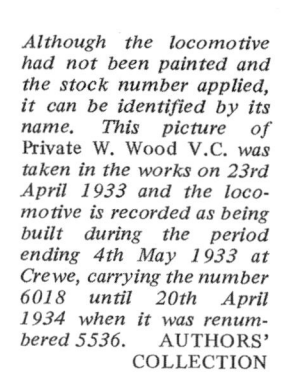

Although the locomotive had not been painted and the stock number applied, it can be identified by its name. This picture of Private W. Wood V.C. *was taken in the works on 23rd April 1933 and the locomotive is recorded as being built during the period ending 4th May 1933 at Crewe, carrying the number 6018 until 20th April 1934 when it was renumbered 5536.* AUTHORS' COLLECTION

the original 5971 had borne. The intention to name the locomotive at some time or another was apparent from the provision of a backing plate above the centre coupled wheel splasher. This plate, curiously, was painted crimson lake with yellow lining and black edging. No. 5902 soon followed and was photographed wearing the photographic grey livery and the name *Sir Frank Ree* on an imitation nameplate somewhat longer than the nameplate proper borne in service. The original 5902 had carried this name since new in 1913. The leading data for the Patriots appears in *Table 11*.

No. 5971 was sent to Leeds Holbeck shed, and joined a batch of reboilered Claughtons (fitted with modified piston valves) which were undertaking good and economical work over the Settle and Carlisle route. The latter, with a load limit of 340 tons, prevailed over the hilly section, had eliminated much of the piloting and a reasonable comparison could be gained with the new locomotive. Actually, the load limit did restrict the potential for comparison because it was a relatively light one. Nevertheless, No. 5971 did prove equal to the work and the signs were very encouraging indeed as experience was gained. The new design gave a very good account of itself.

In February 1931 comparative tests took place between No. 5902, large-boilered Caprotti Claughton No. 5908 and large-boilered and piston valve-modified Claughton No. 5910 over the Euston to Manchester route. The results were even more encouraging with No. 5902 coming out top by a small margin. The tests were conducted using the Horwich dynamometer car and the locomotives used were in almost equally good mechanical condition, but during 1931 it was behind the scenes where economic advantage became apparent. The repair costs proved to be lower and it was here that the improved detail design of the 'Baby Scot' began

to reap benefits over and above the still-unrectified problems of the Claughtons. Indeed, projected over an eight-year period, the new design compared very favourably with a reduction of 50% in maintenance costs over the Claughton. The early results, all round, impressed the LMS authorities and the decision was taken not to pursue the old Claughton design further, but to build 'Baby Scots' instead.

Under Josiah Stamp, the directors and senior managers, often referred to as officers, who were responsible for running the LMS, were gradually changing position, retiring or had newly arrived from outside. This was part of a policy to eliminate allegiances to the constituent companies and to ensure a common aim and purpose directed towards matters in the interest of the LMS. The 'Baby Scots' were to be the last locomotive design produced during Fowler's term of office as Chief Mechanical Engineer because from January 1931 he became the assistant to Sir Harold Hartley, who was the Vice President with special responsibility for research, with the title Director of Scientific Research. Until a man with no pre-grouping allegiances could be secured from elsewhere to become CME, Ernest Lemon was appointed as a caretaker CME from his former post of Carriage and Wagon Engineer. It was left to him to authorise further building of 'Baby Scots', albeit at the expense of any Claughton rebuilding.

In October 1931 the recommendation was made to the LMS Board that forty Claughtons falling due for new cylinders and boilers in 1932 should be withdrawn from service and rebuilt as 'Baby Scots'. This was accepted by the Board. In effect, the forty Claughtons were to be scrapped and replaced, but the myth of rebuilding continued. Those 'Baby Scots' which were built as replacements took running numbers from the Claughtons they replaced (see *Table 11*), but from 1934 they were to be renumbered 5502–41, in

The arrangement of the nameplates on the Patriots varied. Here we show five examples beginning with No. 5501. This locomotive was originally No. 5902 Sir Frank Ree but it was renumbered on 12th April 1934 and renamed St. Dunstan's on 17th April 1937. Patriot No. 5987 was built in 1932 and named Royal Signals and renumbered on 28th June 1934 when it became No. 5504. This right-hand side view also provides a good view of the leading coupled wheel and sand pipes. Unlike the nameplate on No. 5504, which has a badge as part of the plate, there was no badge included in the nameplate Royal Naval Division. Built as No. 5959, the locomotive was renumbered on 28th May 1934, becoming 5502 on 5th June 1937. The final example of a parallel boiler Patriot to be shown is Isle of Man. This name was carried by No. 5511, previously No. 5942, which was named in 1938. This picture shows the left-hand side of the engine. Note the radiused rim between the spokes. Finally, a 1960 view of the nameplate on No. 45527 Southport taken some years after it had been rebuilt with a taper boiler.   L. HANSON
AUTHORS' COLL.
AUTHORS' COLL.
AUTHORS' COLL.
W. POTTER

THE LMS PATRIOTS

order of building, following on from the by then renumbered pair dating from 1930, Nos. 5500/1. The forty locomotives were built at Crewe and Derby Works in 1932/3, the former producing thirty and the latter ten, to Order No. 8179. There were some differences from the original pair worth noting, so far as the main batch is concerned. Plain coupling rods, rather than fluted, were incorporated and two windows in the cab front above the firebox were discontinued. The tenders gained two coal rails in order to increase the coal capacity (although this change also applied to the tenders coupled to other locomotive classes). The L&NWR radial bogie was fitted only to the first ten, the remainder using the bogie modified with side bolsters. The first locomotive was completed at Crewe in June 1932 and by the end of the year fifteen had been built.

By the time the first one had been completed, the LMS had already acquired its new CME from outside. From January 1932 William A. Stanier had taken over, coming straight from the Great Western Railway. The manner of his appointment is told on page 20 of *An Illustrated History of LMS Locomotives* Volume 5, published by Silver Link Publishing; it makes interesting reading. His task was to re-equip the LMS with a standard range of locomotives, but before he could attempt to do this he had to review the stock that he had just inherited. He also had to take into account the current plans which the LMS had regarding the

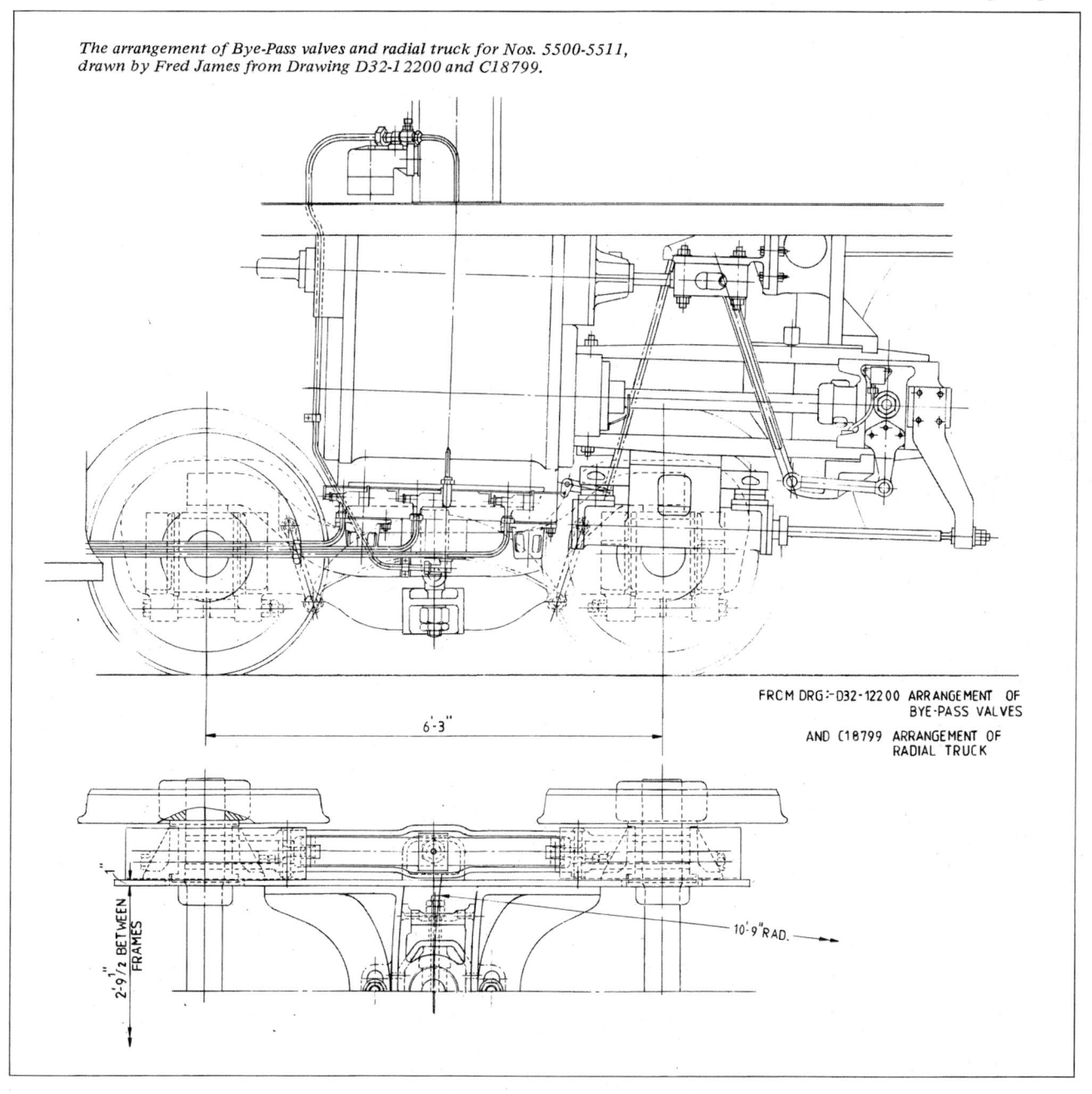

The arrangement of Bye-Pass valves and radial truck for Nos. 5500-5511, drawn by Fred James from Drawing D32-12200 and C18799.

proposed accelerations on the West Coast Main Line for the summer and autumn of 1932. Wherever possible, Stanier considered reboilering existing classes with taper boilers, but where this was not possible he designed anew, incorporating taper boilers. The minute reproduced below summarises the position about seven months into Stanier's term of office.

Mechanical Electrical Engineering Committee Minute 142 27th July 1932
Locomotive Programme 1933 N.W.O. 2844

As a result of experience gained with the No.7 0.8.0 standard freight tender engine it was considered that a material advantage in reliability and haulage capacity would be obtained by the introduction as a standard of a locomotive of the 2.8.0 type instead of the present 0.8.0 and with this object in view only 15 of the 20 0.8.0s authorised in the 1932 programme were being built, the remaining 5 to be included as 2-8-.0 in the 1933 programme.

The programme for 1933:

	Engine	Tender	Total
3 4.6.2	24,225	3,405	£27,630
25 Converted Claughtons	142,500	22,500	£165,000
10 Converted Prince of Wales	56,000	9,000	£65,000
5 2.8.0	27,000	4,500	£31,500
40 2.6.0 mixed traffic	172,000	36,000	£208,000
45 2.6.4 tank	229,500	—	£229,500

The minute also contained a qualifying paragraph which stated:

'In January 1932, the Traffic Committee minute No. 3000 authorised the conversion of 15 "Claughton Locomotives" from four to three cylinders with improved boilers, and the provision of 15 new tenders, at a total estimated cost of £73,365 of which sum £14,805 was in respect of 15 new tenders. The conversion of the locomotives was justified on the

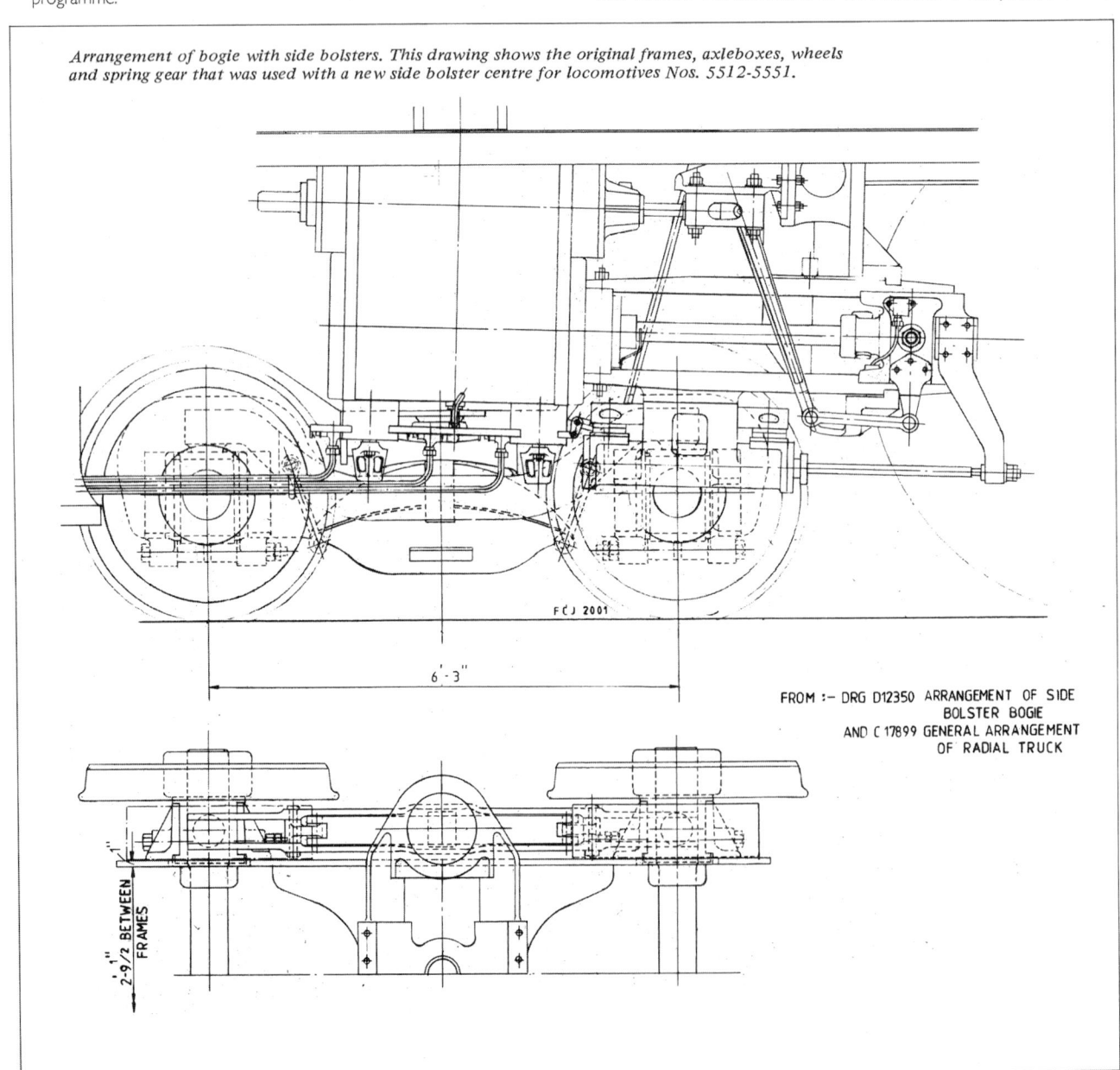

Arrangement of bogie with side bolsters. This drawing shows the original frames, axleboxes, wheels and spring gear that was used with a new side bolster centre for locomotives Nos. 5512-5551.

FROM :- DRG D12350 ARRANGEMENT OF SIDE BOLSTER BOGIE
AND C 17899 GENERAL ARRANGEMENT OF RADIAL TRUCK

THE LMS PATRIOTS

This picture of No. 5516 was taken at Patricroft prior to the locomotive being named The Bedfordshire and Hertfordshire Regiment *in July 1938. Built as No. 5982, it went to Kentish Town shed on the Midland Division and became No. 5516 on 28th May 1934. In April 1935 it was transferred to Patricroft in Manchester, but the stay was short and it came south to Camden in January 1936 and remained on the Western Division until it was withdrawn during the week ending 27th July 1961.*   W. POTTER

grounds of economy and efficiency and it was stipulated that the provision of 15 new tenders would be included in the next renewal programme so as to deal with displacements, and this has been done in the 1933 programme. The expenditure authorised by Minute No. 3000 is therefore reduced from £73,365 to £58,560.'

The final sentence shows something of the way the management of the Company's locomotive stock was driven by strong financial considerations, and that the whims of its officers were not the driving force. There was very little Stanier could do to alter the course of events planned for 1932, so the Royal Scots bore the brunt of the accelerations initially and the 'Baby Scots' were introduced gradually as they were built. On 18th October 1932 the accelerated Up 'Mancunian' was made up of twelve bogie coaches of 355 tons tare, 375 tons loaded, with 'Baby Scot' No. 5959 at the head. It produced a lively run, achieving a maximum of 90 mph on the last leg of the journey.

On 22nd February 1933, Mechanical Electrical Engineering Committee minute 239 approved the fitting of additional balance weights to 70 Royal Scots and 2 Rebuilt Claughtons but prior to this minute we have found nothing else to indicate this was a major problem. Of greater importance was the Traffic Committee Minute No. 3221 and the Mechanical and Electrical Engineering Committee minute 306 of 28th June 1933. They contained details of the 1934 Locomotive Programme under the financial authority DWO 3137. This included the construction of 58 Improved Claughtons at an estimated cost of £382,800. This minute had been preceded by an instruction that said 'Owing to the fact that all Claughton engines now fitted with MM tenders would be rebuilt ultimately and fitted with standard tenders, the CME recommends that the work of modifying the 24 MM tenders authorised by L&EC Minute 1202 dated 28th October 1931 be abandoned and the works order closed.'

The forty locomotives were distributed to sheds around the Western, Northern and Midland Divisions. On the first-named, they positively shone on the old L&NWR services between Euston, Birmingham and Wolverhampton, and between Euston and Manchester. On the Midland they replaced the 4-4-0 Compounds on some jobs, while those based in Scotland worked from Glasgow to Carlisle on the Manchester and Liverpool bound services. The class was a success almost instantaneously, but this did not prevent Stanier from designing a taper-boiler version to develop the design further. It is interesting to note that this move was the antithesis of the desire to reduce the number of classes on the LMS, because there was no chance of economically reboilering the 'Baby Scots' for some years to come because they were all brand new and still being built. In effect, Stanier increased the number of second-line classes by one. The new taper-boiler engines were soon to become better known as the Jubilees; their story is told in *LMS Jubilees* published by Wild Swan Publications. It is interesting to note that the parts of these ten 'Baby Scots' were stamped 6030–9 and that had Stanier not fitted his taper boiler to the remainder, and further altered the building programme, there would have been a run of 'Baby Scots' to 6082 (or 5594) at least. It was fortuitous that the renumbering of 1934 overtook events,

This picture of No. 5907 typifies the Patriot class in their early years before they were renumbered into the 55XX series. Built in 1933 and carrying the name Sir Frederick Harrison, this locomotive became No. 5524 and in 1937 it was renamed Blackpool. Note the vacuum cylinder pump, the 15 Crewe shed plate, and the pristine condition of the locomotive.
AUTHORS' COLLECTION

We have included this picture of No. 5501, which was taken at Manchester Longsight on 25th July 1937, shortly after it was named St. Dunstan's, in order to show the old Claughton driving wheels that were retained when the locomotive was rebuilt in 1930. W. L. GOOD

because the 'Baby Scots' series was in danger of running out of space – No. 6100 was *Royal Scot*.

We believe that most, if not all, from No. 5502 were fitted with crosshead-activated vacuum pumps during the Stanier era, but most, if not all, of these were removed by the time of the outbreak of World War 2. There were three patterns of driving/coupled wheel. Nos. 5500 and 5501 used the original LNWR large-boss wheels and the second pattern was the forerunner of the so-called Stanier pattern which had a radiused rim between the spokes, and a semi-circular gusset between rim and spoke. The second pattern was also the first one to use built-up balance weights. The third was the so-called Stanier pattern with vee rims and they were used on Nos. 5542–5551 from new and subsequently when any wheel required replacing, except for locomotives 5500 and 5501.

The first new fittings to appear on the 'Baby Scots', were smoke deflectors. As early as 1929, because of problems of drifting smoke obscuring the view of drivers, the Royal Scots had been fitted with small devices close to the chimney. The problem had occurred on an increasing scale as larger boilers were designed and chimneys reduced in height. The Leighton Buzzard accident in March 1931, involving Royal Scot No. 6114, was partly caused by the driver's view of the signals and warning notices being obscured by smoke. Among the recommendations which emerged from the enquiry into the accident, was that side shields should be fitted to the Royal Scots. This was implemented, not only to the Royal Scots, but also to the large-boiler Claughtons and the 'Baby Scots'. The first shields were mounted alongside the smokebox and were vertical with the leading upper corner much rounded. Later, cranking inwards the upper edge altered this design. The 'Baby Scots' followed the general pattern and of course some of the 1932 locomotives were built new with the former type. The majority were built new with the latter,

when it was found to be more effective. All 'Baby Scots' eventually had this type fitted. It was, aesthetically, the more pleasing design. The fifty-two 'Baby Scots' collectively displayed a lack of commitment by the LMS with regard to naming all their principal express passenger locomotives. There were, at the time of building, very few named examples and many of the Claughton names disappeared altogether. In later years, naming became intermittent, and appeared to be confused as far as the interested onlooker was concerned.

Following a report by two senior officers, further 'Baby Scots' were to be built. This came about when the 1933 Locomotive Renewal Programme was reviewed and the content of the minute is given below. Notwithstanding what was in the minute, the first ten were to become 'Baby Scots' and the remainder were the first to receive the new Stanier taper boiler, Type 3A. The former were initially allocated the numbers 6030–9, continuing the Claughton series, but, under the 1934 renumbering scheme, they became 5542–51 instead and the taper-boiler version became 5552–6 instead of 6040–4.

Proposed Alterations in Authorised Locomotive Renewal Programme 1933 N.W.O. 2844, as recorded in the Traffic Committee minute 3221 dated 27th July 1932.

The Chief Operating Manager and Chief Mechanical Engineer reported that the 1933 Locomotive Renewal Programme authorised by Traffic Committee Minute No. 3221 dated 27th July, 1932, included ten converted 'Prince of Wales' 4-6-0 engines, and five 2-8-0 Freight engines, the designs for which cannot be completed in time to ensure building this year.

The Chief Operating Manager is anxious to increase the number of three-cylinder 'Claughton' engines, bearing in mind that these engines have proved very satisfactory on our fast heavy expresses and can also be economically used on fast freight trains. Where this inter-working between two services can be arranged the mileage and the usage of the engines per day will be materially increased.

The smoke deflector was more aesthetic as well as being more effective when the top was cranked inwards and we have included this view of No. 5535 before it was named Sir Herbert Walker in 1937 in order to illustrate this point. Furthermore, as we describe in the text, from October 1936 until March 1938 this locomotive was fitted with an experimental top feed that was placed just ahead of the dome and clearly seen in this picture.
AUTHORS' COLLECTION

This is a copy of Derby Locomotive Works drawing No. 33-12816 for side wind plates for the 3-cylinder Claughton.

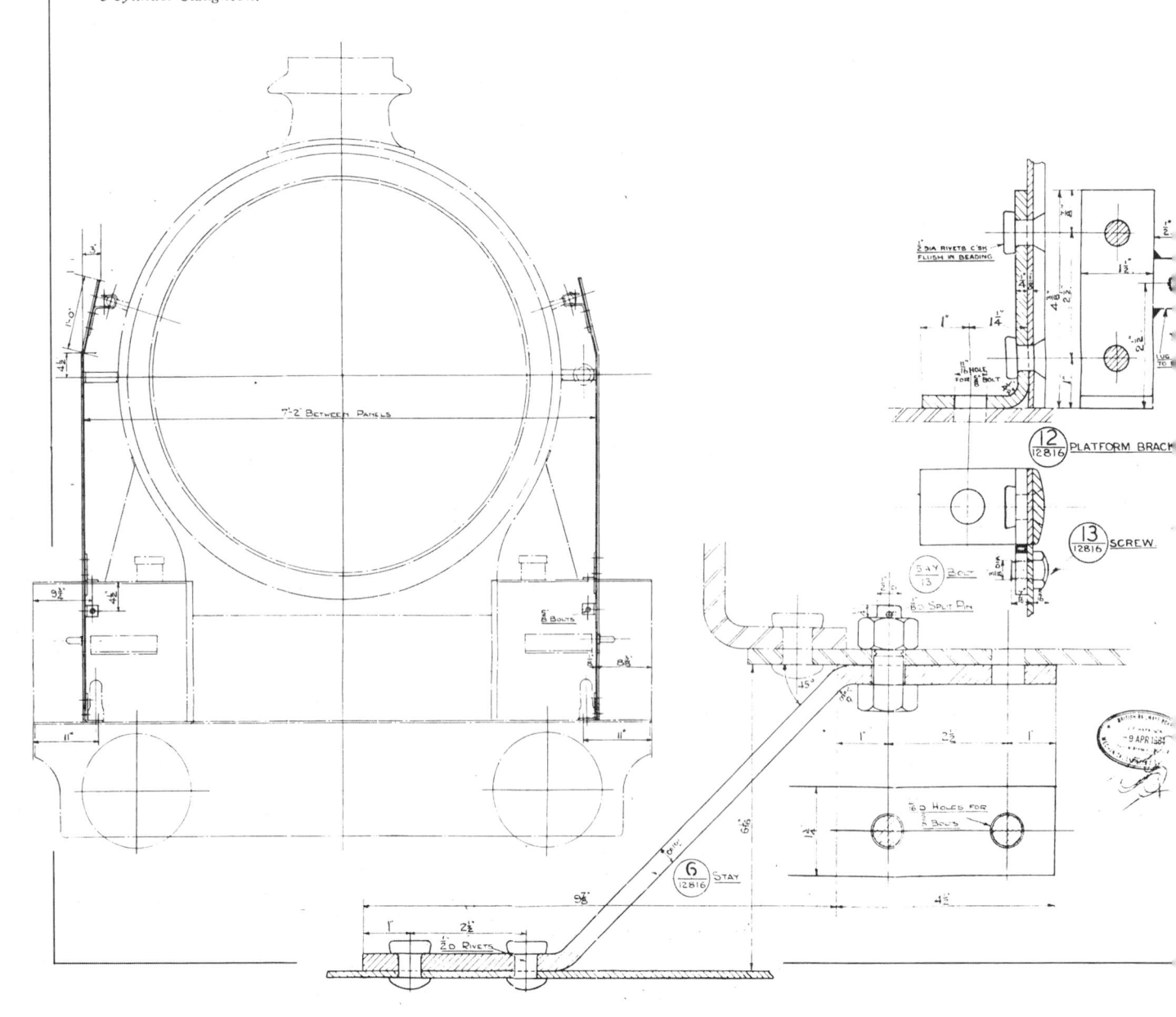

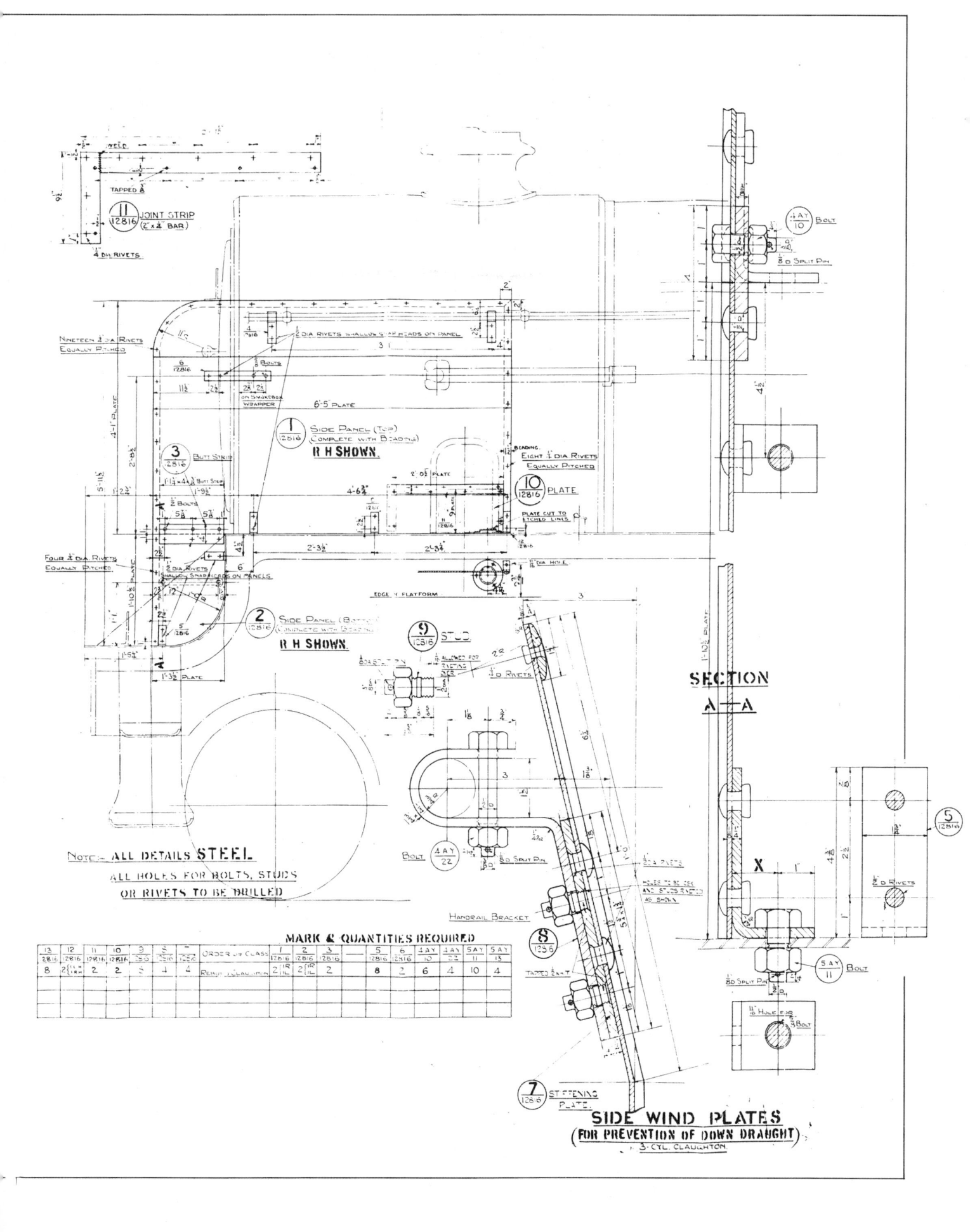

SIDE WIND PLATES
(FOR PREVENTION OF DOWN DRAUGHT)
3-CYL. CLAUGHTON

Derby drawing D29-11590 Smokebox Arrangement. In this view we can see the blastpipe, steam pipes to the inside and outside cylinders, the superheater header and superheater elements.

THE LMS PATRIOTS

It was therefore, recommended, with the approval of the Executive, that 15 additional three-cylinder 'Claughtons' (which it is anticipated can be completed by the end of 1933) be built in the place of the ten 'Prince of Wales' and the five 2-8-0 engines, these to be deferred to the 1934 Programme.

This alteration in the 1933 programme will be taken into account in the 1934 programme, which it is hoped will be submitted next month with revised estimates for 1935 work.

Approved and
Referred to the Board.

Early in 1934 the renumbering scheme commenced; as we have mentioned, the fifty-two locomotives were allocated the series 5500–51 and those below 5542 were renumbered from the Claughton series in order of building. Nos. 5542–51 were to become the last 'Baby Scots' to be built, with the last example appearing in May 1934. That same month No. 5552, the first of the Stanier Jubilees, was also completed. By the end of October over twenty of these taper-boiler locomotives were in service, but were soon to show indifferent

This picture of No. 5514 Holyhead was taken at Wigan Springs Branch in July 1939 when the locomotive was receiving attention from fitters. Note the chain that prevented the smokebox door from swinging open more than was required and the locomotive headlamp still on the left-hand front lamp holder. It was normal practice to remove the lamps when the engine came into the shed. R. F. ROBERTS

A number of Patriots were allocated to the Midland Division. This picture of No. 5954, later renumbered as No. 5520 was taken at Derby in 1933 and shows the locomotive at the head of an express passenger train. The shed plate 16 was for Kentish Town. In 1937 No. 5520 was named Llandudno but was not one of the eighteen that were rebuilt with a 2A taper boiler. AUTHORS' COLLECTION

We have included this picture of No. 5502 Royal Naval Division to show a Patriot painted in the shortlived 1936 block style. Further details will be found in Table 13 and Appendix 2B. Note the vacuum pump below the piston slide bars, which was used to maintain vacuum for the brakes when running, but was later removed from all LMS locomotives. AUTHORS' COLLECTION

steaming. We recorded these problems in our book on the Jubilees. It was only natural that the LMS should wish to compare the 'Baby Scots' with the taper-boiler variants. The last 'Baby Scot' No. 5551 and Jubilee No. 5556 underwent test runs with the dynamometer car attached, during the September and October of 1934, between Birmingham and Euston. The results showed that timings were about equal, but comparative fuel consumption details were not forthcoming – we feel that the 'Baby Scot' won! Between November 1932 and May 1933, Royal Scot No. 6158 had undergone a series of efficiency tests between Crewe and Carlisle. No. 5533 was next selected to undergo a series of tests in October and November 1934. This was done to evaluate fuel consumption better, by analysing the gases inside the smokebox. This determination of combustion efficiency was conducted with the aid of equipment fitted to the locomotive and tended by railway staff from within an indicating shelter mounted on the front end. The results gained from the runs with No. 5533 showed that there was a 29.9% loss of heat when compared with the nominal 100% calorific value of the coal fired. Scientific testing was starting to permeate into the LMS and produce results. Next came a series of tests on the various Jubilee boilers.

One weakness of the 'Baby Scots' concerned leaking smokeboxes. As early as 1934, trouble had been experienced when the Euston to Birmingham trials had taken place. The design of smokebox lent itself to trouble and it was not the 'Baby Scots' alone which experienced this problem; both the Royal Scots and large-boiler Claughtons were troublesome too. The smokebox was the wrapper-plate type forming an inverted 'D' that made awkward junctions with the cylinders and boiler barrel in the lower portions. Stanier soon introduced the barrel type, long-used by the GWR, to the LMS. This was a well-sealed cylindrical 'drumhead' design resting on a saddle, which produced none of the leakages associated with the wrapper design.

In 1935 the LMS wished to accelerate the Birmingham–Euston train service in order to counter increasing competition from road traffic as well as that from the GWR. Following the Grouping in 1923 the new Standard Compound 4-4-0s had replaced ex-L&NWR George the Fifth locomotives, and they in turn were replaced by the 'Baby Scots'. With the arrival of the Jubilees, the LMS sought to replace the Patriots and to improve the service further, but test runs showed that although the latter were good, no startling accelerations were likely. The Jubilees were hamstrung by boiler problems, so they could not possibly be entrusted to do the work satisfactorily, therefore the 'Baby Scots' continued with the good work and accelerations were made in the winter timetable, albeit amounting to a reduction of five minutes from the two-hour schedule. By the autumn of 1935 the 'Baby Scots' were allocated mainly to the Western Division, with three each on the Central and Northern Divisions. For most of their life the class was to be associated with the Western Division, although the Midland Division acquired several from time to time.

Turning now to livery, a variation affected the 'Baby Scots' in 1936. The new block-style of insignia was introduced that year and applied to 'Baby Scots as they passed through the Works. Details of those locomotives recorded by us with this short-lived livery phase are given in *Table 13* and *Appendix 2b*. From October 1936 until March 1938 No. 5535 ran fitted with an experimental top feed, ahead of the dome, on the right-hand side of the top centre line of the boiler. It was fed by the right-hand injector only and presumably it was fitted as a direct comparison with the standard fitting to ascertain if parallel boilers could take them satisfactorily.

In 1937 the LMS finally decided to implement a policy of naming for the class, but it had to be prompted into doing so. The *Railway Magazine* had initiated the move to have the name 'Patriot' transferred from the Claughton on withdrawal, to have it transferred to one of the new 'Baby Scots' and to have it painted black to continue the war memorial locomotive tradition. The LMS made no immediate response, but acted following publication of an article by Mr D.S. Barrie in October 1937, pointing out the dilemma that the LMS had allowed itself to become involved in. No. 5500, still unnamed, was given the name *Patriot* in the standard splasher-mounted

When No. 5500 was named Patriot on 25th February 1937, it received an LMS style of plate which also carried the old L&NWR inscription as shown here.
AUTHORS' COLLECTION

In 1937 there were further comparison trials between Patriots and the new taper-boiler Jubilees. The Patriot used in the trial was No. 5533 and we believe this picture was taken when it was tested against a Jubilee fitted with a Kylchap chimney at Crewe works.
NATIONAL RAILWAY MUSEUM

Patriots were regular visitors to Carlisle Citadel station. Although No. 5535 Sir Herbert Walker was carrying express passenger train headlamps, it was coupled to only one coach. This suggests that the fireman had set his headlamps in readiness to take over an incoming train which it would work forward. The single coach was either a through carriage or a strengthening carriage, probably the latter. Note the experimental top feed.
AUTHORS' COLLECTION

style, but with the old L&NWR inscription below. The livery remained crimson lake and the old L&NWR plates were not transferred because, quite simply, they were not compatible with the features of the newer locomotive. On a more personal note, and with hindsight, it might have been more appropriate if the LMS had dedicated the locomotive not only to the fallen employees of the former L&NWR but to those of all the constituent companies of the LMS en bloc. From this time onward, the class was officially called the Patriot Class, although the 'Baby Scot' name still continued to be used, albeit diminishing as time passed.

It was unfortunate for the LMS that a naming theme was not developed for the class at this time. Already some had been named and others renamed, yet many were to remain anonymous. The class seemed to become a target for random naming and the recipient of names deemed not suitable for other 4–6–0s or 4–6–2s. Of course, to the average traveller, punctuality remained the prime interest and only rarely would he or she gaze in wonder upon the name of the locomotive standing at the head of the train. Conversely, to the LMS publicity department, a naming ceremony provided a chance to promote and publicise the company.

As late as November 1937, a Patriot was engaged in yet further comparative trials with a Jubilee. No. 5533 of Bushbury shed was run against Kylchap chimney Jubilee No. 5684 and fared better. Of course, the LMS was still trying to sort out its Jubilee problems. Gradually, those problems were resolved and the Jubilees began to overshadow the Patriots by their sheer weight of numbers and lower maintenance costs. Other events were to push them out of the limelight – the advent of Pacific locomotives on the West Coast Main Line and the resultant partial relegation of the Royal Scots. The outbreak of World War 2 in 1939 would end the run of good fortune which the class had sustained since new. Thus the end of peacetime schedules, overloading and reduced maintenance set off a new order of events. The war did the Patriots few favours. It was the common wartime problem of stretching everything to the limit, and sometimes beyond. The Patriots suffered perhaps more than their fellow passenger locomotives, such as the Jubilees. The smokebox leaks and corrosion became more than a nuisance, and they gave a rougher ride as the war dragged on. It was a combination of wartime conditions seeking out design weaknesses normally dealt with by peacetime maintenance. The one favour that the war brought was the rebuilding of two Jubilees, Nos. 5735 and 5736, with No. 2A taper boilers – and of course this was extended to the Patriot Class in 1946.

The seeds for rebuilding were sown some time before the war when a large taper boiler had been fitted to the remnants of the experimental 4–6–0 No. 6399 *Fury* in 1935. Designated No. 2, this boiler was mounted on what amounted to a Royal Scot chassis. It therefore followed that there was much scope for improving the Royal Scots when boiler replacements became due, the original parallel boilers having a lifespan of about fifteen years. The resultant locomotive was No. 6170 *British Legion* and although there were initial problems concerning the boiler, Coleman and his men soon corrected them.

Improvements could not only be effected on Royal Scots, but also on Jubilees and Patriots, bearing in mind the shared design similarities of the chassis. The Royal Scots were the clearest case for early improvement, the earlier members dating from 1927; the Jubilees were the last case, being the newest locomotives already fitted with taper boilers, albeit smaller than that fitted to No. 6170. Work eventually started on the Royal Scots during the middle of the war, the first rebuild (No. 6103) emerging in 1943, the year after the two Jubilees had been rebuilt. The intention was to rebuild all the Royal Scots over a short period of seven years, but events took quite a different course and the Patriots were the direct cause of the period being extended considerably, to twelve years.

Between 1943 and 1946, thirty-nine Royal Scots were rebuilt, but then the rate of progress slowed to half, because of a new situation which developed from the troubles which the Patriots had experienced during the war. These troubles were sufficient to cause concern on the LMS to the degree that re-boilering was considered advantageous not only to eliminate the problems, but more so to take the opportunity to uprate the locomotives to 6P. In a Traffic Committee minute dated 28th September 1944 it was summarised thus:

> 7271A Renewal Programme. Conversion of Patriot. N.W.O. 6428. Submitted by the Chief Commercial Manager, Chief Mechanical Engineer, reported: The stock of parallel boilers for 5xp engines is 52 and it is recommended that 18 of them be fitted with taper boilers and a new design of cylinders at an estimated cost of £58,806. These 18 engines are now falling due for renewal of boilers and it is proposed to take this opportunity of fitting taper boilers which together with the new cylinders and new design of smokebox will make these engines identical with the Converted Royal Scots and 5xp taper boiler engines for which authority has already been granted. The following advantages will be obtained by the proposed conversion.
> 1) The smokebox is on the same general design as those fitted to the original Royal Scots and they are similarly difficult to keep airtight resulting in excessive maintenance in the Shops and Shed. The proposed new design will obviate this trouble.
> 2) The taper boiler which it is proposed to fit is of a modern design and high capacity and will avoid the need to perpetuate an obsolete design of boiler that can only be used on this class of 52 engines out of the whole LMS stock.
> 3) As converted the engine will be designated Class 6 and will be capable of their place in the same workings as the Converted Royal Scots and 5xp taper boiler classes, which have proved very satisfactory in service. It has been estimated that a total of 91 Class 6 engines will be required quickly after the war to deal with the acceleration of express passenger services and as the Royal Scot and Class 5xp already account for 73 it is intended to obtain the remaining 18 by means of the conversion of the 5xp parallel engines now proposed.
>
> Proposed to provide 8 boilers in the 1946 and the other 10 in the 1947 Programme.

Although it took six years to complete the Patriot rebuilding programme, it did affect the Royal Scot rebuilding programme by slowing it down after 1946. The locomotives chosen from the Patriot Class were simply those due next for general repair. Additionally, it must be noted that originally

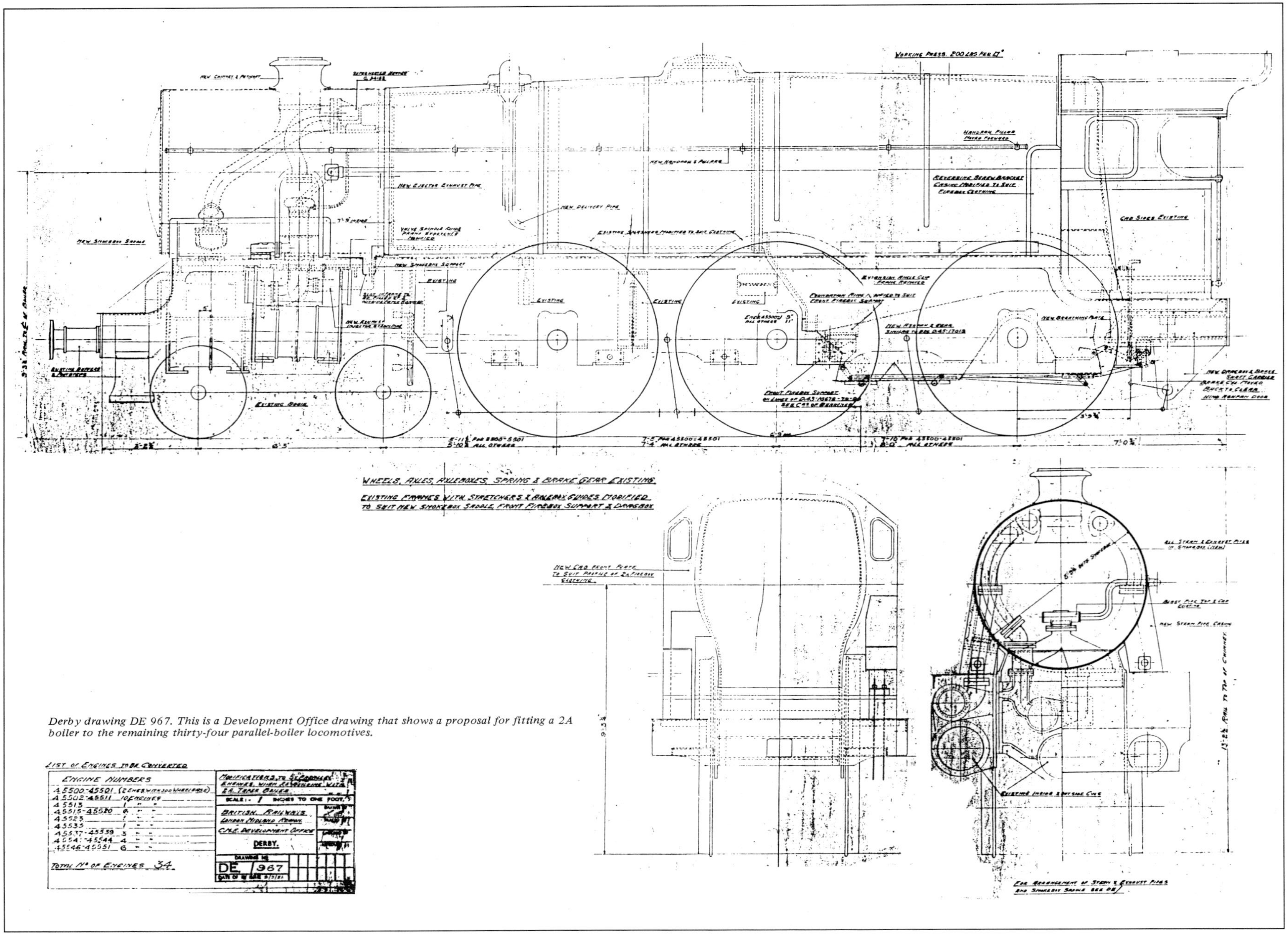

Derby drawing DE 967. This is a Development Office drawing that shows a proposal for fitting a 2A boiler to the remaining thirty-four parallel-boiler locomotives.

The first parallel-boiler Patriot to be rebuilt with a 2A taper boiler was No. 5530 Sir Frank Ree. *The rebuilding or, as it is usually described, conversion, was completed on 19th October 1946. In this picture we see the locomotive at the head of an express passenger train in 1947.*
COLLECTION W. T. STUBBS

there was never a plan to re-boiler more than eighteen Patriots. Work on the No. 2A boiler started in 1939, with the intention of experimentally fitting two examples to a pair of Jubilees, presumably as an extension of the programme to correct the steaming problems of the class. Wartime conditions delayed progress, but during 1942 Nos. 5735/6 returned to service re-boilered. They were not alone; Royal Scot No. 6103, one of ten sanctioned in March 1942, was also converted in July 1943. Another ten were sanctioned in 1943, with the remaining fifty being sanctioned the following year. In practice, it was not until 1955 that the last Royal Scot was converted.

In 1946, the year of the first Patriot rebuild, the LMS announced that all the Royal Scots, Jubilees and Patriots would be rebuilt to produce a fleet of similar, modern locomotives capable of Class 6P duties. They were similar but not identical and the differences among the three classes were minor. History altered those plans; only the Royal Scots achieved a completed full class conversion programme. Nos. 5735/6 remained the only converted Jubilees and the Patriots fell between the two, with eighteen of the fifty-two locomotives being fitted with the 2A boiler. Traffic Committee minute No. 7817 dated 18th December 1946 summarised the position as:

N.W.O. 6428. Submitted with the approval of the Executive and recommended by the Chief Operating Manager and Chief Mechanical Engineer that the estimate of £58,806 authorised by minute 7271a for the conversion of 18 Class 5x parallel boiler engines to Class 6 taper boiler be increased by £9,728 to enable the 18 Class 5x parallel boiler engines to take Royal Scot boilers. Submitted with the approval of the Executive Committee, recommended by the Chief Operating Manager and CME that the expenditure of £58,806 authorised by minute 7271A 28/4/1944, conversion of 18 Class 5x parallel boiler engines to be Class 6 taper boiler be increased by £9,728 to enable 18 engines to be provided with rocking grates, self emptying ashpans and self cleaning smoke boxes. Also provision of new frame plates on 10 engines including the latest design of hornstay, pin-jointed cross stays, and magnesium steel liners to axle boxes and horn block faces.

Although this appears to be a duplication of the recommendation, this is what was recorded and it leaves no doubt as to what was planned when the locomotives were rebuilt. The first Patriot to be rebuilt was No. 5530 *Sir Frank Ree*, in October 1946. It was followed by No. 5521 *Rhyl* the next month, and the remaining sixteen by February 1949. There the conversions ended. Details are listed in *Table 11*.

With the rebuilding with a taper boiler came several differences. The boiler pressure was increased from 200 to 250 lb in^2. The cylinder diameter was reduced to 17 inches, the inside cylinder had the smokebox saddle cast integral with it, and the outside cylinders were the same as that later fitted to the Jubilee 4–6–0s. The old style cab with one window and a cut-out each side was replaced by the Stanier double-window version. A new smokebox with double chimney and self-cleaning plates was fitted, and also a rocking grate and self-emptying ashpan. The first eight locomotives converted retained their original frames, suitably modified.

Of the eighteen parallel-boiler Patriots that were converted to taper boiler, only eight were completed before the LMS became part of British Railways. One of the eight was No. 5526, photographed at Camden carrying the LMS 1946 livery but before any smoke deflector plates were fitted. AUTHORS' COLLECTION

This is another picture of No. 5530 taken after British Railways had renumbered the locomotive during the week ending 10th April 1948. At this time it was not unusual to increase the LMS number by 40000 and to leave the letters 'LMS' on the tender. H. GORDON TIDY

The remaining ten locomotives had new frame plates, the latest design of hornstays, pin-jointed cross stays and manganese steel axlebox liners. The original motion was retained and, finally, the old standard 3,500 gallon tenders were exchanged for Stanier curved-top 4,000 gallon tenders taken from Jubilees. The Jubilees received the old standard tenders as replacement as listed in *Appendix 5*.

Also in 1946 the LMS introduced its postwar livery of glossy black. As express passenger locomotives, the Patriots qualified for the straw-lined version with maroon edging. Block numerals and letters rendered in straw, with an inset maroon line, were also standard. In LMS days any Patriots ex-works received it, but in early BR days it continued to be applied (only with BR markings) until experimental or standard BR liveries replaced it. Details are given in *Appendix 12b* and *Table 13*. An early modification to the rebuilt locomotive was the addition of smoke deflectors due to the old problem of drifting smoke obscuring forward visibility from the cab. Initially, the problem had occurred on the Royal Scots and a very neat design of deflector had been fitted. They were small, rising vertically from the platform and curving outwards to follow the smoke box curvature. A pronounced raked-back leading edge resulted in a very short top edge. Attractive they may have been, but effective they were not always — unless certain speed and weather conditions prevailed. The main problem appeared to be one of smallness and the inclined front restricted their capacity to collect air in front of the smoke box and to guide it back properly before release at the back. On the other hand, photographs have occasionally shown them to be working correctly. Several years later Royal Scot No. 46106 was fitted with BR standard deflectors that were more successful, but it remained the only 6P ex-LMS locomotive so fitted.

Another consideration at this time was to fulfil a long-standing intention to name all members of the class, the convenient time to be when those still unnamed were being rebuilt. Again, the fulfilment never came as sporadic naming continued. At the end of LMS ownership, 31st December 1947, eight of the class had been rebuilt and all were allocated to the Western Division, as one would expect.

Nationalisation brought no sudden changes of policy and for a while the Patriots continued as before. Visible changes, other than rebuilding, concerned renumbering by the addition of 40,000 to the existing numbers and liveries, interim and experimental at first but settling into a BR standard from 1949. No. 45531 was brought into Derby Works paint shop in 1948 and given an experimental livery of apple green with white/black/orange lining applied in L&NWR style. Insignia was painted in 10in. high white Gill Sans numerals and letters, the title 'BRITISH RAILWAYS' on the tender matching the numerals on the cabside and on a level with them. The running number also appeared on a plate affixed to the smoke box door in LMS fashion, but with Gill Sans numerals. The locomotive was very attractive indeed, but not quite LMS! A few Patriots received the revived L&NWR livery of lined black, but as this was reserved for mixed traffic locomotives, it became short-lived on these few. The standard passenger livery adopted was Brunswick Green with GWR-

This undated picture shows No. 5509, which became 45509 The Derbyshire Yeomanry in 1951, at the head of an express freight train.

Research undertaken by one of the authors and the late David Jenkinson during the 1960s suggested that the LMS 1946 livery for locomotives, in its complete form with boiler lining, was introduced about July of that year. There can be little doubt that it was most attractive and we include this picture of No. 5505 The Royal Army Ordnance Corps in order to show a parallel-boiler Patriot painted in this style.
NATIONAL RAILWAY MUSEUM

THE LMS PATRIOTS

inspired lining of orange/black/orange and from 1949, the lion-and-wheel totem. All Patriots received this livery in due course.

As time passed, wartime and postwar restrictions were eased as the backlog of maintenance arrears was slowly cleared. The Patriots never regained their former standing of the 1930s – it was unfortunate, but inevitable. Perhaps only the rebuilt examples snatched a little of the glamour, but then there were fifty-one Stanier Pacifics, the Royal Scots and the Jubilees to divert attention. One unrebuilt Patriot did manage to steal its own private glory – No. 45516, still in its pre-war crimson lake livery, but with its BR number. A little liberty was allowed behind the scenes to enable the old LMS flag to fly under the new regime to commemorate a special event in February 1950. The 1st Battalion of The Bedfordshire and Hertfordshire Regiment was due back in Britain after twenty-five years service abroad, and a special train was laid on to transport the men from the port. No. 45516 bore the name

This is a typical scene at a 'running shed' where locomotives were being prepared for their next turn of duty. This picture shows taper-boiler Patriot No. 45530 Sir Frank Ree *at Camden prior to running light engine to Euston station. Note the 'black smoke' and the safety valves 'lifting'. The locomotive had been renumbered but the tender still displayed the letters 'LMS'.* AUTHORS' COLLECTION

After locomotives went through the shops, or through the works, to use two railwaymen's terms, they were employed on running-in turns. Here we see No. 45536 Private W. Wood V.C. *on an ordinary passenger train at Shrewsbury station in 1948. This locomotive was rebuilt with a taper boiler in November 1948 but the condition of the paintwork, to say nothing of the bright sunshine, suggests this photograph may have been taken in the spring of the following year.*
J. A. G. H. COLTAS

As we describe in the text, this locomotive was specially prepared to work a special train from Southampton carrying men of the Bedfordshire and Hertfordshire Regiment home after 25 years service overseas. This picture of No. 5516, The Beds and Herts, the commonly used nickname for both the locomotive and regiment, was taken c.1939 when the locomotive was still in pre-war LMS livery.
W. POTTER

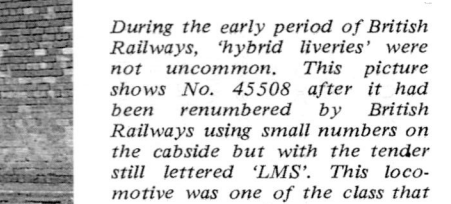

During the early period of British Railways, 'hybrid liveries' were not uncommon. This picture shows No. 45508 after it had been renumbered by British Railways using small numbers on the cabside but with the tender still lettered 'LMS'. This locomotive was one of the class that was never named.
H. C. CASSERLEY

THE LMS PATRIOTS

of that regiment and it was decided that it would haul the special train from Southampton Docks, so it was brought into Crewe Works to be prepared. Of special interest here, is that it still wore the vestiges of the prewar crimson lake livery, but instead of having a repaint into BR livery, someone decided to have the existing livery brightened. It appears that the platform edging lining was re-applied together with that on the lower cabside panels. The BR number was painted on the cab sides in standard BR 10 ins style Gill Sans numerals, but the letters 'LMS' were proudly left on the Fowler 3,500 gallon tender. It was brought up to sparkling condition during the early days of February 1950 and on the 16th hauled the special train of nine LNER coaches and a baggage van. It was almost a pre-war touch – one LMS locomotive wearing crimson lake and all rolling stock in the train, except for one vehicle, still in teak livery.

This picture of No. 455222 Prestatyn *was taken after the locomotive had been renumbered by the addition of 40000 to the LMS stock number and with 'British Railways' on the tender side. It also shows to good effect the handsome appearance of a taper-boiler rebuild without side wind plates.* AUTHORS' COLLECTION

This rather splendid picture of No. 45506 The Royal Pioneer Corps *was taken when the locomotive had been painted in the old LNWR style of livery that was later adopted for mixed traffic locomotives. This engine was both renumbered by British Railways and named during September 1948, so it seems likely that this picture was taken to record the naming.* NATIONAL RAILWAY MUSEUM

This official photograph of slightly work-stained 45534 was taken in the early 1950s, probably during a visit to the works for attention. It is in final condition with smoke deflectors and with 7P power classification. Also of note is the stencilled 5534 on the leading tender footsteps, an aid to the workshops to allocate maintenance and repair costs and ensure that the tender was paired with the correct locomotive afterwards. It was common during BR days for the shops to omit the '4' prefix from the stencilled running number as indeed it was verbally.

One of the authors remembers No. 45509 and can confirm that what we have said in the text was true – The Derbyshire Yeomanry was something of a black sheep and did not enjoy a good reputation. Nevertheless, we feel that this picture, probably taken about the time it was named (10th November 1951), provides a good example of the final British Railways livery style carried by these locomotives.
NATIONAL RAILWAY MUSEUM

The question of BR livery for the Patriots was settled during mid-1949 when Brunswick Green was adopted, together with the lion-and-wheel totem. Except for a change from totem to the revised emblem from 1956, this was to be the standard livery. On the cabsides 10in. Gill Sans numerals were standard, although there may have been occasional applications of 12in. numerals north of the border.

A memorandum from the CME Department, Derby, dated 20th April 1950 concerned the possibility of converting the remaining thirty-four parallel boiler Patriots, as follows:

4–6–0 Class 5X 3-Cylinder Locomotives
Nos. 5500–5551

The 3-cylinder engines (between Nos. 5500–5551) which still retain the original parallel boilers, are dimensionally suitable for reboilering with standard 2A sloping throatplate taper boiler.

The following new details and alterations to the existing engines with parallel boiler will be necessary to make the conversion:-

1. BOILER. The standard 2A sloping throatplate taper boiler, with working pressure reduced from 250 to 200 lb. per sq. inch. The latter pressure enables the engine to retain its existing 5X classification. This boiler includes a rocking grate. Modifications required to foundation ring to suit new carrying arrangements.
2. ASHPAN. New ashpan. To be same as that fitted to Class 6 engines with 2A taper boiler. This ashpan has hopper doors incorporated. Damper gear to be redesigned to suit.
3. CLOTHING. New clothing. To be same as that fitted to 2A taper boiler.
4. SMOKEBOX etc. New circular type smokebox in place of existing flat bottom type. Diameter (5'8½" inside) to be same as for Class 6 engines with 2A taper boiler, but length to be increased to suit. New fabricated smokebox saddle fastened to inside cylinder at front end and resting on existing inside valve spindle guide stretcher casting at back end. New saddle to incorporate existing packing glands round blast pipe connections and inside steam pipe connection, etc. Existing blastpipe to be used again.

   New steam pipes for inside and outside cylinders to suit header on 2A boiler. New steam pipe air tight joints on smokebox. New steam pipe connection pieces to cylinders to suit three bolt steam pipe flanges, and to accommodate new saddle.

   The following new smokebox details which are required will be the same design as for existing Class 6 taper boiler engines:
   Smokebox front end door complete.
   Steam pipe flanges and lens joints.
   Header supporting brackets.

   A new design of single chimney and petticoat will be required as the ejector exhaust ring is incorporated in the existing blast pipe cap which is single. Alternatively a new double blast pipe could be fitted and the Class 6 double chimney retained.
5. CAB. The cut-away in cab front for the 2A firebox is smaller than that necessary for the existing parallel firebox, except on the top. A new cab front plate is therefore required with the profile of the front opening to suit the 2A boiler clothing. Making up pieces will be required for the reversing screw casing on the L.H. side. Wood platform arrangement (cab floor) to be modified to suit new firebox.
6. MAIN FRAMES. Alterations are required to the main frames to suit carrying brackets at front of firebox. A modification is necessary to the front of hind dragbox to accommodate the firebox expansion plate, and to clear the injector steam and vacuum train pipes. This entails moving the vertical front plate back several inches and shortening the horizontal plates to suit.
7. PIPES etc. Injector delivery pipes lengthened to connect up to top feed on taper boiler. Injector steam pipes lengthened to suit manifold. New injector required (same as for taper boiler engines).

Slight modifications will be necessary to the following items:-
Splashers (angles to clothing altered)
Sandbox shield plates.

GENERAL. In assessing the above alterations required, it has been assumed that the minimum amount of alteration will be made to make the conversion.

Additional work to bring the Engine up to date would include fitting of self cleaning smokebox plates and details which would be of new design to suit the internal arrangement of the smokebox.

The weights (in working order) will be approximately as follows:–
On leading bogie	20 ton.	10 cwt.
On leading coupled wheels	20 ton.	15 cwt.
On intermediate coupled wheels	20 ton.	15 cwt.
On trailing coupled wheels	20 ton.	0 cwt.

The question of whether or not to rebuild more Patriots was settled later in 1950 when the London Midland Region (LMR) insisted that it could not justify the continuation of rebuilding because it was considered that there was no operating requirement. Be that as it may, the Royal Scot rebuilding was completed in due course, albeit as boilers became due for replacement. The impending introduction of BR standard designs perhaps had some influence over the decision not to continue rebuilding Patriots.

The first Britannia two-cylinder BR standard 4–6–2s were introduced in early 1951, with the power classification of 7 under a BR scheme, based upon the LMS pattern. Under this scheme, 5XP disappeared to become 6P, the former 6P became 7P and the ex-LMS 7P Pacifics were regraded to 8P. The unrebuilt Patriots therefore became 6P and the rebuilt examples became 7P. Although the first Britannia allocations were to other regions, Holyhead shed received four and Longsight one in late 1952. The former then took on a further five in 1954. Although it post-dated the decision not to continue the Patriot rebuilding, the modernisation intentions of the 1950s certainly reinforced it further.

During the early 1950s, No. 45509 started its own particular affinity with Derby and the Midland Division, where one of the authors knew it well. Named *The Derbyshire Yeomanry*, as if to confirm that affinity, in November 1951, it was to become something of an enigma over the following years. It gained a reputation of being a black sheep during the 1950s, but it is by no means certain that it was fully deserved. Whether or not the Derby and other crews who manned it were able to adapt fully to their single Patriot allocation is uncertain, but they regularly experienced troubles with poor steaming. It was frequently used down to Bristol with occasional forays out on the Midland Main Line into St. Pancras and news frequently emerged through the 'bush telegraph' that it had 'failed again'. Although the reports were probably little more than rumour after repeated retelling, it did not prevent many people from being of the opinion that the 'Derby Yo-Yo' had been dumped on Derby by the Western Division. Whatever the reasons may have been for the less than acceptable performance of No. 45509, other members of the class were still capable of some fine running. Rebuilt Patriot No. 45530 showed what it could achieve in 1954 when it hauled a train of 530 tons over the 158 miles from Crewe to Euston in 150 minutes 59 seconds (149 minutes

From November 1956 until it was withdrawn in the week ending 3rd December 1960, No. 45508 ran with a stovepipe chimney, as seen in this picture taken at Tebay on 23rd April 1960. It was fitted as part of some experiments into smokebox draughting, but it was rather late in the day to consider improving the parallel-boiler Patriots. A. G. ELLIS

This picture of No. 45505 The Royal Army Ordnance Corps was taken in August 1958 on Shap Summit when it was working a Down Class C parcels train made up of vehicles conforming to coaching stock requirements. Note the straight-sided 3500 gallon tender No. 4570 coupled to this engine from May 1958 until it was withdrawn in 1962.
COLLECTION D. F. TEE

There can be little doubt that in their final form with a taper boiler and smoke deflectors, the Patriots were impressive-looking locomotives. This view of No. 45526 shows the engine in its final form when it was photographed at Hest Bank troughs, probably in the early 1950s.
COLLECTION W. T. STUBBS

net) reaching a maximum speed of 82 mph. The usual load allowance for a rebuilt Patriot was 405 tons.

By the mid-1950s the unrebuilt Patriots were twenty years old and still giving good, if unspectacular, service. With the advent of better testing facilities, particularly the Rugby Testing Station, many opportunities to thoroughly test new designs had been made, mainly BR standard locomotives. When time allowed, older pre-nationalisation designs were re-examined and the unrebuilt Patriot was one of them. No. 45508 was chosen as a 'guinea pig' for smokebox draughting experiments to try to implement some improvements. It had been accepted that whilst there was nothing particularly wrong with the parallel boiler, it was not as good as it should be. Boiler tube proportions apart, it was felt that the smokebox draughting had been reasonable pre-war, with skilled crews and good lump coal, but postwar conditions often lacked both of these attributes. The tests on No. 45508 were undertaken on the road and outwardly the only sign of something different was an ugly, but functional, stovepipe chimney. The locomotive ran from late 1956 in this condition until withdrawal in December 1960. Really, it was too late in the day for any improvements to be of a worthwhile nature, because of the impending influx of diesel locomotives.

Although the unrebuilt Patriots had for many years undertaken fast fitted-freight workings, they were used increasingly on lighter duties, often consisting of a handful of milk tank wagons and a full passenger brake, either of the six-wheeled variety or bogie types. In 1957 No. 45550 was actually loaned to Toton shed and spent its time on 'odd jobs' including local trip work and unfitted freight turns. In particular during late 1959 Nos. 45533/7/41 were transferred to Rugby shed specifically for undertaking freight work. By early 1960 three unrebuilt Patriots were reallocated to Preston and six more, plus a rebuilt example, were already allocated to Carnforth. The latter not only worked from Carnforth to Leeds, but also worked from Carnforth to Camden on fitted freights with a similar return working from Camden to Warrington.

The Midland Division by this time had been able to retire many of its elderly and hard-pushed (in more ways than one) 4–4–0s by an influx of displaced Royal Scot and Britannia locomotives. Rebuilt Patriot No. 45532 *Illustrious*, which was allocated to Nottingham shed, joined these engines. Unrebuilt Patriots frequently visited or passed through the Midland Division on various relief or freight workings, and a similar pattern occurred on the Central Division. Perhaps one of the most surprising events of 1959 was the September naming of No. 45528 *R.E.M.E*. It was very late in the Patriot day and the use of initials, rather than the full title Royal Electrical and Mechanical Engineers, was a reminder of when Royal Scot No. 6121 was named *H.L.I.* in 1927. The reason

Although we do not have a date for this picture of No. 45529, it was taken during the early 1960s; note the electrification warning sign, but there is no sign of a strip on the side of the cab. This locomotive, along with most, if not all, of the rebuilds, was fitted with a Stone-Delta speedometer driven off the left-hand trailing wheel crankpin, clearly seen in this view. Following the adoption of the old GWR Brunswick green for express passenger locomotives in 1949, all the taper-boiler locomotives carried this livery, which in this picture appears to have worn reasonably well.
AUTHORS' COLLECTION

THE LMS PATRIOTS

for using this abbreviation was that it was more in keeping with its army-style cognomen, known phonetically as 'Reemy'. For all the brief period that the locomotive carried these initials, No. 45528 was so referred.

September 1960 saw the first Patriot withdrawal. This was No. 45502 of Carlisle Upperby shed, an unrebuilt example as one would expect; the diesel era was beginning to bite. No. 45508 of Bushbury, complete with stovepipe chimney, soon followed it in the November. The following year the first rebuilt Patriot was withdrawn, No. 45514 *Holyhead*, latterly of Derby. It was one of nine Patriots to go that year, and by the end of 1962 all the remaining unrebuilt examples were gone. They went amid the gathering pace of mass withdrawal of steam traction, unsung and with not a thought of preservation in the air. They went as they had served for many years – almost unnoticed. Of the remaining rebuilt examples, seven-

During their final years, the parallel-boiler engines were used on various classes of freight train and we have included three pictures to illustrate them at work. No. 45524 Blackpool was photographed at Greenholme in August 1960 at the head of a Class D express freight train when it was provided with banking assistance.
COLLECTION D. F. TEE

At least two Patriots were coupled to 3500 gallon, high, straight-sided tenders, the confirmed examples being Nos. 45550 and 45551 as seen here. This locomotive was the final Patriot to be built, entering traffic on 2nd May 1934 and being withdrawn on 16th June 1962. The locomotive was never named and ran with tender No. 4570 from 2nd May 1958 until withdrawal. This picture was taken at Polmadie in 1960 when the locomotive was stationed at 12B Carlisle Upperby. We are not sure if all the parallel-boiler Patriots were equipped with AWS but the presence of the timing reservoir just in front of the cab on the left-hand platform confirms this locomotive was fitted with the British Railways standard Automatic Warning System.
W. POTTER

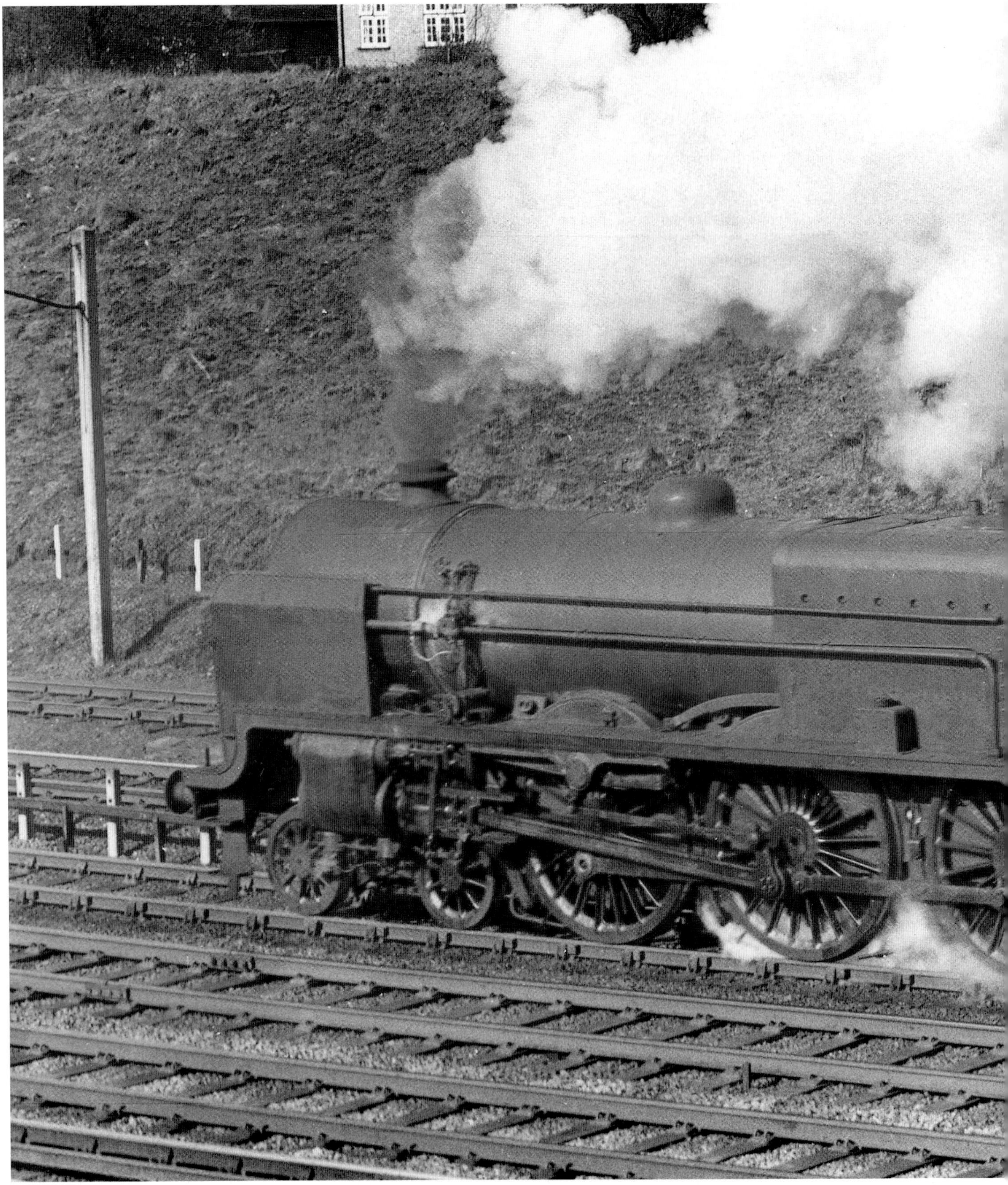

This splendid undated picture of No. 45547, a Patriot that was never named, shows a locomotive at the head of an express freight train. This is confirmed by the vacuum hose connection to the leading vehicle, a container flat with a container, but what class of express freight train is unknown. It could have been a 'Maltese' with four automatic brake vehicles coupled to the engine, a 'semi-fitted' with one third of the vehicle or even a fully-fitted with the vacuum brake operating on at least half of the vehicles. The locomotive is seen in British Railways standard Brunswick green, livery code G14. F. SAUNDERS

teen by 1962, the old Great Central line received an allocation of one, No. 45529, along with various other displaced ex-LMS types. Few were in their best condition, but in early 1964 No. 45529, late of Annesley, was withdrawn.

One of the last rebuilt locomotives to go through an overhaul at Crewe Works was No. 45531 in 1963, and it looked in good condition, retaining its full BR livery with no economy of lining which sometimes occurred during those days. Most of the survivors ended their days allocated to sheds in the north west, particularly Carlisle; the final withdrawal was No. 45530 *Sir Frank Ree*, then of Carlisle Kingmoor, in December 1965. Thus ended an honourable career of thirty-five years for a class of locomotives born of a troubled LMS of the 1920s. They were to fall victim to the modernisation of the 1960s. Again, no example of the rebuilt version was preserved; the nearest examples to a Patriot one can see are two rebuilt Royal Scots, their very close relatives.

In retrospect, the Patriots have been underrated. They resolved, for a time, a locomotive design problem which the LMS had been wrestling with for several years – that of providing a good design of second-line locomotive stud. By the time of nationalisation, further improvements had been effected, but only partially, and it is important to note that the war, its aftermath and the ever-quickening pace of what was termed progress, overtook them. Gone they are, but forgotten they are not.

When this picture was taken at Chester on 11th June 1961, No. 45547 was still in service but close to withdrawal. From November 1961 it was stored at Edge Hill until it was withdrawn during the week ending 15th September 1962. In their final years they carried the electrification warning plates but apart from the green livery, there was little change from their appearance pre-Nationalisation. W. POTTER

In their final years the Patriots were fitted with overhead electrification warning signs, and a diagonal yellow stripe was painted on the cab side, as seen in this picture of No. 45530 with rear coupling rods and nameplate removed at Corkerhill. W. POTTER

TABLES

TABLE I. CLAUGHTONS GENERAL DATES, NUMBERS, NAMES

Order No.	Crewe No.	Date	L&NWR No.	LMS No.	Name	Notes	Date Withdrawn
E249	5117	01/1913	2222	5900	SIR GILBERT CLAUGHTON		03/1935
E249	5138	05/1913	1161	5901	SIR ROBERT TURNBULL	1	05/1933
E249	5139	05/1913	1191	5902	SIR FRANK REE	2	12/1930
E249	5142	06/1913	21	5903	DUKE OF SUTHERLAND	3	05/1933
E249	5143	06/1913	163	5904	HOLLAND HIBBERT	4	12/1934
E249	5144	06/1913	650	5905	LORD RATHMORE	5	02/1933
E249	5145	06/1913	1159	5906	RALPH BROCKLEBANK	6*	03/1937
E249	5140	06/1913	1319	5907	SIR FREDERICK HARRISON	7	01/1933
E249	5141	06/1913	1327	5908	ALFRED FLETCHER	C*	09/1936
E249	5146	06/1913	2046	5909	CHARLES N. LAWRENCE	8	05/1935
E262	5227	08/1914	250	5910	J.A. BRIGHT	*	04/1937
E262	5228	08/1914	260	5911	W.E. DORRINGTON		03/1934
E262	5229	08/1914	1131	5912	LORD FABER		02/1935
E262	5230	09/1914	1429	5913	COLONEL LOCKWOOD		09/1934
E262	5232	09/1914	209	5914	J. BRUCE ISMAY		12/1934
E262	5233	09/1914	668	5915	RUPERT GUINNESS		11/1934
E262	5234	09/1914	856	5916	E. TOOTAL BROADHURST		12/1932
E262	5235	10/1914	1567	5917	CHARLES J. CROPPER		09/1934
E262	5231	09/1914	2239	5918	FREDERICK BAYNES		03/1935
E262	5236	10/1914	2401	5919	LORD KITCHENER	9	09/1934
E266	5337	07/1916	511	5920	GEORGE MACPHERSON		04/1935
E266	5338	07/1916	695	5921	SIR ARTHUR LAWLEY		11/1934
E266	5339	07/1916	968	5922	LORD KENYON		09/1934
E266	5340	07/1916	1093	5923	SIR GUY CALTHROP (SIR added 12/19)		07/1935
E266	5341	08/1916	1345	5924	JAMES BISHOP		09/1934
E266	5342	08/1916	2174	5925	E.C. TRENCH		03/1933
E266	5343	08/1916	2204	5926	SIR HERBERT WALKER (K.C.B. added 03/17)		01/1933
E266	5344	08/1916	2221	5927	SIR FRANCIS DENT	C*	12/1936
E266	5345	08/1916	2338	5928	CHARLES H. DENT		01/1934
E266	5346	09/1916	2395	5929	J.A.F. ASPINALL		03/1935
E277	5367	02/1917	37	5930	G.R. JEBB		10/1934
E277	5368	03/1917	154	5931	CAPTAIN FRYATT		05/1934
E277	5369	03/1917	155	5932	SIR THOMAS WILLIAMS (I.T. WILLIAMS until 12/19)		04/1935
E277	5370	03/1917	162	5933			12/1933
E277	5371	03/1917	186	5934			01/1935
E277	5372	03/1917	713	5935			02/1933
E277	5373	04/1917	1334	5936			08/1932
E277	5374	04/1917	2042	5937			11/1934
E277	5375	04/1917	2097	5938			02/1935
E277	5376	05/1917	2230	5939	CLIO (07/22)		06/1935
E278	5377	05/1917	1019	5940	COLUMBUS (02/22)		09/1934
E278	5378	05/1917	1335	5941			08/1934
E278	5379	05/1917	2366	5942			09/1932
E278	5380	05/1917	2373	5943	TENNYSON (01/22)		08/1934
E278	5381	06/1917	2411	5944		10	04/1933
E278	5382	06/1917	2420	5945			04/1934
E278	5383	06/1917	2427	5946	DUKE OF CONNAUGHT. (01/22)	C*	02/1941
E278	5384	06/1917	2431	5947		11	02/1935
E278	5385	07/1917	2445	5948	BALTIC (07/23)	C*	04/1937
E278	5386	07/1917	2450	5949			08/1932
E279	5387	08/1917	116	5950			10/1934
E279	5388	08/1917	159	5951			10/1935
E279	5389	08/1917	171	5952			11/1932
E279	5390	08/1917	986	5953	BUCKINGHAM. (02/22)	*	09/1936
E279	5391	08/1917	1085	5954			12/1932
E279	5392	09/1917	1103	5955			05/1935
E279	5393	09/1917	2122	5956			03/1934
E279	5394	09/1917	2368	5957		C*	02/1936
E279	5395	09/1917	2416	5958			10/1932
E279	5396	10/1917	2426	5959			06/1932
E290	5503	01/1920	69	5960			03/1934
E290	5504	01/1920	178	5961			10/1934
E290	5505	01/1920	194	5962		C*	12/1935
E290	5506	01/1920	972	5963			12/1932
E290	5502	01/1920	69 then 1914	5964	PATRIOT IN MEMORY OF THE FALLEN L&NWR EMPLOYEES 1914-1919		07/1934
E291	5512	02/1920	484	5965			09/1934
E290	5507	01/1920	1177	5966	BUNSEN (02/22)		10/1932
E291	5513	02/1920	1407	5967	L/CORPL. J.A. CHRISTIE V.C. (01/22)		11/1934
E290	5511	02/1920	1599	5968	JOHN O' GROAT (06/22)		01/1935
E290	5508	01/1920	2179	5969			09/1934
E290	5509	02/1920	2499	5970	PATIENCE (06/22)	*	12/1935
E290	5510	02/1920	2511	5971	CROXTETH (06/23)		12/1930
E291	5514	03/1920	1726	5972		*	05/1937
E291	5515	03/1920	1741	5973			12/1932
E291	5516	03/1920	1747	5974		12	08/1932
E291	5521	04/1920	12	5975	TALISMAN (01/23)	C*	06/1937
E291	5517	03/1920	2035	5976	PRIVATE E. SYKES V.C. (01/22 to 04/1926)		03/1935

E291	5518	03/1920	2083	5977			04/1929
E291	5519	03/1920	2231	5978			05/1934
E291	5520	03/1920	2268	5979	FROBISHER (06/22)		04/1934
E292	5522	04/1920	85	5980			01/1935
E292	5523	04/1920	98	5981			06/1934
E292	5524	04/1920	103	5982			11/1932
E292	5525	04/1920	201	5983			10/1932
E292	5526	05/1920	499	5984			10/1935
E292	5527	05/1920	808	5985			06/1932
E292	5528	05/1920	1092	5986		*	11/1935
E292	5529	05/1920	1096	5987			08/1932
E292	5530	05/1920	1097	5988	PRIVATE W. WOOD V.C. (01/22 to 04/26)		06/1935
E292	5531	05/1920	1133	5989			11/1934
E293	5533	06/1920	1326	5990			04/1935
E293	5532	05/1920	2059	5991	C.J. BOWEN COOKE (10/20)	D	02/1935
E293	5534	06/1920	2090	5992			10/1932
E293	5535	06/1920	2095	5993		*	05/1936
E293	5537	06/1920	6	5994			06/1935
E293	5538	06/1920	8	5995			02/1934
E293	5539	07/1920	10	5996			02/1933
E293	5540	07/1920	11	5997			03/1933
E293	5536	06/1920	2101	5998			08/1934
E293	5541	07/1920	13,2430	5999	VINDICTIVE (06/22 to 08/36)	+*	06/1937
E294	5542	07/1920	15	6000			03/1933
E294	5543	08/1920	23	6001			10/1934
E294	5544	08/1920	30	6002	THALABA (04/23)		09/1934
E294	5545	08/1920	32	6003			10/1934
E294	5546	08/1920	42	6004	PRINCESS LOUISE (02/22 TO 09/35)	*	04/1949
E294	5547	084920	63	6005			09/1932
E294	5548	08/1920	68	6006			11/1932
E294	5549	08/1920	102	6007			10/1934
E294	5550	09/1920	110	6008	LADY GODIVA (05/23)		12/1932
E294	5551	09/1920	119	6009			05/1934
E295	5552	03/1921	149	6010			08/1932
E295	5553	03/1921	150	6011	ILLUSTRIOUS (05/23)	13	02/1933
E295	5554	03/1921	152	6012			09/1932
E295	5555	03/1921	156	6013		C*	03/1936
E295	5556	04/1921	157	6014			09/1934
E295	5557	04/1921	158	6015	PRIVATE E. SYKES V.C. (04/26)		03/1933
E295	5558	04/1921	161	6016		14	01/1935
E295	5559	04/1921	169	6017	BREADALBANE (03/23)	*	10/1940
E295	5560	04/1921	179	6018	PRIVATE W. WOOD V.C. (04/26)	15	02/1933
E295	5561	04/1921	180	6019	LLEWELLYN (04/23)		12/1934
E296	5562	05/1921	183	6020			07/1935
E296	5563	05/1921	192	6021	BEVERE (07/23)		02/1934
E296	5564	05/1921	205	6022		16	04/1933
E296	5565	05/1921	207	6023	SIR CHARLES CUST (12/21)	C*	07/1941
E296	5566	05/1921	208	6024			03/1935
E296	5567	05/1921	210	6025			08/1935
E296	5568	06/1921	211	6026			12/1932
E296	5569	06/1921	517	6027			04/1933
E296	5570	06/1921	1216	6028			09/1934
E296	5571	06/1921	1220	6029		C*	12/1935

NOTES
Locomotives listed in order of LMS running numbers.

* Rebuilt with larger boiler and reclassified 5XP.
C Rebuilt with Caprotti valve gear.
D Date on nameplate altered to OCTR. 1920 to coincide with Bowen Cooke's death.

Intended names
1 LORD STALBRIDGE
2 RALPH BROCKLEBANK
3 A.H. HOLLAND HIBBERT
4 J. BRUCE ISMAY
5 LORD RATHMORE
6 COLONEL LOCKWOOD
7 W.E. DORRINGTON
8 SIR FREDERICK HARRISON
9 LORD KENYON

Temporary namings
10 COLONEL LOCKWOOD for working the Royal Train 08.08.1922.
11 CHARLES N. LAWRENCE for working the Royal Train 08.08.1922.
12 SIR CHARLES CUST and temporarily renumbered 207 for working the Royal Trains 08.08.1922 and 10.10.1922.
13 HOLLAND HIBBERT for working the Royal Train 08.10.1921.
14 RALPH BROCKLEBANK for working the Royal Train 08.10.1921.
15 J.A.F. ASPINALL for working the Royal Train 08.10.1921.
16 CHARLES N. LAWRENCE for working the Royal Train 08.10.1921.

+ Renumbered 2430 10/1922. No. 13 was regarded as potential bad luck when combined with the name VINDICTIVE. This was the name of the old warship sunk deliberately at Zeebrugge in 1918.

The names PRIVATE E. SYKES V.C. and PRIVATE W. WOOD V.C. were transferred from 5976 and 5988 to 6015 and 6018 respectively in April 1926. This occurred when the original locomotives bearing them were transferred away from the Manchester area. To ensure that the names would continue to be associated with their home city, they were transferred to locomotives remaining based in the area.

In 1922 further names were chosen but not used, as follows:

DUKE OF ALBANY	MAGDALA
EDEN	MARCHIONESS OF STAFFORD
FIREFLY	OUTRAM
HARDMAN	PLUCK
JOSHUA RADCLIFFE	QUERNMORE

TABLE 2. CLAUGHTONS – PRINCIPAL DATA (USE WITH ENGINE DIAGRAM)

	Original Condition	Rebuilt Condition
Locomotive weight in full working order	77 tons 5cwt	79 tons 1cwt
Tender weight laden	39 tons 5cwt	
Boiler barrel length	14ft 5⅞in	
Boiler diameter front	4ft 11½in	5ft 5⅛in max
Boiler diameter rear	5ft 2in	
Boiler centre line above rail level	8ft 9in	8ft 9¼in
Boiler pressure	175lb/in²	200lb/in²
Firebox length (outside)	9ft 6in	
Firebox width	4ft 1in	4ft ⅞in
Tractive effort	27,072lb	29,570lb
Height from rail to top of chimney	13ft 4⁷⁄₁₆in	
Maximum width	8ft 7in	
Locomotive length	40ft 4in	
Tender length	23ft 0in	
Tender capacity – coal	6tons	
Tender capacity – water	3,000 gallons	
Wheelbase		
bogie	6ft 3in	
bogie to leading coupled wheel (dr)	7ft 6in	
l.c.w. to second coupled wheel	7ft 5in	
s.c.w. to rear coupled wheel	7ft 10in	
tender	13ft 6in	
Total locomotive	29ft 0in	
Bogie wheel diameter	3ft 3in	
Coupled wheel diameter	6ft 9in	
Cylinders (four) 1914 batches	16in x 26in	
	15in x 26in	
	15½in x 26in	
standard	15in x 26in	

Walschaerts valve gear (see *Table 3* for subsequent changes)

N.B. Some of the above may vary according to condition of individual locomotives at any one given time; for example, ex-GCR tenders, oil firing, valve gear, and modifications to clear Northern and Midland Divisions loading gauges.

TABLE 3. CLAUGHTON LOCOMOTIVES REBOILERED WITH LARGER BOILER/FITTED WITH CAPROTTI VALVE GEAR

LMS No.	Date Reboilered	Date of Caprotti Valve Gear
5906	05/1928	
5908	12/1928	08/1926
5910	05/1928	
5927	07/1928	07/1928
5946	06/1928	06/1928
5948	06/1928	06/1928
5953	05/1928	
5957	09/1928	09/1928
5962	07/1928	07/1928
5970	07/1928	
5972	04/1928	
5975	06/1928	06/1928
5986	04/1928	
5993	05/1928	
5999	04/1928	
6004	04/1928	
6013	07/1928	07/1928
6017	08/1928	
6023	08/1928	08/1928
6029	05/1928	05/1928

TABLE 4. CLAUGHTON LOCOMOTIVES TEMPORARILY CONVERTED TO OIL BURNING

1920 conversion
2222

1926 conversions (37)
LMS Nos

5900	5911	5939	5972	5994
5901	5912	5941	5980	6003
5904	5918	5943	5983	6005
5907	5922	5947	5984	6009
5909	5924	5950	5986	6012
	5926	5959	5989	6015
	5931	5960	5990	6024
	5936	5964	5992	6028

All locomotives were converted to the Scarab system.

TABLE 5A. CLAUGHTON LOCOMOTIVES KNOWN TO US TO HAVE BEEN ALTERED TO CONFORM TO THE LMS MIDLAND DIVISION LOADING GAUGE

5900	5934	5963	5979	6005
5902	5935	5964	5982	6009
5906	5938	5970	5983	6011
5908	5944	5971	5984	6012
5910	5948	5973	5992	6018
5916	5949	5974	5993	6025
5917	5954	5975	5997	6029
5923	5955	5977	6000	(43 locomotives)
5932	5960	5978	6001	

TABLE 5B. CLAUGHTON LOCOMOTIVES KNOWN TO US TO HAVE BEEN ALTERED TO CONFORM TO THE LMS NORTHERN DIVISION LOADING GAUGE

5905	5933	5968	5999*
5906*	5940	5970*	6004*
5908*	5942	5972*	6013*
5910*	5946*	5975*	6017*
5912	5948*	5976	6023*
5915	5953*	5979	6029*
5917	5957*	5986*	
5927*	5962*	5993*	

*Reboilered with a larger boiler.

TABLE 6. CLAUGHTONS DATES OF LMS RENUMBERING

5900	06.1925	5934	05.1927	5968	11.1926	6002	03.1927
5901	12.1925	5935	01.1927	5969	01.1927	6003	06.1926
5902	12.1926	5936	12.1926	5970	02.1927	6004	10.1926
5903	04.1927	5937	03.1927	5971	07.1923	6005	02.1927
5904	07.1926	5938	01.1927	5972	03.1927	6006	11.1926
5905	05.1927	5939	03.1924	5973	08.1926	6007	12.1926
5906	02.1926	5940	02.1927	5974	09.1926	6008	02.1927
5907	06.1926	5941	03.1927	5975	01.1927	6009	06.1927
5908	08.1926	5942	05.1927	5976	01.1927	6010	08.1926
5909	03.1927	5943	07.1926	5977	02.1927	6011	01.1927
5910	04.1927	5944	09.1923	5978	12.1926	6012	06.1926
5911	05.1926	5945	06.1927	5979	03.1924	6013	03.1927
5912	02.1926	5946	05.1927	5980	05.1926	6014	01.1927
5913	06.1927	5947	03.1924	5981	01.1927	6015	05.1926
5914	12.1926	5948	03.1927	5982	06.1927	6016	08.1927
5915	06.1927	5949	04.1926	5983	04.1926	6017	11.1926
5916	06.1927	5950	09.1923	5984	04.1926	6018	01.1928
5917	08.1926	5951	02.1927	5985	05.1927	6019	04.1926
5918	04.1927	5952	02.1927	5986	04.1926	6020	06.1928
5919	04.1927	5953	02.1927	5987	01.1927	6021	05.1927
5920	01.1927	5954	03.1927	5988	01.1927	6022	11.1926
5921	01.1927	5955	03.1927	5989	03.1926	6023	06.1927
5922	12.1926	5956	03.1927	5990	07.1927	6024	12.1926
5923	03.1928	5957	05.1927	5991	07.1928	6025	05.1927
5924	02.1927	5958	06.1927	5992	06.1926	6026	03.1927
5925	02.1927	5959	10.1926	5993	01.1927	6027	09.1926
5926	06.1926	5960	06.1926	5994	06.1926	6028	04.1926
5927	06.1926	5961	09.1923	5995	04.1927	6029	01.1927
5928	09.1926	5962	02.1927	5996	01.1923		
5929	12.1926	5963	01.1927	5997	06.1927		
5930	03.1927	5964	06.1926	5998	12.1926		
5931	04.1926	5965	11.1926	5999	03.1927		
5932	02.1927	5966	02.1927	6000	02.1927		
5933	06.1927	5967	02.1927	6001	04.1926		

TABLE 7. LMS LOCOMOTIVE LIVERY KEY LIST

Crimson Lake Livery variations

A1	Pre-1928 standard	18" figures	LMS Coat of Arms
A2	Pre-1928 standard	18" figures	Individual letters 'LMS'
A3	Pre-1928 standard	14" figures	LMS Coat of Arms
A4	Pre-1928 standard	14" figures	Individual letters 'LMS'
A5	Post-1927 standard	Gold/black insignia	10" numerals
A6	Post-1927 standard	Gold/black insignia	12" numerals
A7	Post-1927 standard	Gold/black insignia	14" numerals, Midland pattern
A8	Post-1927 standard	Straw/black insignia	10" numerals
A9	Post-1927 standard	Straw/black insignia	12" numerals
A10	Post-1927 standard	Straw/black insignia	14" numerals, Standard pattern
A11	Post-1927 standard	Gold/red insignia	12" numerals
A12	Post-1927 standard	Gold/red insignia	1936 pattern
A13	Post-1927 standard	Yellow/red insignia	10" numerals
A14	Post-1927 standard	Yellow/red insignia	12" numerals
A15	Post-1927 standard	Yellow/red insignia	14" numerals, Midland pattern

Lined Black Livery variations

B1	Lined black, Horwich/St. Rollox style		18" Midland numerals
B2	Post-1927 standard	Gold/red insignia	10" numerals
B3	Post-1927 standard	Gold/red insignia	12" numerals
B4	Post-1927 standard	Gold/red insignia	14" numerals, Midland pattern
B5	Post-1927 standard	Gold/black insignia	10" numerals
B6	Post-1927 standard	Gold/black insignia	12" numerals
B7	Post-1927 standard	Gold/black insignia	14" numerals, Midland pattern
B8	Post-1927 standard	Yellow/red insignia	10" numerals
B9	Post-1927 standard	Yellow/red insignia	12" numerals
B10	Post-1927 standard	Yellow/red insignia	14" numerals, Midland pattern
B11	Post-1927 standard	Gold/red insignia	1936 pattern
B12	1946 standard livery	Full lining style	
B13	1946 standard livery	Simpler original lining style	

Plain Black Livery variations

C1	Pre-1928 standard	18" figures	Standard cab/bunker panel
C2	Pre-1928 standard	18" figures	Rounded corner cab/bunker panel
C3	Pre-1928 standard	18" figures	Individual letters 'LMS'
C4	Pre-1928 standard	14" figures	Standard cab/bunker panel
C5	Pre-1928 standard	14" figures	Rounded corner cab/bunker panel
C6	Pre-1928 standard	14" figures	Individual letters 'LMS'
C7	Crewe 'hybrid' style	18" figures	LMS Coat of Arms
C8	Crewe 'hybrid' style	14" figures	(Midland pattern), LMS Coat of Arms
C9	Crewe 'hybrid' style	14" figures	(Standard pattern-straw), LMS Coat of Arms
C10	Crewe 'hybrid' style	18" figures	Individual letters 'LMS'
C11	Crewe 'hybrid' style	14" figures	(Midland pattern), Individual letters 'LMS'
C12	Crewe 'hybrid' style	14" figures	(Standard pattern), Individual letters 'LMS'
C13	Post-1927 standard	Gold/black insignia	10" numerals
C14	Post-1927 standard	Gold/black insignia	12" numerals
C15	Post-1927 standard	Gold/black insignia	14" numerals, Midland pattern
C16	Post-1927 standard	Plain straw insignia	10" numerals
C17	Post-1927 standard	Plain straw insignia	12" numerals
C18	Post-1927 standard	Plain straw insignia	14" numerals, Standard pattern
C19	Post-1927 standard	Gold/red insignia	1936 pattern
C20	Post-1927 standard	Gold/black insignia	1936 pattern
C21	Post-1927 standard	Yellow/red insignia	10" numerals
C22	Post-1927 standard	Yellow/red insignia	12" numerals
C23	Post-1927 standard	Yellow/red insignia	14" numerals, Midland pattern
C24	Post-1927 standard	Plain Yellow insignia	10" numerals
C25	Post-1927 standard	Plain Yellow insignia	12" numerals
C26	Post-1927 standard	Plain Yellow insignia	14" numerals, Midland pattern
C27	1946 standard insignia	Smaller size	
C28	1946 standard insignia	Larger size	

Post-1922 hybrid LNWR liveries

H1　LNWR lined black with LMS Coat of Arms on cab, No. on tender.
H2　LNWR lined black with LMS Coat of Arms on cab, tender not numbered
H3　LNWR lined black with LMS No. stencilled on cab
H4　LNWR plain black with LMS No. stencilled on cab

N.B. On the above LNWR liveries, freshly painted 'patches' usually obliterated Coat of Arms and renovated areas evacuated by number plates.

FOOTNOTE

The above key list should adequately define the vast majority of liveries applied during LMS days with the exception of letter spacing in the post-1927 period. It is based upon the code created by the late David Jenkinson and used by him and Bob Essery in the *Illustrated History of LMS Locomotives* series published by the Oxford Publishing Company and Silver Link Publishing.

TABLE 8. CLAUGHTONS – RECORDED LMS LIVERIES

LMS No.	Livery key/date
5900	A1 08.1925; A8-; A10 c1932;
5901	H3 02.1926; A7 1931;
5902	C18-;
5903	
5904	
5905	A7 ROD;
5906	H3-; A10 LB SD 07.1934
5907	
5908	C7-; C16-; C18 LB c1928; A10 LB SD 1932 onwards
5909	A7-;
5910	C7*; A7 LB SD 08.1933; A7 LB SD c1934;
5911	A1 (but with post 1927 red tender); A7 03.1929; A7 1932;
5912	A7 ROD;
5913	C16-; A7-;
5914	
5915	A7-;
5916	A10 ROD 07.1932
5917	C16-;
5918	A10-;
5919	A7 07.1932
5920	
5921	A7-;
5922	A7-;
5923	C16*-; A7-;
5924	A7-;
5925	C7*-; A7 ROD-;
5926	A1-;
5927	A10 LB c1930; A7 LB SD 1935;
5928	
5929	C16-; A7-;
5930	A7-;
5931	C18-; A7-;
5932	A10 ROD 1935;
5933	A7 ROD-; A7 LB ROD-;
5934	A7-;
5935	

5936	A7-;
5937	A1-; A7-; A7 09.1933;
5938	C18-; A7-;
5939	A2 1924; A10 03.1934
5940	A7 06.1933; A10
5941	A2-; A1-; A7-;
5942	A7 ROD
5943	C16-; A7-;
5944	A2 1925; A1 1926;
5945	C16-; A10-;
5946	A10 LB-; A10 LB SD-; A11 LB SD 1933; A7 LB SD-; A15 LB SD-
5947	A2-; A5 05.1928; A8-; A7 12.1933
5948	A10 LB-; A10 LB SD 09.1932
5949	A7 ROD-;
5950	A8-;
5951	A7 08.1935
5952	A7-;
5953	C18* LB c1928; A10 LB c1930; A7 LB SD-
5954	C18-; A7 ROD-;
5955	A7 02.1933
5956	H4 1927
5957	A10 LB-; A7 LB SD 04.1933;
5958	A7 SB 1931;
5959	A7 ROD-;
5960	
5961	A1-; A8-;
5962	A10 LB 1929; A7 LB SD 1935;
5963	C18- ; A7-;
5964	A9 09.1928; A7 ROD 06.1931;
5965	A7 1932
5966	
5967	C18-; A1-;
5968	C18-; A7 ROD-;
5969	A1-;
5970	C7-; C18 LB-; A7 LB 05.1928; A7 LB SD-;
5971	A2 10.1923; A1 1925; A10 ROD-;
5972	C18 LB 1929; A7 LB SD 06.1935
5973	A7 ROD-;
5974	C18
5975	A10 LB 06.1928; A10 LB SD-; A7 LB SD 08.1936;
5976	A7 ROD-;
5977	C7*-;
5978	A7 ROD-;
5979	A2 1924; A2 07.1925; A7-;
5980	C16*-; A7-;
5981	A7 pre 1934;
5982	C18-;
5983	A7-;
5984	A7-; A7 c1932;
5985	
5986	C7-; A10 LB pre 1930; A10 LB SD 1932;
5987	C18-;
5988	A7-;
5989	H3-; A7-;
5990	A7 pre 1935;
5991	A7 6.1933
5992	A7-;
5993	A7-,
5994	A7-;
5995	A10-; A7-;
5996	A2-; A1-;
5997	A7 04.1930
5998	A7-;
5999	A5 LB 1929; A8 LB-; A10 LB-;
6000	C7-; A10-; A7-;
6001	A7C ROD-; A11C ROD-;
6002	A7-;
6003	
6004	A7 LB-; A7 LB SD-; A10 LB SD pre 1935; A15 LB SD 05.1939; A15 LB SD 1949.
6005	A10 ROD 1932;
6006	
6007	A7-;
6008	C18 SB* 1928/9;
6009	A7 ROD pre 1934; A7 05.1932
6010	A7-;
6011	
6012	A7 ROD-;
6013	A7 LB SD pre 1935;
6014	C18-;
6015	A7-;
6016	C18-;
6017	A10 LB-; A7 LB-; A7 LB SD-;
6018	A7 1928; A7 pre 1933;
6019	H4 04.1926;
6020	A7 pre 1934;
6021	C7*; A10 pre1934;
6022	
6023	C7*; A10 LB-; A7 LB SD pre 1933 and 04.1935; A15 05.1938;
6024	A10-;
6025	A7 ROD 06.1935;
6026	
6027	C18-;
6028	C18-;
6029	C18-; A7 LB SD 07.1932;

For livery key codes, see Table 7.
*	LNWR lining on tender
C	Countershading
ROD	Ex ROD tender
LB	Large boiler
SD	Smoke deflectors

TABLE 9. CLAUGHTON LOCOMOTIVES KNOWN TO HAVE BEEN COUPLED TO EX-ROD (GCR TYPE) TENDERS

5900	5931	5955	5976	6017*
5905	5932	5959	5977	6025
5912	5933	5960	5978	
5916	5940	5964	5984	
5917	5942	5968	6001	
5923	5944	5971	6005	
5925	5949	5973	6009	
5930	5954	5974	6012	

* When reboilered.

N.B. Not all pairings were concurrent, due to the tender pool being twenty plus two spares. See Appendix 3.

TABLE 10. CLAUGHTON LOCOMOTIVES REPLACED BY PATRIOTS WHICH ACQUIRED THEIR NUMBERS

Pre-1934 No.	Post-1934 No.		
5901	5540	5974	5506
5902	5501	5982	5516
5903	5541	5983	5514
5905	5533	5985	5503
5907	5524	5987	5504
5916	5525	5992	5515
5925	5539	5996	5528
5926	5529	5997	5535
5933	5521	6000	5538
5935	5534	6005	5509
5936	5507	6006	5518
5942	5511	6008	5519
5944	5527	6010	5508
5949	5505	6011	5532
5952	5517	6012	5510
5954	5520	6015	5537
5958	5513	6018	5536
5959	5502	6022	5530
5963	5526	6026	5523
5966	5512	6027	5531
5971	5500	Total: 42 locomotives.	
5973	5522		

TABLE 11. PATRIOT 4-6-0 GENERAL DATES, NUMBERS
Table 11a. Order Details

Loco No.	Year	Order No.	Lot No.	Works	Works No.
5500	1930	O/7560	74	Derby	
5501	1930	O/7560	74	Derby	
5502	1932	X934(B369)	87	Crewe	56
5503	1932	X934(B369)	87	Crewe	57
5504	1932	X934(B369)	87	Crewe	58
5505	1932	X934(B369)	87	Crewe	59
5506	1932	X934(B369)	87	Crewe	60
5507	1932	X934(B369)	87	Crewe	62
5508	1932	X934(B369)	87	Crewe	61
5509	1932	X934(B369)	87	Crewe	63
5510	1932	X934(B369)	87	Crewe	64
5511	1932	X934(B369)	87	Crewe	65
5512	1932	X33(B370)	88	Crewe	66
5513	1932	X33(B370)	88	Crewe	67
5514	1932	X33(B370)	88	Crewe	68
5515	1932	X33(B370)	88	Crewe	69
5516	1932	X33(B370)	88	Crewe	70
5517	1932	X33(B370)	95	Crewe	96
5518	1932	X33(B370)	95	Crewe	97
5519	1932	X33(B370)	95	Crewe	98
5520	1933	O/8179	98	Derby	
5521	1933	O/8179	98	Derby	
5522	1933	O/8179	98	Derby	
5523	1933	X33(B370)	95	Crewe	99
5524	1933	X33(B370)	95	Crewe	100
5525	1933	O/8179	98	Derby	
5526	1933	O/8179	98	Derby	
5527	1933	O/8179	98	Derby	
5528	1933	O/8179	98	Derby	
5529	1933	379	95	Crewe	102
5530	1933	379	95	Crewe	101
5531	1933	379	95	Crewe	103
5532	1933	379	95	Crewe	104
5533	1933	O/8179	98	Derby	
5534	1933	O/8179	98	Derby	
5535	1933	O/8179	98	Derby	
5536	1933	379	95	Crewe	105
5537	1933	379	95	Crewe	108
5538	1933	379	95	Crewe	109
5539	1933	379	95	Crewe	110
5540	1933	379	95	Crewe	111
5541	1933	379	95	Crewe	112
5542	1934	380	96	Crewe	153
5543	1934	380	96	Crewe	154
5544	1934	380	96	Crewe	155
5545	1934	380	96	Crewe	156
5546	1934	380	96	Crewe	157
5547	1934	380	96	Crewe	158
5548	1934	380	96	Crewe	159
5549	1934	380	96	Crewe	160
5550	1934	380	96	Crewe	161
5551	1934	380	96	Crewe	162

TABLE 11B BUILDING, REBUILDING AND WITHDRAWAL DETAILS

Orig. No.	Second No.	Date Built	Loco. Cost	Date Rebuilt with taper boiler	Small Smoke Deflectors Fitted	Date Withdrawn	Date Scrapped
5971	5500	08.11.30	£5401			11.03.61	04.1961
5902	5501	13.11.30	£5401			26.08.61	09.1961
5959	5502	01.07.32	£5172			03.09.60	10.1960
5985	5503	14.07.32	£5172			12.08.61	09.1961
5987	5504	18.07.32	£5172			17.03.62	03.1962
5949	5505	26.07.32	£5172			02.06.62	08.1962
5974	5506	01.08.32	£5172			17.03.62	03.1962
5936	5507	12.08.32	£5172			20.10.62	03.1963
6010	5508	09.08.32	£5172			03.12.60	12.1960
6005	5509	19.08.32	£5172			12.08.61	09.1961
6012	5510	24.08.32	£5172			09.06.62	07.1962
5942	5511	31.08.32	£5172			11.02.61	03.1961
5966	5512	14.09.32	£5172	26.07.48	14.06.52	27.03.65	07.1965
5958	5513	19.09.32	£5172			15.09.62	10.1962
5983	5514	21.09.32	£5172	26.03.47	30.12.50	27.05.61	06.1961
5992	5515	27.09.32	£5172			09.06.62	08.1962
5982	5516	10.10.32	£5107			22.07.61	09.1961
5952	5517	06.02.33	£5107			09.06.62	07.1962
6006	5518	20.02.33	£5107			20.10.62	02.1963
6008	5519	25.02.33	£5107			17.03.62	03.1962
5954	5520	17.02.33	£5468			19.05.62	06.1962
5933	5521	04.03.33	£5468	31.10.46	05.11.49	28.09.63	11.1963
5973	5522	03.03.33	£5468	07.02.49	17.05.52	19.09.64	06.1965
6026	5523	08.03.33	£5107	08.10.48	25.03.52	25.01.64	03.1964
5907	5524	14.03.33	£5107			15.09.62	10.1962
5916	5525	22.03.33	£5468	20.08.48	21.02.53	11.05.63	06.1963
5963	5526	22.03.33	£5468	06.02.47	10.12.53	24.10.64	02.1965
5944	5527	27.03.33	£5468	13.09.48	23.11.51	05.12.64	04.1964
5996	5528	04.04.33	£5468	21.08.47	06.09.52	19.01.63	03.1963
5926	5529	06.04.33	£5107	05.07.47	15.09.51	22.02.64	02.1964
6022	5530	03.04.33	£5107	19.10.46	12.05.50	01.01.65	07.1966
6027	5531	07.04.33	£5107	13.12.47	11.08.51	30.10.65	03.1966
6011	5532	11.04.33	£5468	03.07.48	?	01.02.64	01.1965
5905	5533	10.04.33	£5468			15.09.62	10.1962
5935	5534	25.04.33	£5468	31.12.48	?	09.05.64	06.1964
5997	5535	04.05.33	£5468	25.09.48	12.01.52	26.10.63	09.1964
6018	5536	04.05.33	£5107	12.11.48	27.12.52	29.12.62	03.1964
6015	5537	19.07.33	£5224			09.06.62	09.1962
6000	5538	21.07.33	£5224			22.09.62	11.1962
5925	5539	27.07.33	£5224			16.09.61	10.1961
5901	5540	07.08.33	£5224	01.11.47	?	06.04.63	07.1963
5903	5541	15.08.33	£5224			09.06.62	09.1962
	5542	13.03.34	£5143			09.06.62	09.1962
	5543	16.03.34	£5143			17.11.62	09.1963
	5544	22.03.34	£5143			09.12.61	03.1962
	5545	27.03.34	£5143	05.11.48	23.02.52	30.05.64	11.1964
	5546	29.03.34	£5143			09.06.62	08.1962
	5547	09.04.34	£5143			15.09.62	11.1962
	5548	27.04.34	£5143			09.06.62	10.1962
	5549	27.04.34	£5143			16.06.62	08.1962
	5550	01.05.34	£5143			01.12.62	08.1963
	5551	02.05.34	£5143			16.06.62	10.1962

5542–5551, but for the 1934 renumbering scheme, would have been completed as 6030–6039.

TABLE 11C PATRIOT 4-6-0 NAMES

Number	Date of Naming	Name
5500	11.1933	CROXTETH
	25.02.1937	PATRIOT
5501	11.1930	SIR FRANK REE
	17.04.1937	ST. DUNSTAN'S
5502	05.06.1937	ROYAL NAVAL DIVISION
5503	08.07.1938	THE LEICESTERSHIRE REGIMENT
	03.11.1948	THE ROYAL LEICESTERSHIRE REGIMENT
5504	10.04.1937	ROYAL SIGNALS
5505	08.1947	THE ROYAL ARMY ORDNANCE CORPS
5506	15.09.1948	THE ROYAL PIONEER CORPS
5507	20.11.1937	ROYAL TANK CORPS
5508		
5509	10.11.1951	THE DERBYSHIRE YEOMANRY
5510		
5511	By 01.1938	ISLE OF MAN
5512	Late 1933	BUNSEN
5513		
5514	07.1938 &	HOLYHEAD
	26.03.1947	(un-named 1942–1947)
5515	15.01.1939	CAERNARVON
5516	31.07.1938	THE BEDFORDSHIRE AND HERTFORDSHIRE REGIMENT
5517		
5518	06.1939 &	BRADSHAW
	03.1947	(un-named 1942–1947)
5519	02.1933	LADY GODIVA
5520	By 01.1937	LLANDUDNO
5521	By 01.1938	RHYL
5522	22.03.1939	PRESTATYN
5523	03.1938	BANGOR
5524	03.1933	SIR FREDERICK HARRISON
	22.03.1937	BLACKPOOL
5525	03.1933–08.1937	E. TOOTAL BROADHURST
	01.1938	COLWYN BAY
5526	06.10.1937	MORECAMBE AND HEYSHAM
5527	09.1937	SOUTHPORT
5528	02.10.1959	R.E.M.E.
5529	04.1933–09.1937	SIR HERBERT WALKER K.C.B.
	24.07.1948	STEPHENSON
5530	10.03.1937	SIR FRANK REE
5531	01.1938	SIR FREDERICK HARRISON
5532	04.1933	ILLUSTRIOUS
5533	04.1933	LORD RATHMORE
5534	08.1937	E. TOOTAL BROADHURST
5535	04.1938	SIR HERBERT WALKER K.C.B.
5536	05.1933	PRIVATE W. WOOD, V.C.
5537	07.1933	PRIVATE E. SYKES V.C.
5538	04.11.1938	GIGGLESWICK
5539	07.1933	E.C. TRENCH
5540	08.1933	SIR ROBERT TURNBULL
5541	08.1933	DUKE OF SUTHERLAND
5542		
5543	30.07.1940	HOME GUARD
5544		
5545	03.11.1948	PLANET
5546	18.07.1938	FLEETWOOD
5547		
5548	18.12.1937	LYTHAM ST. ANNES
5549		
5550		
5551		

NOTES

Names chosen for Patriots remaining un-named by 1943.

No.	Name
5505	WEMYSS BAY
5509	COMMANDO
5513	SIR W.A. STANIER
5529	AIR TRAINING CORPS
5542	DUNOON
5545	THE ROYAL MARINE
5549	R.A.M.C.
5550	SIR HENRY FOWLER
5551	ROTHESAY

Names chosen for intended rebuilt Patriots, but not used.
VULCAN, GOLIATH, COURIER, VELOCIPEDE, CHAMPION, DRAGON, HARLEQUIN

TABLE 12. PATRIOT 4-6-0 – PRINCIPAL DATA

	Original Condition	Rebuilt Condition
Locomotive weight in full working order	80 tons 15cwt	82 tons 0cwt
Tender weight, laden. Old standard	44 tons 14cwt	
Modified old standard	44 tons 4cwt	
New standard +		53 tons 13 cwt
Boiler designation *	G9 ½ S	2A
Boiler barrel length front	5ft 3¹¹⁄₁₆in	5ft 5in
rear	5ft 5⅛in	5ft 10½in
Boiler centre height above rail level	8ft 11½in	9ft 3¼in
Boiler pressure	200 lb/in²	250 lb/in²
Tractive effort at 85% boiler pressure	26,520 lb	29,590 lb
Height from rail to top of chimney	13ft 2½in	13ft 2¼in
Maximum width	8ft 7in	5ft 7in
Length of locomotive	39ft 7in	39ft 7in
Wheelbase		
Bogie	6ft 3in	6ft 3in
Bogie to leading coupled wheel	5ft 10½in	5ft 9in
L.C.W. to second coupled wheel (dr)	7ft 4in	7ft 4in
S.C.W. to rear coupled wheel	8ft 0in	8ft 0in
Total, locomotive	27ft 5½in	27ft 7in
Bogie wheel diameter	3ft 3in	3ft 3in
Coupled wheel diameter	6ft 9in	6ft 9in
Three cylinders (diameter x stroke)	18in x 26in	17in x 26in

Walschaerts valve gear.
* Crewe Works designation: Scheme 3 Claughton
+ welded tank: 53 tons 13 cwt.

At page 124 we show Engine Diagrams for both the parallel and taper boiler Patriot.

TABLE 13. PATRIOT – RECORDED LMS LIVERIES (A) PRE-1934 NUMBERING

No.	Livery Key/date
5901	A6
5902	A7 named 1931; A7 08.1932 straight deflectors
5903	
5905	A7 c1933, angled smoke deflectors
5907	A7 (grey, with false nameplate) new; A7 pre 1935, A6
5916	A7
5925	A6
5926	A6
5933	A7 02.1933 straight deflectors; A7 09.1933 angled smoke deflectors
5935	A7
5936	A6 straight deflectors
5942	A6
5944	
5949	A6
5952	
5954	A7 new 1933
5958	A6
5959	A6 c1932/4 straight deflectors; A6 angled deflectors c1935
5963	A7
5966	A6 pre 1934
5971	A7 un-named 1931; A7 un-named, straight deflectors
5973	A7
5974	A6 new and straight deflectors
5982	A6
5983	A6
5985	A7 un-named
5987	A6
5992	A6
5996	A7
5997	A7 un-named
6000	A7 1933
6005	A6 straight deflectors pre 1935
6006	A6 05.1934
6008	A6
6010	
6011	
6012	A6 un-named, A7 un-named angled deflectors new, 05.1933
6015	A7
6018	A6
6022	A6
6026	A6 c1932
6027	

See Table 7 for livery key details.

PATRIOT – RECORDED LMS LIVERIES (B) 1934 NUMBERING

No.	Livery Key/date
5500	A6 03.1935; A6 04.1937; A14
5501	A7 05.1934; C25, C22 wartime onwards; B12
5502	A6 un-named; A12 1937; A12 10.1938
5503	A6
5504	A6 un-named 09.1935; A12 1937; B12 1947
5505	A12 1935; A12 1937; B12 c1946
5506	
5507	A11 post 1935; A12 un-named late 1930s; A14-; B12 1947
5508	A7 un-named, A14 07.1948
5509	A6-; plain black, unlined, 1936 block Nos. (black-shaded?) 1945
5510	A6 10.1934
5511	A11 01.1938; A7 1945
5512	A6 08.1935; B2 09.1948
5513	A6 06.1936; A11-;
5514	A6 09.1936; A14-; A11-; B12 08.1947
5515	A6-; A14 c1945
5516	A6 05.1934; red livery 1949/50
5517	A6 1935
5518	A6 03.1935; B12 1947
5519	A6
5520	A6 c1934; A7 03.1935; A14 1938; red livery 12.1948
5521	A14 05.1938; B12 1947
5522	A12 08.1937; A14 08.1938; A14
5523	A6-; A14 1938; A14 05.1939
5524	A12 1938; A14 1938
5525	A6 1935
5526	A7 04.1935; A14 01.1938; B12 03.1947
5527	A6 06.1934; A12 08.1937
5528	A6-; B12 1947
5529	A6-; C27 1947; B12 1947
5530	A6-; B12 1947
5531	A6-; A14 1939; B12 1947
5532	A6-; A12 1938
5533	A6 or A9 10.1934; A12 11.1937; A14 05.1939
5534	A6 pre 1935
5535	A6 pre 1935; A6 1936-8 period
5536	A7 1936; A12-; A14-;
5537	A6 06.1936; red livery 10.1948
5538	A6 1935; A14 c1938; A14 10.1938; B12 06.1947
5539	
5540	A6 10.1936; B12 1947
5541	A6 1935; B11 1947; B12 1947
5542	A6-;
5543	A6 pre 1935
5544	A6-; A14
5545	A6 pre 1935; A6 05.1937
5546	
5547	A6-;
5548	
5549	A6-;
5550	A6-; C22 06.1946 (high sided tender)
5551	A6 new; B12 1947

See Table 7 for livery key details.

TABLE 14. LOCOMOTIVE LIVERY KEY (BRITISH RAILWAYS)

Key	Livery	Numerals	Lettering/Emblem
B1	LMS 1946 black	12" block numerals with M prefix/suffix	BRITISH RAILWAYS, block letters
B2	LMS 1946 black	10" block numerals 4XXXX	BRITISH RAILWAYS, block letters
B3	LMS 1946 black	10" block numerals 4XXXX	1946 LMS on tender
B4	LMS 1946 black	8" Gill Sans numerals 4XXXX	1946 LMS on tender
B5	LMS 1946 black	8" Gill Sans numerals 4XXXX	BRITISH RAILWAYS, block letters
B6	LMS plain black	10" LMS scroll numerals 4XXXX	LMS on tender, serif letters
R7	LMS red	10" LMS scroll numerals 4XXXX	LMS on tender, serif letters
B8	BR plain black	8" Gill Sans numerals	BRITISH RAILWAYS, Gill Sans
B9	BR mixed traffic black, lined	8" Gill Sans numerals	BRITISH RAILWAYS, Gill Sans
B10	BR mixed traffic black, lined	8" Gill Sans numerals	1949 lion & wheel totem
G11	BR experimental light green, lined	8" Gill Sans numerals	BRITISH RAILWAYS, Gill Sans
G12	BR std. Brunswick green, lined	8" Gill Sans numerals	1949 lion & wheel totem
G13	BR std. Brunswick green, lined	10" Gill Sans numerals	1949 lion & wheel totem
G14	BR std. Brunswick green, lined	8" Gill Sans numerals	1956 lion & wheel emblem
G15	BR std. Brunswick green, lined	10" Gill Sans numerals	1956 lion & wheel emblem
G16	BR std. Brunswick green, lined, yellow stripe on cabsides	8" Gill Sans numerals	1956 lion & wheel emblem
G17	BR Brunswick green, unlined yellow stripe on cabsides	8" Gill Sans numerals	1956 lion & wheel emblem
G17A	BR Brunswick green, probably unlined, no stripe on cabsides	8" Gill Sans numerals	1956 lion & wheel emblem

TABLE 15. PATRIOTS – RECORDED BR LIVERIES

No.	Livery Key/date recorded
45500	G12 08.1950; G14 05.1957; G14 08.1958; G14 04.1959; G14 06.1959; G14 10.1959
45501	G17A-;
45502	B3 04.1949; G12 1951; G14 06.1960
45503	B3-; G12 mid 1950s; G14-;
45504	G16-;
45505	G12-;
45506	B9 09.1948; G12 08.1955; G12 09.1955; G12 05.1956
45507	10" Nos., tender blank, probably plain black; G14 06.1961; G14 04.1962;
45508	B4 c1948; G12 06.1957; G14 1960
45509	G12 05.1951; G12 03.1953; G12 03.1957; G12 c1959
45510	Plain black, LMS on tender; G12 30.06.1951; G12 03.1953; G12 04.1958; G14 08.1960
45511	G12 06.1956; G14 08.1959
45512	B2 c1949; G14 mid 1961; G14 09.1963
45513	B9 1948; B9 c1950; G14 1960; G14 06.1961; G14 07.1961
45514	B3 c1949
45515	B5 c1948; G12 (high-sided tender) 11.1957
45516	R7 (but with 8" Gill Sans numbers) 1949/50
45517	A14 03.1948; R7 (but with Gill Sans numbers) 1949/50; G14 1957; G14 07.1959
45518	G14-;
45519	G12 early 1950s; G12 06.1953; G14 05.1959
45520	B9 c1948/9
45521	G12 c1956/7
45522	B5 02.1949; B9 1951; G12 early 1950s; G14 08.1961
45523	G14 05.1963
45524	G14 10.1957
45525	B5 05.1948; B9; G14 10.1958
45526	G12 1950; G12 1950s; G16 10.1964
45527	G12 early 1950s; G14 1962; G16 07.1964; G16 09.1964
45528	B4 c1949; G12 10.1959
45529	B9 1948/9; B9 1951; G12 mid 1952; G12 08.1957; G14 1963
45530	B3-; G14 04.1963; G14 08.1963
45531	G11 06.1948; G12 mid 1950s; G14 07.1962; G14 05.1963; G16 11.1964
45532	B2 (scroll front numberplate) c1948/9; B2 (no boiler bands) 04.1950; G12-; G14 05.1963
45533	B9 05.1953; B9 08.1953; G14 1959
45534	B5
45535	B9 c1949/50; G12 1950s
45536	B5-; B9 1952
45537	G12 1950; G14 1960; G14 03.1961
45538	G14 06.1962
45539	G12 (high-sided tender) 1950s
45540	B5-; G12 08.1959; G12 09.1960; G12 08.1962
45541	Red, block numbers, LMS on tender 08.1950; G12 early 1950s; G14 1960
45542	Plain black, 8" block numbers, tender blank; G12 04.1954
45543	G12 08.1953; G14 08.1962
45544	B8, tender blank; G12 1951; G12 1957
45545	B5-; B9 11.1948; G14 12.1963
45546	G14-;
45547	G14-;
45548	B8, tender blank
45549	B9 c1950; G12 04.1954
45550	B9 (high-sided tender) 09.1954, G12 (high-sided tender) 05.1955
45551	B3 c1948; B3 1949; G12-; G14 (high-sided tender) 06.1959

See Table 14 for BR livery key description.

TABLE 16. RENUMBERING OF PATRIOT 4–6–0s

Orig. LMS No.	2nd LMS No.	Date of renumbering	Date of BR renumbering into 455xx series
5971	5500	03.05.34	23.04.49
5902	5501	12.04.34	26.03.49
5959	5502	28.05.34	20.11.48
5985	5503	14.07.34	15.05.48
5987	5504	28.06.34	02.10.48
5949	5505	19.06.34	26.06.48
5974	5506	14.07.34	04.09.48
5936	5507	23.07.34	23.10.48
6010	5508	17.04.34	08.01.49
6005	5509	10.08.34	17.09.49
6012	5510	25.06.34	26.06.48
5942	5511	03.08.34	21.05.49
5966	5512	14.07.34	31.07.48
5958	5513	25.07.34	12.06.48
5983	5514	02.08.34	22.05.48
5992	5515	21.08.34	24.04.48
5982	5516	28.05.34	12.02.49
5952	5517	14.07.34	17.09.49
6006	5518	22.05.34	03.07.48
6008	5519	28.06.34	04.12.48
5954	5520	25.09.34	05.07.48
5933	5521	26.07.34	14.08.48
5973	5522	29.05.34	12.02.49
6026	5523	07.05.34	09.10.48
5907	5524	19.07.34	12.02.49
5916	5525	24.07.34	21.08.48
5963	5526	25.07.35	02.07.49
5944	5527	26.04.34	18.09.48
5996	5528	14.07.34	12.03.49
5926	5529	21.05.34	07.08.48
6022	5530	02.08.34	10.04.48
6027	5531	01.06.34	22.05.48
6011	5532	14.08.34	01.07.48
5905	5533	18.09.34	05.02.49
5935	5534	13.07.34	31.12.48
5997	5535	11.05.34	25.09.48
6018	5536	20.04.34	13.11.48
6015	5537	25.06.34	08.05.48
6000	5538	03.08.34	26.06.48
5925	5539	30.06.34	24.09.49
5901	5540	18.07.34	22.05.48
5903	5541	18.05.34	01.05.48
	5542		25.06.49
	5543		28.05.49
	5544		18.09.48
	5545		06.11.48
	5546		08.01.49
	5547		26.02.49
	5548		02.04.49
	5549		12.02.49
	5550		22.10.49
	5551		29.05.48

TABLE 17. PATRIOT 4–6–0 ALLOCATIONS (TAKEN FROM ENGINE HISTORY CARDS)

Loco No.	Allocations
5500	Leeds 08.11.30, Kentish Town 21.05.32, Camden 16.02.35, Crewe 20.02.37, Camden 10.04.37, Willesden 20.11.37, Edge Hill 03.05.47, Longsight 05.06.48, Carlisle Upperby 06.11.54, Blackpool 26.07.58, Willesden 04.10.58, Carnforth 03.10.59, Newton Heath 26.03.60 & 28.05.60
5501	Crewe undated, Kentish Town 18.06.32, Leeds 30.10.33, Camden 11.35, Crewe 20.02.37, Camden 10.04.37, Crewe 26.11.38, Camden (loan) 10.12.38, Camden 31.12.38, Willesden 10.06.39, Crewe 22.03.41, Longsight (loan) 14.03.42, Crewe 28.03.42, Preston 11.04.42, Patricroft 06.06.42, Edge Hill 03.10.42, Willesden 16.06.45, Edge Hill 03.05.47, Longsight 05.06.48, Crewe North 14.06.53, Carnforth 07.11.59, Mold Junction 28.01.60, Warrington 23.01.60, Carlisle Upperby 10.09.60
5502	Camden 29.07.33, Longsight 08.06.34, Camden no date, Edge Hill 08.06.35, Camden 06.07.35, Longsight 23.11.40, Rugby 31.05.41, Willesden 05.06.43, Bushbury 20.05.44, Carlisle Upperby 09.03.46, Carlisle Kingmoor (loan) 07.09.46, Carlisle Upperby (loan) 12.10.46, Carlisle Upperby 02.11.46, Preston 16.11.46, Carlisle Upperby 01.10.49, Crewe North 10.06.50, Willesden 29.11.52, Camden 10.01.53, Carlisle Upperby 21.02.53, Preston 21.11.59, Carlisle Upperby 23.04.60
5503	Camden 13.05.33, Crewe 02.02.35, Edge Hill 20.04.35, Camden 06.07.35, Aston 25.09.37, Preston 11.03.39, Carlisle Upperby 29.07.39, Patricroft 04.10.41, Preston 11.04.42, Edge Hill 09.05.47, Willesden 05.06.43, Camden 08.06.46, Crewe North 18.10.47, Longsight 29.04.50, Crewe North 24.06.50, Carlisle Upperby 22.09.56, Crewe North 03.11.56, Newton Heath 26.07.58, Crewe North 04.10.58, Warrington 04.07.59, Carnforth 18.06.60, Carlisle Upperby 10.09.60
5504	Preston 22.07.33, Edge Hill 23.09.33, Camden 06.07.35, Camden 08.03.38, Willesden 11.10.41, Camden 05.06.43, Willesden 09.10.43, Camden 03.05.47, Crewe North 11.10.47, Carlisle 29.01.55, Western Region 15.11.58
5505	Edge Hill 14.08.32, Crewe 07.09.32, Edge Hill 20.04.35, Camden 06.07.35, Rugby 09.11.35, Camden 16.11.35, Willesden 11.10.41, Camden 05.06.43, Carlisle Upperby 11.01.47, Preston 11.10.47, Carlisle Upperby 01.10.49, Preston 07.07.51, Carlisle Upperby 15.09.51, Preston 12.06.54, Longsight 18.09.54, Carlisle Upperby 10.09.60, Lancaster 10.02.62
5506	Camden 14.08.32, Bushbury 20.04.35, Camden 25.07.36, Willesden 10.06.39, Rugby 29.11.40, Willesden 05.06.43, Edge Hill 16.06.45, Longsight 25.01.47, Preston 05.04.47, Carlisle Upperby 21.06.47, Crewe North 28.05.49, Willesden 05.07.52, Crewe North 20.09.52, Carlisle 29.01.55, Western Region 15.11.58
5507	Crewe from new?, Longsight 06.10.34, Leeds 01.12.34, Camden 06.04.35, Bushbury 20.04.35, Bescot 25.09.37, Crewe 11.03.39, Rugby 28.10.39, Willesden 05.06.43, Camden 02.10.43, Crewe North 18.10.47, Preston (on loan) 05.02.49, Crewe North 26.02.49, Carlisle Upperby 20.09.53, Preston 21.11.59, Carlisle Upperby 09.01.60, Lancaster 10.02.62
5508	Longsight 21.10.33, Derby 01.12.34, Camden 16.02.35, Bushbury 04.05.35, Camden 28.08.37, Longsight 23.08.41, Rugby 16.05.42, Willesden 02.10.43, Camden 18.03.44, Edge Hill 17.06.44, Crewe North 30.11.46, Carlisle Upperby 24.07.48, Preston 19.02.49, Preston 12.06.54, Longsight 18.09.54, Preston 02.10.54, Carlisle Upperby 01.09.56, Preston 21.11.59, Carlisle Upperby 23.04.60
5509	Crewe 28.08.32, Longsight 04.11.33, Derby 01.12.34, Camden 16.02.35, Willesden 09.05.36, Longsight 23.08.41, Rugby 16.05.42, Camden 05.06.43, Edge Hill 03.05.47, Willesden 21.06.47, Crewe North (on loan) 09.06.51, Crewe North 28.07.51, Derby (on loan) 20.10.51, Derby 10.11.51, Newton Heath 30.08.58, Newton Heath 03.01.59
5510	Carlisle 30.10.33, Leeds 03.11.34, Camden 06.04.35, Crewe 28.08.35, Camden 28.09.35, Longsight 23.08.41, Rugby 16.05.42, Willesden 05.06.43, Edge Hill 03.05.47, Willesden 21.06.47, Crewe North 28.05.49, Edge Hill 10.02.51, Crewe North 24.03.51, Willesden 05.07.52, Crewe North 20.09.52, Willesden 29.01.55, Carnforth 03.10.59, Carlisle Upperby 10.09.60, Lancaster 10.02.62
5511	Crewe no date, Longsight 11.08.34, Bristol 01.12.34, Edge Hill 20.04.35, Camden 06.07.35, Edge Hill 05.10.35, Camden 02.12.39, Longsight 23.08.41, Crewe 18.07.42, Bushbury 05.06.43, Crewe North 09.03.46, Edge Hill 24.01.48, Crewe North 14.02.48, Edge Hill (on loan) 28.08.48, Crewe North 13.11.48, Carlisle Upperby 29.04.50, Crewe North 24.06.50, Edge Hill (on loan) 31.03.51, Crewe North 07.04.51, Willesden 28.07.51, Carnforth 17.10.59, Mold Junction 23.01.60, Warrington 23.04.60, Carlisle Upperby 10.09.60

5512 Camden no date, Crewe 02.02.35, Edge Hill 20.04.35, Camden 06.07.35, Longsight 26.07.35, Camden 04.01.36, Bushbury (on loan) 20.11.37, Longsight 23.11.40, Crewe 18.07.42, Preston 30.01.43, Bushbury 05.06.43, Crewe North 09.03.46, Bushbury 02.10.48, Carlisle Upperby 28.05.49

5513 Kentish Town 06.11.32, Leeds 25.03.33, Kentish Town 30.10.33, Camden 16.02.35, Longsight 14.06.41, Crewe North 18.07.42, Bushbury 05.06.43, Edge Hill 09.03.46, Longsight 25.01.47, Preston 18.10.47, Crewe North 21.01.50, Carlisle Upperby 29.01.55, Carnforth 10.09.60, Edge Hill 09.09.61

5514 Leeds 06.11.32, Camden 16.02.35, Shrewsbury 23.03.35, Aston 20.04.33, Preston 20.04.35, Carlisle 29.07.39, Longsight 31.05.41, Crewe 18.07.42, Edge Hill 13.05.44, Longsight (on loan) 24.08.46, Edge Hill 21.09.46, Holyhead 07.05.47, Crewe North 21.06.47, Bushbury 19.07.47, Holyhead 07.08.48, Bushbury 02.10.48, Carlisle Upperby 28.05.49, Bushbury 01.10.49, Camden 10.06.50, Derby 27.05.61

5515 Leeds 06.11.32, Carlisle 30.10.33, Leeds 03.11.34, Camden 16.02.35, Shrewsbury 23.03.35, Aston 20.04.35

5516 Kentish Town 06.11.32, Patricroft 20.04.35, Camden 04.01.36, Longsight 03.05.41, Preston 28.03.42, Crewe 03.10.42, Preston 05.06.43, Carlisle Upperby 15.09.51, Preston 05.07.52, Crewe North 20.09.52, Edge Hill 29.01.55, Crewe North 07.09.57, Edge Hill 21.09.57, Warrington 06.02.60

5517 Camden 13.05.33, Edge Hill 16.03.35, Camden 06.07.35, Longsight 13.07.35, Aston 30.11.35, Preston 18.07.36, Crewe 25.02.39, Preston (on loan) 11.03.39, Preston 01.04.39, Carlisle 16.09.39, Aston 06.01.40, Rugby 20.01.40, Longsight 31.05.41, Aston 25.04.42, Crewe 23.05.42, Edge Hill 13.05.44, Crewe North 14.02.48, Carlisle Upperby 05.06.48, Willesden 13.06.53, Bank Hall 26.07.58, Bank Hall 08.11.58

5518 Camden 13.05.33, Longsight 07.10.39, Aston 28.03.42, Willesden 02.05.42, Crewe North 03.05.47, Carlisle Upperby 16.08.47, Preston 13.06.53, Edge Hill 19.09.53, Warrington 06.02.60, Aston 18.06.60, Edge Hill 09.09.61, Lancaster 10.02.62

5519 Camden 13.05.33, Crewe 17.06.33, Edge Hill 23.09.33, Crewe 02.01.37, Preston 01.05.37, Carlisle Upperby 16.09.39, Crewe 08.01.40, Rugby 11.01.41, Longsight 28.02.42, Aston 21.03.42, Willesden 02.05.42, Camden 08.06.46, Carlisle Upperby 11.01.47, Preston 24.03.51, Longsight 02.10.54, Carlisle Upperby 25.08.56, Preston 20.10.56, Longsight 17.11.56, Carlisle Upperby 20.09.58, Western Region

5520 Kentish Town 25.02.33, Edge Hill 06.04.35, Edge Hill 28.09.35, Longsight 05.06.48, Preston 18.06.55, Longsight 17.09.55, Edge Hill 31.12.60

5521 Kentish Town 25.03.33, Edge Hill 16.02.35, Bushbury 11.09.37, Crewe 11.03.39, Rugby 28.10.39, Crewe 05.06.43, Longsight 05.04.47, Holyhead 17.05.47, Edge Hill 21.06.47, Springs Branch 16.09.61

5522 Kentish Town 25.03.33, Bushbury 16.02.35, Crewe 11.03.39, Rugby 14.12.40, Crewe 05.06.43, Bushbury (on loan) 06.10.45, Crewe North 05.01.46, Preston 27.11.48, Crewe North 12.04.49, Longsight 18.06.49, Bushbury 01.10.49, Camden 10.06.50

5523 Camden 25.03.33, Camden 13.05.33, Bushbury 23.03.35, Crewe 06.04.35, Bushbury 28.09.35, Crewe 11.03.39, Edge Hill 17.5.40, Crewe 17.05.41, Edge Hill 29.12.45, Carlisle Upperby 05.06.48, Crewe North 16.10.48, Camden 07.07.51, Willesden 21.01.61

5524 Patricroft 13.05.33, Camden 04.01.36, Preston 10.04.37, Carlisle Upperby 03.02.51, Preston 24.03.51, Carlisle Upperby 15.09.51, Carlisle Kingmoor 05.07.52, Crewe 02.08.52, Carlisle 29.01.55, Warrington 10.09.60, Edge Hill 10.06.61

5525 Kentish Town 25.03.33, Bushbury 28.09.35, Crewe 08.03.38, Preston 11.03.39, Preston 04.10.41, Edge Hill 03.10.42, Longsight 25.01.47, Willesden 21.06.47, Crewe North 21.08.48, Bushbury 02.10.48, Carlisle Upperby 28.05.49, Bushbury 01.10.49, Carlisle Upperby 10.06.50, Crewe North 03.09.50, Camden 07.07.51, Crewe North 15.09.51, Camden 05.07.52, Crewe North 20.09.52, Edge Hill (on loan) 04.10.52, Edge Hill 03.01.53, Willesden 14.01.61, Llandudno Junction 23.09.61

5526 Leeds 25.03.33, Bushbury 16.02.35, Crewe 11.03.39, Rugby 18.01.41, Edge Hill 05.06.43, Leeds (on loan) 28.06.47, Bushbury 01.10.49, Carlisle Upperby 10.06.50

5527 Camden 13.05.33, Edge Hill 16.12.33, Bushbury 04.03.61, Holyhead 06.05.61, Bushbury 10.06.61, Llandudno Junction 10.06.61, Holyhead 09.09.61, Willesden 22.06.63

5528 Camden no date, Polmadie 11.05.35, Patricroft (on loan) 28.01.34, Patricroft 01.02.41, Edge Hill 27.09.46, Longsight 25.01.47, Bushbury 23.08.47, Crewe North 05.06.48, Longsight (on loan) 23.10.48, Crewe North 25.03.50, Camden 07.07.51, Crewe North 15.09.51, Camden 13.06.53, Crewe North 18.09.54, Longsight 19.02.55, Holyhead 26.03.55, Crewe North 07.05.55, Longsight 14.01.56, Crewe North 21.04.56, Holyhead no date, Crewe North 20.04.57, Willesden 14.01.61

5529 Patricroft 13.05.33, Camden 04.01.36, Aston 25.09.37, Crewe 11.03.39, Patricroft 06.06.42, Edge Hill 03.10.42, Bushbury 19.07.47, Camden 05.06.48, Bushbury 02.10.48, Crewe North 28.05.49, Camden 05.07.52, Crewe North 20.09.52, Camden 13.06.53, Crewe North 19.09.53, Camden 21.11.53, Crewe North 02.01.54, Camden 29.03.58, Willesden 14.01.61, Annesley 12.10.63

5530 Patricroft 13.05.33, Camden 04.01.36, Crewe 20.02.37, Camden 10.04.37, Crewe 10.08.40, Longsight 05.04.47, Leeds (on loan) 17.04.48, Longsight 15.05.48, Northwich 25.04.59, Longsight 13.06.59, Camden 10.09.60, Willesden 10.06.61, Llandudno Junction 23.09.61, Willesden 07.07.62

5531 Patricroft 05.03.33, Bushbury 06.04.35, Camden 28.09.35, Willesden 20.11.37, Aston 11.06.38, Willesden 11.03.39, Camden 05.06.43, Bushbury 20.05.44, Crewe North 09.03.46, Longsight (on loan) 24.08.46, Crewe North 28.09.46, Bushbury 20.12.47, Camden 28.05.49, Bushbury 01.10.49, Edge Hill 10.06.50, Springs Branch 19.10.63

5532 Leeds 11.04.33, Bushbury 28.09.35, Crewe (on loan) 20.11.37, Bushbury 11.12.37, Crewe 11.03.39, Holyhead (on loan) 17.07.48, Bushbury 07.08.48, Camden 28.05.49, Holyhead (on loan) 15.07.50, Camden 12.08.50, Nottingham 21.11.59, Saltley 17.06.61, Derby 07.04.62, Carlisle Upperby 30.06.62

5533 Kentish Town 10.04.33, Bushbury 16.02.35, Crewe 11.03.39, Patricroft 30.09.39, Springs Branch 11.03.40, Crewe 08.06.40, Preston 22.06.40, Edge Hill 03.10.42, Willesden 23.10.42, Camden 05.06.43, Bushbury 20.05.44, Edge Hill 09.03.46, Carlisle Upperby 27.09.58, Rugby 21.11.59, Nuneaton 31.12.60, Edge Hill 16.09.61

5534 Leeds undated, Longsight, 16.02.35, Leeds 25.07.36, Edge Hill (on loan) 21.08.48, Edge Hill 11.09.48, Crewe 04.12.48, Bushbury 01.10.49, Longsight 10.06.50, Holyhead (on loan) 15.07.50, Longsight 14.10.50, Camden 11.08.51, Edge Hill 10.11.51, Llandudno Junction 07.11.59, Longsight 18.06.60, Crewe 10.09.60, Willesden 10.06.61, Llandudno Junction 23.09.61, Crewe 22.06.63

5535 Leeds 30.10.33, Longsight 16.02.35, Leeds 25.07.36, Crewe North (on loan) 02.04.48, Crewe North 06.11.48, Camden (on loan) 30.09.50, Edge Hill 18.11.50, Crewe North 02.12.50, Camden 07.07.51, Crewe North 15.09.51, Edge Hill (on loan) 11.10.52, Crewe North 29.11.52, Edge Hill 12.06.54, Carlisle Kingmoor 03.11.62

5536 Longsight 28.09.35, Crewe 27.11.37, Longsight (on loan) 18.12.37, Crewe 01.01.38, Longsight (on loan) 15.01.38, Longsight 26.02.38, Crewe 26.11.38, Longsight 10.12.38, Carlisle Upperby 31.05.41, Preston 04.10.41, Longsight 27.11.48, Bushbury 01.10.49, Longsight 10.06.50

5537 Longsight 29.07.33, Preston 18.07.36, Carlisle Upperby 15.09.51, Preston 05.07.52, Carlisle Upperby 20.09.52, Rugby 21.11.59, Rugby 02.01.60, Nuneaton 31.12.60

5538 Leeds 30.10.33, Longsight 16.02.35, Leeds 25.07.36, Willesden (on loan) 21.08.48, Willesden 11.9.48, Edge Hill 28.05.49, Preston 22.06.57, Willesden 20.06.59, Nuneaton 14.01.61

5539 Preston 19.08.33, Aston 23.09.33, Longsight 07.06.35, Aston 28.09.35, Crewe 11.03.39, Preston 05.06.48, Crewe North 02.10.48, Longsight 29.04.50, Edge Hill 27.10.56, Willesden 20.06.59, Carnforth 08.10.59, Newton Heath 26.03.60, Newton Heath 28.05.60

5540 Preston 19.08.33, Aston 23.09.33, Crewe 11.03.39, Edge Hill 29.12.45, Bushbury 08.11.47, Willesden 28.05.49, Bushbury 01.10.49, Longsight 10.06.50

5541	Longsight 21.07.34, Camden 14.06.41, Edge Hill 03.01.42, Willesden 23.10.42, Camden 28.04.45, Carlisle Upperby 11.01.47, Preston 11.10.47, Carlisle Upperby 25.10.47, Rugby (on loan) 21.11.59, Rugby 02.01.60, Nuneaton 31.12.60
5542	Kentish Town 24.03.34, Longsight 20.04.35, Crewe 28.05.35, Longsight 28.09.35, Carlisle Upperby 26.10.40, Patricroft 04.10.41, Crewe North 27.07.46, Carlisle Upperby 05.06.48, Preston 15.11.58, Nuneaton 22.07.61
5543	Kentish Town 24.03.34, Crewe 16.02.35, Longsight 20.04.35, Crewe 27.11.39, Camden (on loan) 18.12.37, Crewe 01.01.38, Longsight (on loan) 12.03.38, Longsight 19.03.38, Carlisle Upperby 23.09.39, Patricroft 04.10.41, Edge Hill 27.07.46, Crewe North 02.10.48, Carlisle Upperby 04.10.52, Crewe North 25.10.52, Carlisle Upperby 18.09.54, Preston 15.11.58, Longsight 10.01.59, Edge Hill 31.12.60, Lancaster 05.05.62, Carnforth 02.06.62
5544	Kentish Town 24.03.34, Leeds 03.11.34, Crewe 16.02.35, Longsight 20.04.35, Preston 18.07.36, Patricroft (on loan) 08.12.38, Preston 31.12.38, Crewe North 20.09.52, Edge Hill 29.01.55, Carlisle Upperby 20.06.59, Warrington 10.09.60
5545	Kentish Town 21.04.34, Carlisle 16.06.34, Leeds 03.11.34, Crewe 16.02.35, Longsight 27.05.35, Camden 31.05.41, Willesden 31.01.42, Camden 05.02.44, Willesden 10.11.45, Edge Hill 03.05.47, Longsight 13.11.48, Bushbury 27.11.48, Camden 28.05.49, Crewe 15.09.56, Camden 28.02.57, Crewe 04.05.57, Carlisle Upperby 10.06.61
5546	Kentish Town 21.04.34, Carlisle 16.06.34, Leeds 03.11.34, Crewe 16.02.35, Edge Hill 20.04.35, Newton Heath 08.06.35, Crewe (on loan) 23.10.42, Crewe 16.01.43, Willesden 18.11.50, Crewe 24.11.56, Carlisle Upperby 15.12.56, Crewe 05.01.57, Warrington 27.06.59, Crewe 04.07.59, Carnforth 07.11.59, Mold Junction 23.01.60, Warrington 23.04.60
5547	Preston 28.04.34, Newton Heath 11.08.34, Crewe (on loan) 05.12.42, Crewe 16.01.43, Edge Hill (on loan) 23.01.43, Edge Hill 27.02.43, Crewe 02.10.48, Preston (on loan) 19.08.50, Crewe 14.10.50, Edge Hill (on loan) 19.08.50, Crewe 14.10.50, Edge Hill 11.11.50, Crewe 06.01.51, Willesden 29.01.55, Carnforth 02.10.59, Willesden 17.10.59, Llandudno Junction 07.01.61, Edge Hill 10.06.61
5548	Preston 28.04.34, Newton Heath 11.08.34, Crewe (on loan) 02.01.43, Crewe 16.01.43, Carnforth 07.11.59, Rugby 23.04.60, Nuneaton 31.12.60
5549	Polmadie 06.07.34, Crewe (on loan) 18.01.41, Crewe 01.02.41, Willesden 28.08.48, Longsight 28.05.49, Crewe 18.06.49, Carlisle Upperby 29.04.50, Edge Hill 15.11.58, Carlisle Upperby 20.06.59, Warrington 23.04.60
5550	Preston 05.05.34, Polmadie 06.07.34, Crewe 07.12.40, Preston (on loan) 11.01.41, Preston 01.02.41, Patricroft 06.06.42, Carlisle 27.07.46, Preston 13.06.53, Edge Hill 19.09.53, Carlisle Upperby 20.06.59, Aston 18.06.60, Warrington 05.08.61, Lancaster 05.05.62, Carnforth 02.06.62
5551	Preston 05.05.34, Camden 23.06.34, Willesden 10.06.39, Crewe 22.03.41, Carlisle Upperby 14.01.50, Camden 25.06.60, Willesden 09.7.60, Edge Hill 10.06.61

APPENDIX I
L&NWR LIVERY, WITH SPECIAL REGARD TO THE CLAUGHTON CLASS

The standard locomotive livery of the L&NWR in 1913 was black with red, cream and grey lining. It was a long-established livery dating back to the Webb era. It had been introduced in early 1873 and continued with few exceptions or variations until the outbreak of The Great War, when lining, varnishing and the application of the coat of arms ceased 'for the duration', although the coat of arms may have continued to be applied in many cases, as some photographs tend to indicate. A resumption of the full livery application came in 1921/2 (after the completion of the last Claughton) as a result of a Minute of the Locomotive and Engineering Committee dated 20 October 1921. This was to be short-lived, due to the grouping of the railways which came into effect on 1st January 1923, although the infant LMS continued the L&NWR livery for a while (minus the coat of arms) until it agreed a new passenger locomotive livery, which was to be based upon Midland Railway practice.

Application of the standard lined L&NWR livery for new Claughton locomotives, therefore, would appear to be limited to the first twelve locomotives delivered from Crewe (for which see Table 1). Some later locomotives received the standard lined livery during repaints, before the L&NWR ceased to exist.

The basic shade was drop black; the term 'shade' is correct when describing either black or white. To lineside observers and railway enthusiasts alike, it became known as 'blackberry' black, due to the depth and quality given to it by varnish and the attention of cleaners armed with oily cloths. One notable exception to this appearance was the ever-hot and unvarnished smokebox.

The observed red, cream and grey lining was actually specified as red, cream and pale blue, the difference in colour being due to the application of a golden brown varnish. As the livery weathered and wore, further changes in shade would be noticeable.

So far as the Claughtons are concerned, those which received the livery before the war had the three-colour lining applied to the upper cabside panels, the rectangular cabside sheets, footplate, platform edging, wheel splashers and the slots in the long motion and coupling rod splashers. An extra inner red line was applied to the wheel splashers and which followed their general shape. The tender side panels received this treatment, together with the frame lower edges and slots, the rear panel remaining unlined.

Boiler bands received two red lines each, the lighter colours having proved to lose their original hues in the past, due to the effects of heat from the boiler.

The front buffer plank was painted red and had a black border all around the edge. A narrower black line was painted between the buffers to form a rectangular panel. The tender buffer plank was plain black.

The LNWR coat of arms was applied in transfer form to the wheel splashers, some 1ft 7in ahead of the centre coupled axle. The running number appeared on a rectangular cast brass or iron plate affixed centrally to the lower cab side sheets. This plate measured 33in by 11⅝in and bore scroll running numbers 6in tall, together with the legend 'CREWE WORKS,' the month and year below rendered in letters and numerals ¾in tall. The background was painted vermilion or black and the raised portions were polished.

The tender was fitted with a cast plate 11in by 4⅞in bearing the initials 'L & NWR' and the tender number in letters and numerals 1⅜in tall. The letters and numerals were sometimes picked out in white paint.

The straight nameplates fitted to the Claughtons were, with one exception, to the standard design for horizontal wheel splashers. The length varied, but they were usually six feet long and inscribed with the company initials, the name and 'CREWE WORKS' along the main portion. A smaller portion below had the date inscribed. The name was rendered in sans serif, upper case, letters 2¼in tall. Those plates fitted after the Grouping had 'LMS' inscribed in place of 'L & NWR Co.' The exception was that of 'PATRIOT', fitted to No. 1914, the war memorial locomotive. This plate was inscribed in a similar style to the standard, but the name was on an extended upper portion and boldly underlined. Below, on the central portion, was inscribed in exactly the standard and in two rows, the legend 'IN MEMORY OF THE FALLEN' on the upper, 'L&NWR EMPLOYEES' on the lower. The extended lower portion was inscribed '1914–1919'. The whole plate was inscribed with a line around the edge. It was usual to fill the incised letters and numerals with black engine stopping wax and then paint over it with black Japan paint.

Some photographic evidence of L&NWR livery (dated where possible) is as follows:

Standard lined
2222 new and 1922
1161 new
1191 new
163 early years
650 early years
1159 early years
1327 early years
154 c1922
2420 c1923
2450 c1923/4
1407 05.1924
8 1922
42 undated
161 undated
1216 06.1922
149 undated
1319 c1924
21 c1915
32 undated

Unlined with coat of arms
2401 undated
713 undated
2366 1920
2431 undated
2450 undated
2416 c1923
1407 04.1922
499 1922
1097 undated
8 1920/1
2430 1922/3
23 undated
32 08.1923
158 1922
183 undated
192 10.1921
207 12.1921
208 08.1926
2122 (as LMS 5956) 1927 tender had LNWR lining

Unlined, no coat of arms
1429 1923
1567 undated
968 1924
2221 1920, 07.1924
1914 new until LMS livery
1599 undated
2059 undated
154 undated
2174 undated

This splendid picture of No. 32 was taken when the locomotive was piloting the Royal Train. Note the distinctive 4-headlamp code. This locomotive was built in 1920 and became No. 6003 when renumbered by the LMS in June 1926 and was withdrawn from service in October 1934. We have included this picture to show lined L&NWR livery.
AUTHORS' COLLECTION

No. 2174 was built in August 1916 and named E. C. Trench. This picture shows a Claughton in unlined black livery but with a lined buffer beam. As LMS No. 5925, it was withdrawn in March 1933.
REAL PHOTOGRAPHS

APPENDIX 2
LMS LIVERY, WITH SPECIAL REGARD TO THE CLAUGHTON CLASS

Taken at Crewe South on 9th March, this photograph shows a Claughton No. 5911 W. E. Dorrington *in LMS Crimson Lake livery. Built in August 1914, it was not rebuilt and was withdrawn in March 1934.*
W. H. WHITWORTH

The standard express passenger locomotive livery until 1941 was crimson lake with yellow or cream lining edged with black. It was inherited from the Midland Railway and very little altered on its adoption by the LMS in 1923.

Although the subject of LMS locomotive liveries is not always straightforward, that regarding its proper application to the Claughtons is reasonably straightforward. The most concerning aspect is its lack of proper application or its non-application prior to 1930.

In May 1923 the first passenger locomotive livery was decided upon by the LMS Rolling Stock Committee Meeting. It was to be crimson lake, with full yellow lining and with black edging. The first known ex-L&NWR locomotive to appear in the new colours was Claughton No. 5971 *Croxteth*, in July 1923. The running number appeared on the tender in 18in tall gold numerals of Midland scroll style, shaded black to the right and below. The letters 'LMS' were placed on the cabside panel in a small, well-spaced serif style in gold with black shading. The running number also appeared on a small cast-iron smokebox door plate, placed just above the wheel and dart door tightening device. Our livery code for this style is listed in *Table 7* as A2. The correct, standard livery (code A1) was identical except for the substitution of the small letters 'LMS' by the new LMS circular emblem.

This latter livery was confirmed as standard in December 1923, so the letters 'LMS' on *Croxteth* were a temporary expedient until emblem transfers became available. Officially, two sizes of tender numerals were made available, 14in and 18in, both in the Midland style. Those Claughtons which were to receive a complete repaint usually received the 18in numerals. This livery had one disadvantage in that the running number appearing on the tender conflicted with the Crewe Works practice of pairing the locomotive with the next available and suitable tender. The works staff now had to endeavour to pair the locomotive with its correspondingly-numbered tender – this caused delays or, in certain cases of expediency, locomotive and tender running numbers not agreeing out on the line. The potential for confusion among depot staff and signalmen can be appreciated. Indeed, with the slow renumbering of the former LNWR fleet, it was not unusual to see an LNWR number on the locomotive and an LMS number on the tender!

The standard livery was officially revised during the winter of 1927/8. The positions of the displaying company ownership and the running number were reversed, with the LMS emblem being replaced by the letters 'LMS', 14in tall. The running number was to be 'imitation gold with black shading' as were the letters 'LMS'. The sizes of numerals were 10, 12 and 14in. In practice there were two styles of numerals, the standard style and the Midland style, with the latter being common in 14in gold numerals. In addition to gold, a 'straw' colour was used, but all three sizes were in the standard pattern. The main reason for the differences in colour (and style for the 14in numerals) was that Crewe made much use of painted numerals rendered in the straw colour and standard pattern, probably with the aid of stencils to permit a regularity of style otherwise achieved with transfers. The livery key codes for these variations are listed in *Table 7*. Only the rebuilt Claughtons were without smokebox door number plates from 1928.

As an aside to the above, about 1931/2 a book *Locomotives of the LMS, Past & Present* was published. In this, various colour plates depicted various LMS locomotives. The artist was M. Secretan, and his beautiful illustrations were based upon official photographs, but the interesting feature of the insignia is that it has plain red shading, not black. Claughton No. 5953 *Buckingham* is featured and has red-shaded, straw insignia with the 14in numerals in standard style.

Red shading had been authorised in 1929, but it was not a plain style, rather it was a blending of vermilion and crimson to simulate the apparent change in colour experienced when light is reflected differently over a uniformly-coloured surface, partly in the shade. Almost a year later the decision was made to revert to black shading for red locomotives. When one adds to this that red-shaded transfers, properly intended for lined black locomotives, were used on red locomotives the confusion is compounded further. The LMS has only been equalled (surpassed?) by BR in the 1980s and 1990s for a confused scenario of liveries and insignia; how the pendulum swings. The best layout of the post-1927 red livery is depicted in the official photograph of rebuilt Claughton No. 5999 *Vindictive*, photographed in 1928. It has 10in standard numerals and is in photographic grey, but neither detract.

The 1936 sans serif, or block style, of insignia does not appear to have affected the few remaining Claughtons, although the 1937 reversion to scroll/serif style may have been applied to some locomotives. Chrome yellow with plain bright vermilion shading became the standard colours for the insignia, with the lining colour of the locomotives now matching the chrome yellow. The war would have affected painting styles, but since there were few Claughtons which entered the period in question and only one survived (No. 6004) the Claughtons were barely affected. No. 6004 may have had odd areas touched up as a matter of expediency.

Having dealt with the course of events concerning the diverse standard liveries, we must consider the hybrid liveries, so common between 1923 and the early 1930s. It will be remembered that the standard lined black LNWR livery had been reintroduced before the Grouping and that there were still many unlined Claughtons to be seen at the same time. Despite the early application of the new LMS livery of crimson lake to No. 5971, there were several factors which led to the application and perpetuation of black on the Claughtons in LMS days.

During the first few months of 1923, lined black livery, but without the L&NWR coat of arms, would have been normal for locomotive repaints. Once red had been decided upon as the new colour, then application should have followed as a matter of course, but it did not. Crewe Works normally dealt with the larger needs of the Claughtons, the heaviest repairs normally necessitating a full repaint, lesser repairs perhaps a lesser treatment. The latter would encourage perpetuation of black and, in some cases, hold back renumbering.

How much resentment at Crewe of things Midland/Derby affected the repainting and renumbering cannot be judged, but the aforementioned difficulties caused by pairing tenders and the reorganisation of the works in the mid 1920s may be judged from some photographic evidence. Red was still not a common livery for the Claughtons by 1927, nor were LMS numbers a common feature until 1926/7, and then only after Euston had sent out an edict to have it done, on shed if necessary. One effect of the edict was that many ex-L&NWR locomotives were in service with their L&NWR plates removed and the vacated space taken up by the new LMS number rendered in paint, by means of free-hand or stencil, in the style and size of the former L&NWR numbers. Otherwise, it had been quite common for the plates to be removed, and a patch of black paint applied in preparation for receiving the LMS circular emblem. The L&NWR coat of arms also would be obliterated by a patch of black paint. The running number would be applied to the tender sides and smokebox door in many cases. All these foregoing combinations appeared on either a plain or lined black livery, or a combination of both if tenders had been exchanged. Indeed, it was possible to have red tenders with black locomotives and vice versa! In this work we have included as many livery variations as space permits.

Even after the 1927/8 livery changes, this state of affairs persisted and even the larger-boilered Claughtons were known to have re-entered service in plain black livery. Furthermore, one (No. 5908) still sported a buffer plank lined L&NWR-style in 1930/1!

As a result of the foregoing, it will be appreciated that certain photographic evidence may be difficult to analyse, on dirty locomotives or locomotives photographed at widely differing angles and reflecting light. The photographic emulsions of the time sometimes eliminated lining evidence, so this effect must also be taken into consideration. Anyone wishing to model a Claughton should tread very carefully. It is appreciated that it is difficult to decide whether or not a locomotive in plain black livery circa 1929 was an LMS repaint or old plain black L&NWR livery.

Where the old livery was retained, but patch-painted, we have coded as follows:

H1 L&NWR lined black livery with LMS emblem on cabside and running number on tender.
H2 L&NWR lined black livery with LMS emblem on cabside, but no running number on tender.
H3 L&NWR lined black livery with LMS running number stencilled on cabside.
H4 Plain black livery with LMS running number stencilled on cabside.

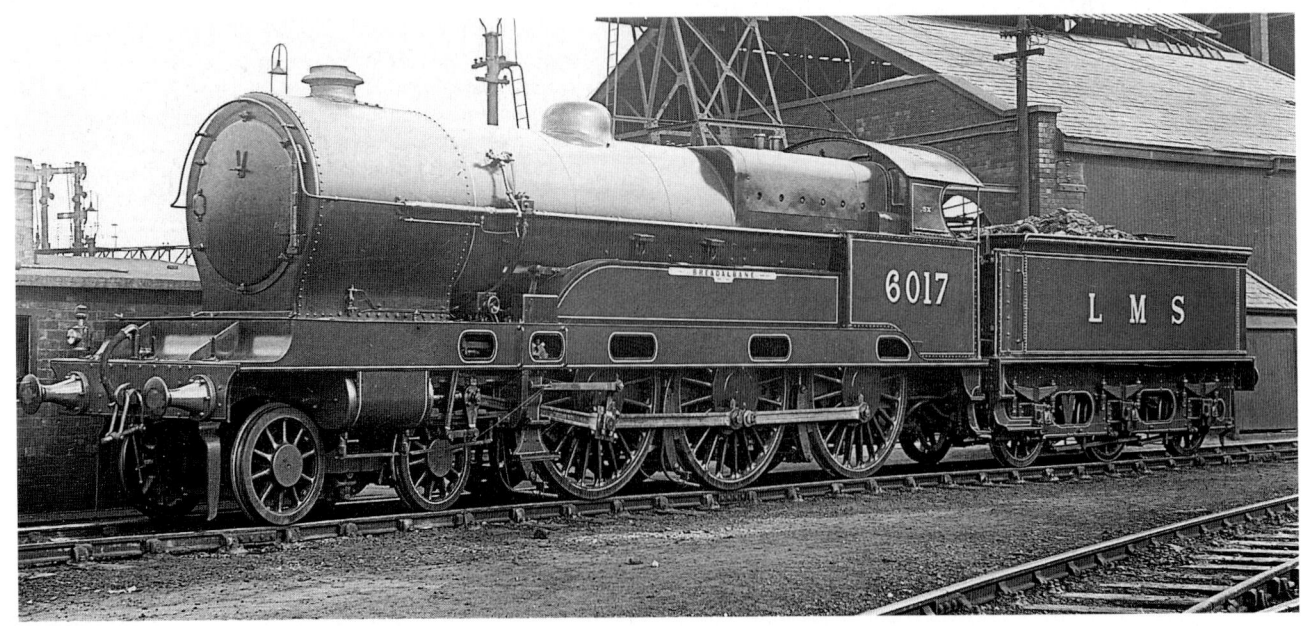

This picture of No. 6017 Breadalbane *at Edge Hill was taken after it had been rebuilt in August 1928 with a large boiler and reclassified 5XP. It shows a locomotive in immaculate condition in red livery with full lining. Although undated, it was probably taken shortly after the locomotive returned to traffic with the large boiler.*
AUTHORS' COLLECTION

APPENDIX 2b
LMS LIVERIES WITH SPECIAL REGARD TO THE PATRIOT CLASS

The Patriots were introduced in late 1930 and therefore featured none of the early LMS liveries, these being discontinued from 1928. This simplifies the situation when compared to other LMS classes predating the Patriots. The 1928 passenger locomotive livery, therefore, was the first livery which they received. This crimson lake livery was lined in yellow and edged in black. It saw the introduction of cabside numerals in scroll style and appeared in several variations. The letters 'LMS' were serif style and appeared on the tender sides. Sometimes the numerals and letters were in gold and sometimes in yellow, both colours generally having shading to the right and below, in black or sometimes red.

The Patriots built at Crewe Works generally received the livery version (our code A6) consisting of 12in standard cabside numerals of gold, shaded black. The LMS letters on the tender sides were 14in high, but often offset from the vertical centreline towards the rear to avoid rivets. Those built at Derby generally received livery Code A7, consisting of 14in Midland-pattern numerals of gold, shaded black. The LMS matched these numerals in size and were not usually offset towards the rear of the tender, rivets apparently posing no problem to the Derby paint shops. While it must be noted that the foregoing is a general guideline to Crewe and Derby practices, photographic evidence sometimes indicates the opposite regarding these styles. It may be that locomotives received attention to paintwork and insignia at the works within two years of being built. Certainly on and after renumbering into the 55XX series, the styles changed more often and can be more readily attributed to repaints and renumbering.

The power classification was 5XP, but it was common for Patriots to bear '5X' during their early days. Nos. 5902 and 5971 when new had '5XP' in line and centrally positioned ahead of the cabside window. Others had '5X' in this position, but it was not unusual for the '5XP' to have the '5X' in line and the 'P' below. Alternatively, '5X' and '5XP' could be found situated between the window and cut-out, again the latter with the 'P' below the '5X'. This confused situation was usually resolved during the 1930s, when the glass shields were fitted between the window and cut-out, the power classification consistently being '5XP' and positioned below the window, midway between the front and rear of the cab. This position was to remain standard until around 1945.

In 1936 the LMS introduced a block style of insignia. It was short-lived, but a few Patriots received it as they passed through the works for overhaul. It had gold characters with red shading to the right and below. We have coded it A12. It is believed that it was not popular with signalmen who, among others, were required to

We believe this undated picture of Patriot No. 5997 was taken at Derby where it was built in April 1933. This engine was later renumbered 5535 and in 1938 named Sir Herbert Walker KCB.
AUTHORS' COLLECTION

111

This photo taken at Edge Hill in June 1931 shows No. 5531 Sir Frederick Harrison when it was painted in what we describe as livery code A14. The locomotive was carrying a code 1A Camden shedplate, which suggests that No. 5531 was employed on London to Liverpool express services.
AUTHORS' COLLECTION

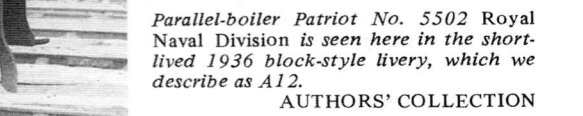

Parallel-boiler Patriot No. 5502 Royal Naval Division is seen here in the short-lived 1936 block-style livery, which we describe as A12.
AUTHORS' COLLECTION

APPENDICES

record the locomotive numbers. Its unpopularity was due to mistaken identity of similar numerals when observed at speed or in reduced lighting conditions. One main difference was that the '3' was round-topped, opposite to usual LMS practice for locomotives. By 1938 a reversion to the old pattern had been made, but with chrome yellow replacing gold, and red shading replacing black.

This was the last livery change to occur before the outbreak of war in 1939. By 1942, wartime economy had dictated an abandonment of crimson lake for complete repaints in favour of unlined black. Generally, the insignia applied was that of the 1938 style, but, due to wartime shortages of transfers, resort was made to obsolete transfer stock and hand painting. The latter was very evident on those locomotives which did not receive complete repaints, but renovation of the existing livery.

From about 1945, cabside numbers were applied in a higher position on the cabside and the power classification was moved to a

Taken at Crewe on 6th September 1947 when it was working an express passenger train, this picture shows taper-boiler Patriot No. 5529 in LMS 1946 livery prior to being named Stephenson *in 1948.*
COLLECTION V. R. ANDERSON

No. 5551 was to have been named Rothesay *but the name was not applied. This is an example of a parallel-boiler Patriot carrying the LMS 1946 black livery with full lining.*
REAL PHOTOGRAPHS

position just below it. This position was applied regardless of livery and was continued and incorporated into the new post-war express passenger livery introduced by the LMS in 1946.

After some experiments on other classes the Patriots soon received this livery as they passed through the works. The basic livery was black, with straw lining and maroon edging. Insignia was applied in an attractive block style, in straw, but with a thin, inset, maroon line on the letters and numerals. The platform angle was maroon with straw lining on both sides, as were the first and last boiler bands. To envisage how this livery appeared on a rebuilt Patriot, the reader is advised to view a colour print of the superbly restored Royal Scot No. 6115, which bore this livery for some years in preservation. The round-topped '3' was re-introduced for cabside numerals. We have coded this livery B12.

As a purely LMS scheme, the 1946 livery was short-lived, being curtailed in application by nationalisation of the railways on 1st January 1948. In modified form it continued into 1948, but as a basic LMS livery it saw only two years of application and was to add to an already much-varied livery situation.

Two further examples of taper-boiler Patriots are shown on this page. The first is No. 5528, which was rebuilt with a taper boiler in August 1947 and named R.E.M.E. in 1959. We believe this picture was taken shortly after the locomotive had returned to traffic following rebuilding.
AUTHORS' COLLECTION

For a few months following nationalisation in January 1948, locomotives that had been renumbered displayed 'British Railways' in full on the side of the tender. This picture shows No. 45525 Colwyn Bay *waiting to take over an express train when the correct express passenger train headcode would be set.*
AUTHOR'S COLLECTION

APPENDIX 3
R.O.D. TENDERS

The Claughtons acquired ex-ROD tenders in a curious way, to meet their changed circumstances upon transfer away from the Western Division. The tender design was that of Robinson, CME of the Great Central Railway. Naturally these tenders were coupled to various GCR locomotive types, perhaps the most notable being the Class 8K 2-8-0 freight locomotive, otherwise known as the ROD for its exploits in military service. Hundreds were built purely for war service during the Great War under the auspices of the Ministry of Munitions and were operated by the Railway Operating Division. Many carried their running numbers preceded by the letters ROD in large characters painted on their tender sides – hence the familiar title RODs.

After the cessation of hostilities, these locomotives saw loan service on several British railways and many more were sold to them. Many others were stored as war surplus.

The L&NWR had some on loan and also bought some. The LMS bought a batch of seventy-five at rock-bottom prices in April and May 1927, solely for their tenders. This last decision resulted from a shortage of tenders, probably caused by the reorganisation of Crewe Works during the 1926/7 period. It was recorded that ex-L&NWR locomotives freshly repaired had to stand for several days waiting for tenders to emerge from the shops, due to the fact that L&NWR policy had not been to have one tender per locomotive. This policy was based upon the belief that tenders were returned to traffic more quickly than locomotives, hence they did not need as many tenders as locomotives.

Each locomotive and tender had cost the LMS £340 and a further £400 was required to make each tender suitable for traffic. After purchase, twenty locomotives were placed in service with ROD tenders (LMS Nos. 6271–89, 6339), leaving fifty-five tenders for use elsewhere. Forty-nine tenders were actually used for pairing with ex-L&NWR locomotives, twenty-two of which were made suitable for pairing with Claughtons, tender Nos. being (6296/8/9/6303–6/9/13/14/21–3/6/8/32–8).

An initial modification was a reduction of water capacity from 4,000 gallons to 3,800 gallons, but further modifications were authorised for those paired with Claughtons and which proved a little unsatisfactory. Improvements included the fitting of standard LMS tender coal doors, zinc sieves across the tanks to prevent water swilling away from the feed valves, and the provision of food lockers for the footplate crews. By 1932 only four had been fully modified.

Details of ROD tenders are as follows:

1927-purchase tenders added to LMS stock

Tender Nos (LMS std. series)	Total	Locomotives attached to	Fuel Capacity
6271–89 6339	20	9646–65 (ex-ROD 2–8–0s)	Coal 6 tons, water 4,000 gallons.
6290–6338	49	Claughtons, other LNWR 4–6–0s, 4–4–0s 0–8–0s.	Coal 6 tons, water 3,800 gallons.

N.B. 6 tenders were never taken into running stock.

1930 list of 22 tenders suitable for use with Claughtons
(on an allocation of 20, plus 2 nominal spares)

6296	6306	6323	6335
6298	6309	6326	6336
6299	6313	6328	6337
6303	6314	6332	6338
6304	6321	6333	
6305	6322	6334	

Twenty Claughtons were paired with tenders from the above pool in 1930 as follows. Order of pairing not known.

5900	5971
5928	5973
5929	5974
5932	5978
5933	5984
5944	5995
5949	6000
5959	6001
5960	6005
5964	6025

N.B. One of the spare tenders had been paired with No. 5971 when it was damaged at Doe Hill in 1929. Some ROD tenders saw further service as departmental sludge tenders, well into BR times. The gain in water capacity over Bowen Cooke tenders was 800 gallons of water.

ROD TENDER DATA (in unmodified form)

Weight unladen	24 tons 6cwt.
Wheelbase	6ft 6in + 6ft 6in
Coal capacity	6 tons
Water capacity	4,000 gallons

APPENDIX 4
BOWEN COOKE TENDERS

As previously stated, the Bowen Cooke tender had a long ancestry. As with L&NWR locomotives, the history of L&NWR tenders was one of continuous development associated with a very distinctive style, and easily recognisable.

The origins even predated the L&NWR itself, with certain design features taking shape on Crewe-built tenders of the early 1840s. Indeed, by the turn of the century much of the original idea of what a tender should be still held good. The tender outline was already apparent by the late 1830s as a four-wheeled vehicle coupled to Stephenson 'Patentee' 2–2–2s of the Grand Junction Railway, and it was further developed by Crewe Works from 1841, when the railway transferred its locomotive building activities there. In 1846 the L&NWR was formed and inherited various influences from its constituent companies.

During the early L&NWR days, a Crewe-designed tender differed from a Wolverton-designed example. This emanated from the differing working practices of the L&NWR constituent companies which continued during the early years of the L&NWR when it was divided into two divisions Northern and Southern). Each was provided with parallel facilities, including design and works. The Crewe tender featured a wooden frame and rounded tank corners, whereas the Wolverton product favoured iron frames and squared tank corners. The Crewe version eventually dominated, particularly after the strict divisions were eliminated and particularly when John Ramsbottom took overall charge of locomotive design (based at Crewe) for all the L&NWR system in 1857.

Francis Webb, who succeeded him in 1871, continued what was by then a traditional L&NWR style. The size of tender increased with the need to supply more fuel to match the increased size of locomotives, but the wooden frames were still incorporated in the design, often of increased size and depth. By this time six-wheeled tenders were standard. Water pickup gear was another additional feature, brought about by the introduction of water troughs on the L&NWR.

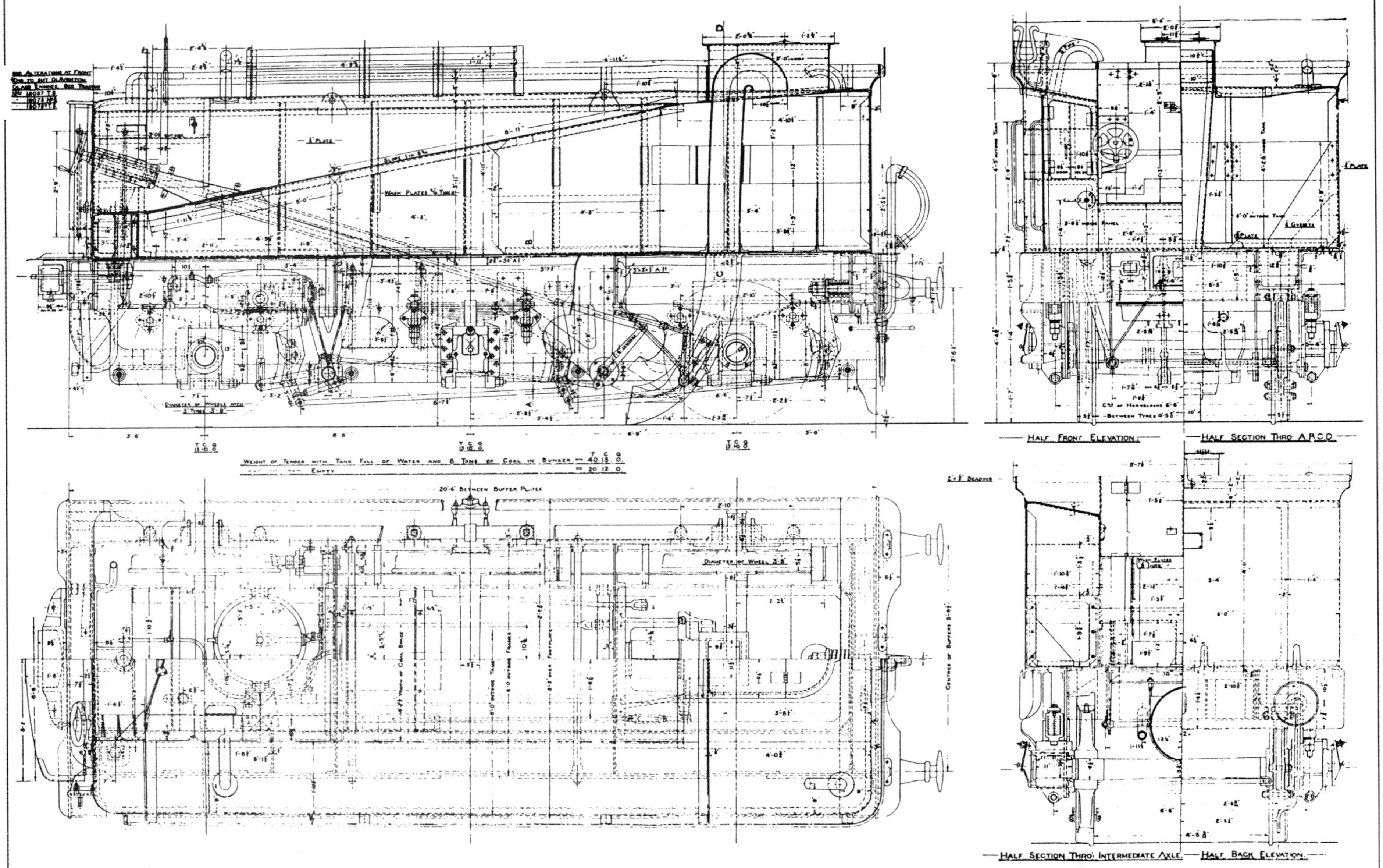

Official drawing of final type of Bowen Cooke tender.

The drawing for the Patriot 3,500 gallon tender appears in LMS Locomotive Profile No. 2 — The Horwich Moguls and Profile No. 10 — The Midland and LMS Standard Class 4 Freight Engines, so we have not repeated it in this work.

L&NWR SOCIETY

APPENDICES

Changes after Webb's time dictated that there should be further alterations. The major change came in 1904 when Whale introduced steel frames to replace the old wooden frames which were becoming insufficient to withstand the heavier loads and shocks consequent upon the introduction of heavier trains and locomotives.

The old 'U'-shaped water tank (plan view) continued in use for a few years and it was left to Whale's successor to design the ultimate L&NWR tender type.

Bowen Cooke continued the modernisation of the L&NWR tender by further developing the Whale version. To the lineside observer there appeared little difference. The tender side and rear appeared almost the same, the frames were the same and still provided with large 'D'-shaped slots, and the leading footsteps were stylishly raked back to join the leading axlebox guides. The two coal rails of the Whale tender gave way to one, and there were differences in axlebox design.

The most fundamental change lay in the redesign of the tank and coal space. The 'U'-shaped tank was replaced as the coal space was re-profiled to allow for a degree of self-trimming. A sloping floor was incorporated from the rear full tank height down towards a shovelling plate at the front. The coal space sides were also inclined and this, combined with the sloping floor, was intended to reduce the fireman's lot by depositing the coal nearer to him by use of gravity combined with the vibration and movement of the tender when in motion. At the front, a retaining plate fitted with doors reduced the spillage of coal onto the footplate and provided access to the coal space when required. The toolboxes were taken from their previous positions on top and replaced by side cupboards mounted on the front of the tank wings. This basically was the mainstream Bowen Cooke tender. Over the years some changes were made to the design, but these were mostly of a minor detail nature.

Concurrent with and partly for the introduction of the Claughtons, several changes occurred. The decision was made that express locomotives should be fitted with vacuum-operated brakes instead of steam-operated ones, No. 2222 *Sir Gilbert Claughton* being the first to appear as such. Brake blocks were positioned behind the wheels rather than in front and the associated pull rod layout was altered to facilitate easier maintenance. Additionally, those tenders coupled to Claughtons were further different to their contemporaries inasmuch that they had a footplate 9 inches higher than normal to match the footplate of these locomotives. This in turn was due to the Claughton-design firehole being 9 inches higher above rail level than on previous designs. Tender side doors and handrails of the stanchion type also matched those on the locomotive. These Claughton tenders were not readily interchangeable with those coupled to other classes and therefore became one of the exceptions to the L&NWR policy of common-user tenders.

The tender first coupled to No. 2222 was unique because it had a double beaded coping; those coupled to later Claughtons had a single bead around the top of a now partly vertical coping.

In June 1916 there appeared another variation. Gone were the 'D'-shaped frame slots, replaced by lozenge-shaped slots instead. Quite why this change occurred is not apparent, but maintenance access may have become lessened in an attempt to strengthen the frames. Additionally, the rear end of the frames were squared off rather than upwards-swept as previously and the lower edge reinforced with a steel strip. The Claughton tenders, whether with 'D' or lozenge slots, were strictly coupled to the Claughtons and never to other classes until the advent of the ROD tenders in LMS days. Those displaced were then modified and ran with other ex-L&NWR classes on a common-user basis, notable recipients being the 'Super D' 0–8–0s. Years later, some passed into departmental use.

The main subsequent alteration to Claughton tenders was the fitting of oil tanks, together with associated equipment, to some examples in the 1920s. The large cylindrical oil tank sat, in some ungainly fashion, above the coal space.

The main details of the Bowen Cooke Claughton tender were as follows:

Wheelbase	6ft 9in + 6ft 9in
Length (overall)	23ft 0in
Weight, empty	20 tons 12cwt
Weight, full	40 tons 15cwt
Coal capacity	6 tons
Water capacity	3,000 gallons

We have included this rear view of No. 5988 Private W. Wood V.C., *which was taken at Willesden in 1932, in order to show the rear of an L&NWR 3000 gallon tender. In 1928 the LMS allocated numbers to all LMS tenders that did not carry an individual number, and the renumbering was referred to as 'Distinctive Tender Numberplate'. The tender numberplate seen in this picture reads L&NWR No. 1114.*
J. A. G. COLTAS

APPENDIX 5
TENDERS COUPLED TO PATRIOTS

During their lifetime the Patriots were paired with three types of tender, the old standard (Fowler 3,500 gallons/5½ tons), the modified old standard with high sides (3,500 gallons/7 tons) and the new standard (Stanier 4,000 gallon/9 tons) tender. In unrebuilt condition they were paired with the first two and the latter following rebuilding. One exception was the fitting of ROD tender No. 6309 to 5971 for the first few weeks following its release to traffic following rebuilding into a Patriot. It had been paired with this tender during its final days as a Claughton.

The Fowler type was the first LMS standard and was derived from the Midland Railway design used in conjunction with the Midland Compound 4–4–0s. It was paired with most of the LMS tender locomotives of Fowler design, together with the Horwich 2–6–0s. It was neat in appearance and a good visual match for many Midland-style locomotives. In common with most tender designs, the tank/bunker portion was of riveted construction, but the rivet heads were not visible. The front bulkhead was solid, with very limited through access from the footplate to the bunker, but some were equipped with doors to the coal space. Two mushroom-shaped air ventilators were positioned within the bunker space, rising from the water tank. The bunker floor was partly sloped to aid self-trimming of coal during runs. Coal capacity was officially four tons, and often more, although even more was carried as a matter of course. Later, coal rails were added to increase coal capacity. The water capacity was 3,500 gallons. The six wheels were each 4ft 3in diameter and the wheel spacing was 6ft 6in + 6ft 6in.

The first two Patriots of 1930 were paired with tenders conforming generally to the above, but fitted with a proper doorway access through the front bulkhead. Officially the coal capacity had increased to five tons. The remaining Patriots had an improved version of this tender from new, the improvements being the addition of coal rails around the top of the bunker space and the air ventilators repositioned to the rear of the bunker space rear bulkhead, well away from coal detritus. Not necessarily an improvement was the use of round-head rivets, which were prominent on the tank/bunker. This riveted style was applied to the final batches built, and tenders of this style were coupled to Standard 2P 4–4–0s, Standard Class 7 0–8–0s and Standard Class 5P4F 2–6–0s. Coal capacity was 5½ tons.

Nos. 5502–5541 received tenders numbered 4474 to 4513 inclusive, probably in the order of 5502–19/23/24/29–32/36/20–2/5–8/33–5/7–41. The remaining ten Patriots 5542–51 received tenders numbered 4554–63, probably in numerical order.

Once in service, the Patriots eventually experienced tender exchanges, usually with each other. The most notable change which concerned unrebuilt examples was the acquisition of the modified Fowler tender type with the high sides. With a seven tons coal capacity and holding 3,500 gallons of water, this type entered service behind Jubilees Nos. 5607–16. They bore tender numbers 4564 to 4573 inclusive and only these ten examples were built. Two of them saw service behind Patriots as outlined below: 4569; 45551 July 1958–April 1960, then 45505 April 1960–June 1962. 4573; 5550 May 1946–April 1956, then 45539 April 1956–January 1958, then reverted to Jubilee usage.

When the eighteen Patriots were rebuilt with taper boilers in 1946–9, they were provided with Stanier 4,000 gallons/9 tons capacity tenders, obtained in an exchange with Jubilee 4–6–0s. This was a logical step, in keeping with their uprating and consequent increased fuel requirements. Unfortunately, it further complicated the prolonged and unfulfilled efforts to provide all the Jubilees with Stanier tenders.

The tenders transferred to Jubilees are listed below, but it must be noted that as the rebuilding programme spanned both the late LMS and early BR periods, LMS locomotive numbers are quoted for convenience.

Transferred from	Tender No.	Transferred to
5512	4484	5722
5514	4486	5557
5521	4485	5596
5522	4492	5561
5523	4501	5721
5525	4503	5556
5526	4502	5611
5527	4507	5591
5528	4505	5726
5529	4495	5598
5530	4494	5600
5531	4496	5563
5532	4497	5740
5534	4507	5587
5535	4508	5724
5536	4498	5585
5540	4512	5723
5545	4472	5698

Loco No.	Cost of Tender	Tender allocations
5500	£865	6309 from new, 3187 24.12.30, 4488 23.02.35, 4483 05.02.54, 3933 17.03.55, 4557 16.06.56
5501	£865	4190 from new, 3190 26.12.31, 4511 16.05.52
5502	£865	4474 01.07.32, 3190 23.06.52, 4488 13.03.54, 3904 14.09.56, 3909 14.09.57
5503	£865	4475 21.07.32, 4484 21.07.34, 4475 21.09.34, 4493 03.05.58, 4487 23.04.59
5504	£865	4476 18.07.32, 4477 26.07.32, 3190 09.03.54, 4236 05.11.54, 4569* 02.04.60
5505	£865	4477 26.07.32, 3190 09.03.54, 4236 05.11.54, 4569* 02.04.60
5506	£865	4478 01.08.32
5507	£865	4480 12.08.32, 4473 15.10.54, 4248 15.05.59
5508	£865	4479 09.08.32, 3922 13.01.55, 4488 07.12.56
5509	£865	4481 19.08.32
5510	£865	4482 24.08.32, 4505 13.05.61
5511	£865	4483 31.08.32, 3931 10.10.53, 3937 03.03.55, 3933 22.02.58, 4252 02.09.60
5512	£865	4484 14.09.32, 4505 07.07.34, 4475 21.07.34, 4484 21.09.34, 9759 26.07.48, 9342 21.01.52, 9759 11.03.52
5513	£865	4485 19.09.32, 4500 05.11.41, 3927 05.10.50, 4236 03.12.53, 3190 05.11.54, 3907 04.06.57, 4490 05.02.59
5514	£865	4486 21.09.32, 9761 15.03.47
5515	£865	4487 27.09.32, 4505 29.07.53, 4509 04.01.56, 4573* 10.01.51, 3898 09.02.57, 4570* 17.08.57, 4487 15.03.58, 4493 03.04.59, 4489 25.10.60, 3927 19.11.60
5516	£865	4488 10.10.32, 3187 23.02.35, 3929 07.02.52, 4554 29.12.53, 3933 10.12.57, 4554 22.02.58
5517	£843	4489 06.02.33, 4493 25.10.60
5518	£843	4490 20.02.33, 3922 24.10.58, 3913 13.10.59
5519	£843	4491 25.02.33
5520	£1011	4499 17.02.33, 4474 14.10.52, 4479 07.03.55, 4505 23.01.56, 4482 13.05.61
5521	£1011	4500 24.02.33, 4485 22.10.41, 9779 31.10.46, 9453 24.02.53
5522	£1011	4501 03.03.33, 4492 08.03.45, 9762 31.12.48
5523	£843	4492 08.03.33, 4501 08.03.45, 9755 08.10.48, 9370 04.08.52, 9756 27.11.56

APPENDICES

5524	£843	4493 14.03.33, 4509 17.08.54, 4512 26.11.55
5525	£1011	4503 22.03.33, 9757 20.08.48
5526	£1011	4502 22.03.33, 9754 28.12.46
5527	£1011	4504 27.03.33, 9753 13.09.48, 9779 24.02.53, 9765 22.06.59, 9761 30.03.62
5528	£1011	4505 04.04.33, 4484 07.07.34, 4505 21.07.34, 4469 30.01.44, 4505 22.03.44, 9782 21.08.47, 9013 12.07.52, 9782 05.11.52
5529	£843	4495 06.04.33, 3931 05.10.45, 4495 02.05.46, 9767 05.07.47
5530	£843	4494 03.04.33, 9772 19.10.46
5531	£843	4496 07.04.33, 9756 13.12.47, 9370 27.11.56
5532	£843	4497 new, 9760 03.07.48
5533	£1011	4506 10.04.33, 4488 15.03.61
5534	£1011	4507 25.04.33, 9765 31.12.48, 9037 30.04.53, 9781 29.09.60
5535	£1011	4508 04.05.33, 9771 25.09.48
5536	£843	4498 04.05.33, 4469 13.12.38, 4498 11.01.39, 9781 12.11.48, 9037 25.07.60
5537	£832	4509 19.07.33, 4487 29.06.54, 3943 29.03.58, 3899 04.03.60
5538	£832	4510 21.07.33, 4558 23.08.56, 3909 07.10.60
5539	£832	4511 27.07.33, 3937 18.02.52, 3922 05.08.53, 3899 04.12.54, 4573* 01.05.56, 4509 10.01.57
5540	£832	4512 07.08.33, 9758 01.11.47
5541	£832	4513 new, 4248 17.04.50, 4499 04.12.52, 4477 28.04.54, 4469 18.08.55, 3187 08.11.58, 4500 21.02.59
5542	£805	4469 13.03.34, 4498 13.12.38, 4469 11.01.39, 4505 30.01.44, 4469 22.03.44, 3927 09.06.55, 4489 19.11.60
5543	£805	4470 16.03.34, 4471 15.12.35, 4479 29.06.56
5544	£805	4471 22.03.34, 4470 15.12.35, 4561 06.03.50, 4497 03.04.54, 3909 02.07.56, 3898 17.08.57, 3931 05.12.57, 4475 01.06.59
5545	£805	4472 27.03.34, 3331 06.04.48, 9773 05.11.48
5546	£805	4473 29.03.34, 4480 15.10.54
5547	£805	4554 09.04.34, 3927 07.12.53, 4492 28.04.55, 4238 17.01.59, 3943 27.02.60
5548	£805	4555 27.04.34
5549	£805	4556 27.04.34
5550	£805	4557 01.05.34, 4573* 29.12.42, 4242 23.01.56, 4558 31.07.56, 4510 23.08.56, 4475 03.05.58, 3931 01.06.59
5551	£805	4560 20.09.34, 4558 04.10.34, 4242 31.07.56, 4570* 02.05.58

* High straight-sided 3500 gallon tender of the ten examples 4564–4573. Patriots rebuilt with taper boiler were paired with Stanier 4000 gallon tenders.

APPENDIX 6
BR LIVERIES WITH SPECIAL REGARD TO THE PATRIOTS

At nationalisation, British Railways inherited a varied assortment of LMS liveries, those of the Patriots showing an appreciable variation.

For the first few months the 1946 livery continued in modified form, adding further variation, due to changes in numbering and ownership identification. Locomotives ex-works initially had numbers prefixed by the letter 'M', indicating London Midland Region. These numbers were rendered in a style clearly derived from the 1946 style, but without the inset maroon line. Where applied, the title 'BRITISH RAILWAYS' in full was the order of the day. This was rendered in block capitals on the tender sides. From March 1948 all Patriot LMS running numbers were increased by 40,000, although it took time to implement.

During visits for light service repairs or on shed, partial repaints or patch painting cab sides allowed renumbering to take place, but often the letters 'LMS' remained on the tender sides. This resulted in many variations during 1948, based upon the 1946 livery, wartime liveries and a few pre-war varieties. Perhaps the most celebrated was the late sprucing up of the old crimson lake livery of 45516, described previously, in BR days. Smokebox door numberplates exhibited some variety also. Apart from the purely LMS scroll pattern prefixed 'M', there was the five-figure BR number in the same style, a BR block version and BR standard Gill Sans, the last style being retained as standard until the end of steam traction.

During 1948 many livery experiments took place, though most did not involve Patriots. Various line-ups of locomotives were staged for officials to view and inwardly digest. Meanwhile, Crewe Works started to outshop Patriots (and other classes) in L&NWR-style black livery. Two points are worth noting. Riddles (originally of the L&NWR in his early railway career and in 1948 a member of the Railway Executive) arranged for three Class 5 4–6–0s to be prepared in various green liveries to aid the Executive in choosing standard liveries. Knowing that each member had personal preferences but a certain disinterest in liveries to the point of accepting black as a compromise for most locomotives, he had one extra Class 5 locomotive specially prepared on a surprise basis in lined L&NWR black livery for one of the displays, so there was an element of pushing his favoured choice. Secondly, unlike the other former company workshops, Crewe did not stock any other colour in appreciable quantities – black had been used universally on the LMS for repaints since 1941/2 and as standard since 1946, together with some maroon for express passenger locomotives. The opportunity arose therefore, to send out locomotives in the old L&NWR livery – and this is just what happened. From an early date BR does appear to have adopted Gill Sans numbers and letters, so most, if not all, those locomotives which received neo-L&NWR livery had this style of insignia. Most Patriots rebuilt during 1948/9 received it as did several unrebuilt examples. No-one in authority could have failed to notice what was happening!

Two rebuilt Patriots were repainted in LNER light green, with L&NWR style lining. It was an unhappy marriage. No. 45531 together with No. 45540, both rebuilds of late 1947, appeared a year later in this livery. Both matched Jubilee 4–6–0 Nos. 45565, 45604 and 45694. The two Patriots were put to work on the Euston–Wolverhampton services, together with a train of coaches painted in 'plum and spilt milk' livery. On 20th December 1948 No. 45540 was exhibited in this livery, together with 4–6–2 No. 46201 in neo-L&NWR black livery, at Marylebone Station. The light green does not appear to have gained any favour at this time and receded, although No. 45540 did retain it until 1950.

In March 1949 the dark green of the old Great Western was chosen as the livery for selected passenger classes, including the Patriots. This livery included the orange/black/orange lining, but of course none of the brasswork associated with the native GWR style. Gill Sans insignia continued as previously.

During April and May 1949 various experiments occurred to establish a satisfactory BR totem to replace the words 'BRITISH RAILWAYS' on locomotives. Within several months a totem was selected. It consisted of a stylised lion astride a locomotive wheel, with the words 'BRITISH RAILWAYS' in a band across the centre. Produced in several sizes, this totem was to be used until 1956. It was produced in two versions, both identical except that each was a mirror image of the other to ensure that the device could face forward at all times. From mid-1949 the Patriots generally received the dark green (Brunswick Green) livery bearing this device. A smaller size was applied to Fowler tenders and a larger size to the high-sided and Stanier tenders, where there was more uninterrupted space. Locomotives shopped in England received 8in high cabside numerals and locomotives shopped at St. Rollox Works, Glasgow, received 10in numerals. Although quite a few Jubilees were given the 10in size, it is thought that Patriots so treated were very rare.

The only significant change in ownership marking occurred from June 1956 when a heraldic lion and wheel device was introduced as a replacement for the 1949 totem. This device was truly heraldic, having office approval from the College of Arms in England and the Lyon Court of Scotland. A red British demi-lion issued rampant from a golden yellow heraldic crown. It, correctly, faced left and held a golden railway wheel between its forepaws. The crown had arranged on its band the two leeks of Wales, a thistle of Scotland and a rose of England. Between the latter was an oak leaf. The lion, wheel and crown were circumscribed by a circle from which two horizontal bars issued. Inside the left was the word 'BRITISH' and inside the right was 'RAILWAYS', both words being rendered in serif characters. The background was always that of the locomotive colour, the result of the transfers having clear backgrounds themselves. Despite the above, many locomotives did run with right and left-facing versions, a situation eventually rectified when the error was realised. Quite simply, this was a continuation of existing practice, albeit heraldically incorrect for the new emblem. This livery, with the left-facing lion, was the last official livery and one that most Patriots bore until their demise.

Late survivors did appear in unlined green, a practical move in an age when all were living on borrowed time. Some received the yellow diagonal cabside stripes indicating that they were barred from certain electrified sections of the West Coast Main Line.

Sources and further reading

LMS Engine History Cards for the Patriot Class held at the National Railway Museum, York.
National Archive Kew. Various files in the Rail 418, 422,491 series.
Copies of E.S. Cox reports in the author's collection.
National Railway Museum, York. Various files held in the library.
Leicester University Library, Leicester, archives of contemporary railway journals.
Locomotive Panorama Vol. 1 by E.S. Cox, Ian Allan Ltd 1965.
Chronicles of Steam by E.S. Cox, Ian Allan 1967.
The Lancashire & Yorkshire Railway in the Twentieth Century by Eric Mason, Ian Allan Ltd 1954.
West Coast 4–6–0s at Work by C.P. Atkins, Ian Allan Ltd 1981.
LNWR Locomotives of C.J. Bowen Cooke by O.S. Nock, D Bradford Barton Ltd 1977.
A Compendium of LNWR Locomotives 1912–1949, Part 1 Passenger Tender Engines, by Willie B Yeadon, Challenger Publications 1995.
Stephenson Locomotive Society Journal, various issues.
Railway Observer, the journal of the Railway Correspondence & Travel Society, various issues.
The Railway Magazine, various issues.
Premier News, the journal of the LNWR Society, various issues.

This tender behind No. 5945 Ingestre *(previously No. 2420) provides an example of what we have described as the lozenge-shape cut-outs.*
AUTHORS' COLLECTION

Side, end and plan elevation of the Patriot with parallel boiler.

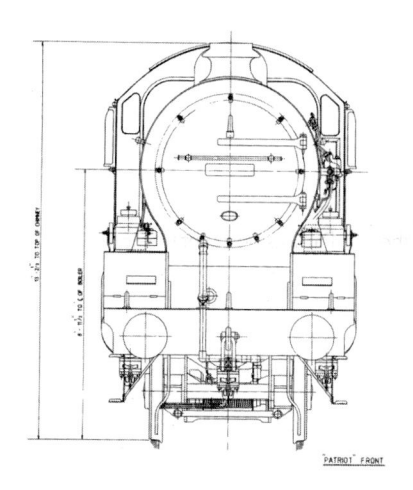

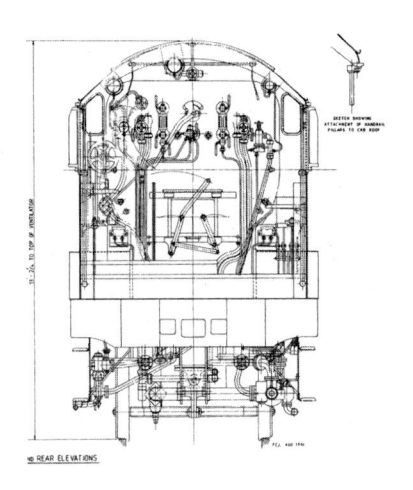

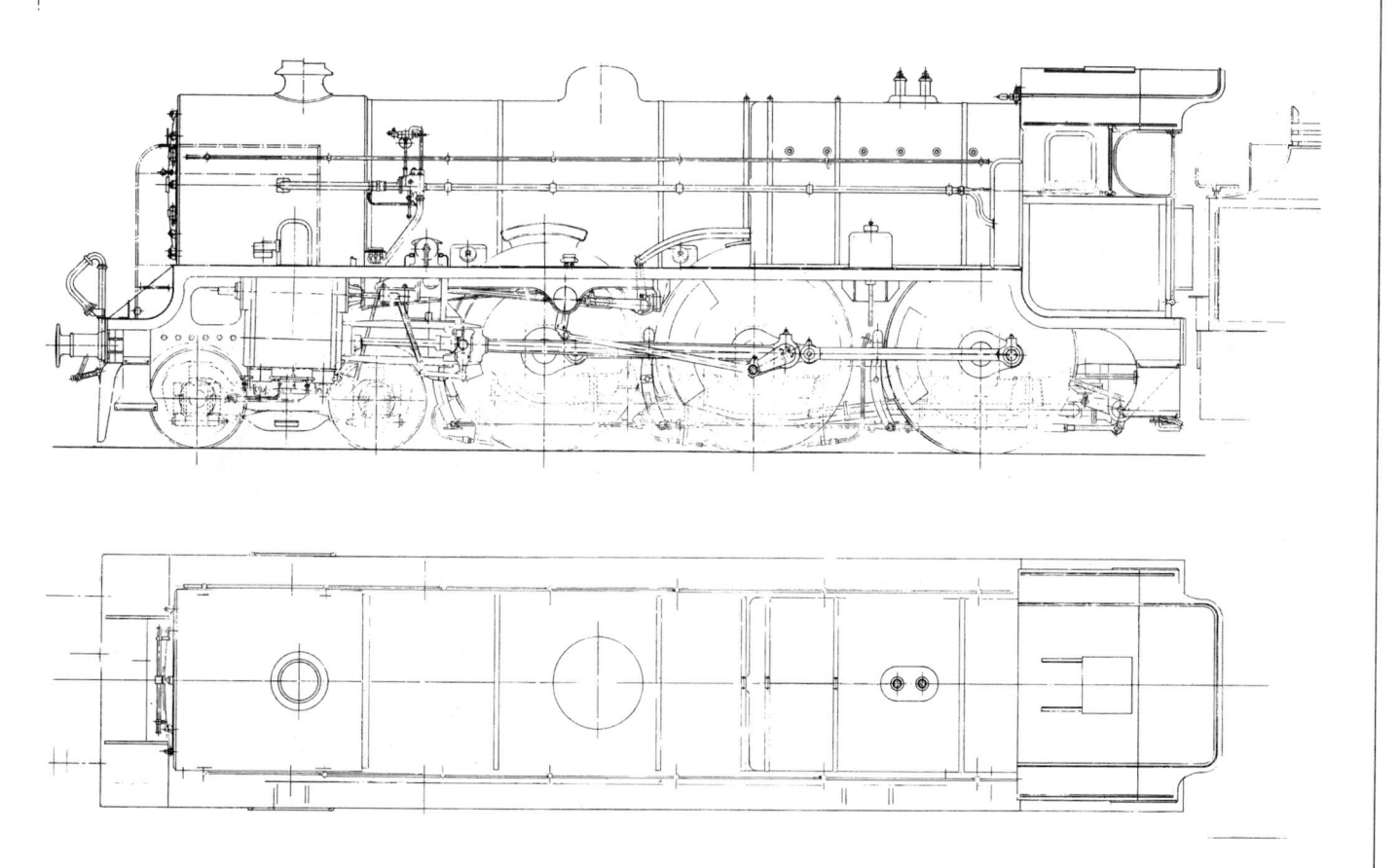

Side elevations of taper-boiler Patriots with single and double chimneys. The top one is our impression of what the remaining parallel-boiler locomotives would look like if they had been modified to drawing DE 967 (see page 78).

6'-6" SIX COUPLED "CLAUGHTON" CLASS.
5'-5" DIA. BOILER.

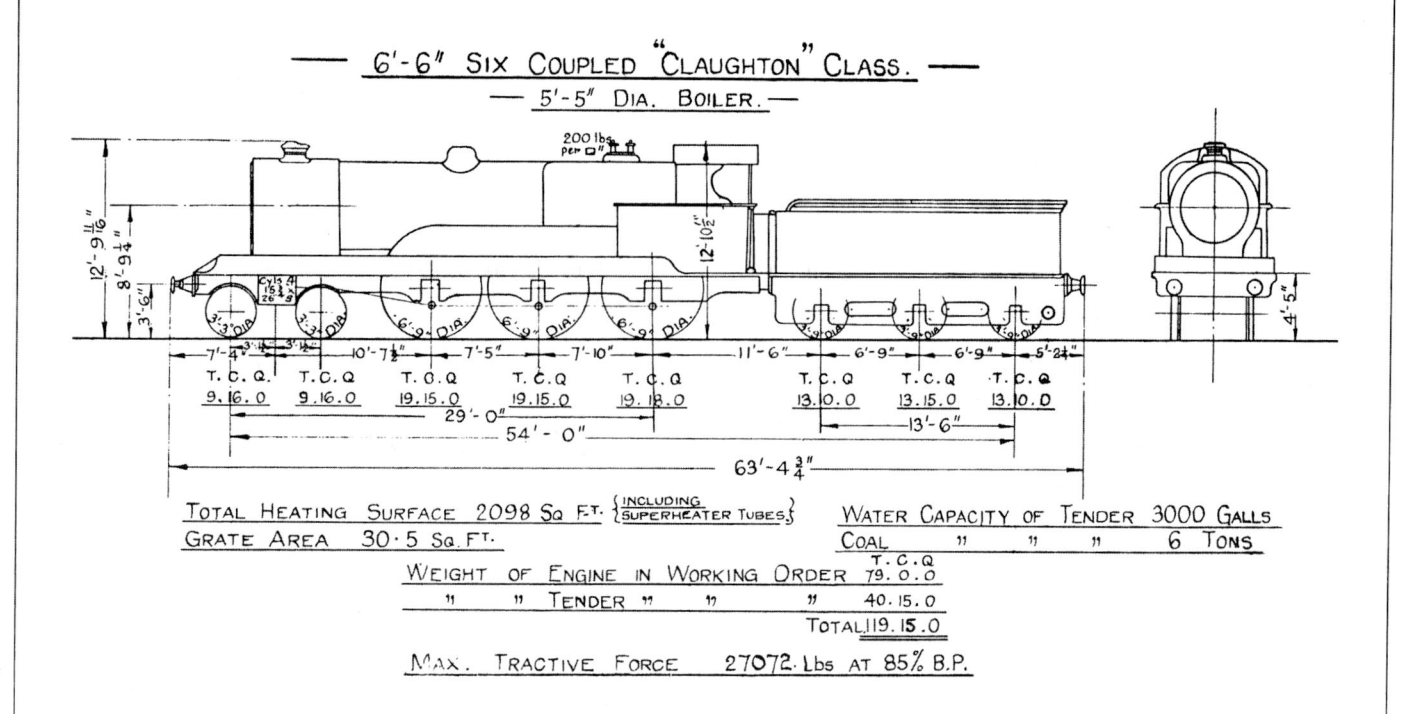

TOTAL HEATING SURFACE 2098 SQ. FT. (INCLUDING SUPERHEATER TUBES)
GRATE AREA 30·5 SQ. FT.
WATER CAPACITY OF TENDER 3000 GALLS
COAL " " " 6 TONS

WEIGHT OF ENGINE IN WORKING ORDER   T.C.Q   79. 0. 0
"   "   TENDER   "   "   "   40.15. 0
                                      TOTAL 119.15. 0

MAX. TRACTIVE FORCE 27072 LBS AT 85% B.P.

4-6-0 SUPER^{HR} PASSENGER ENGINE
(REBUILT "CLAUGHTON") 5X.

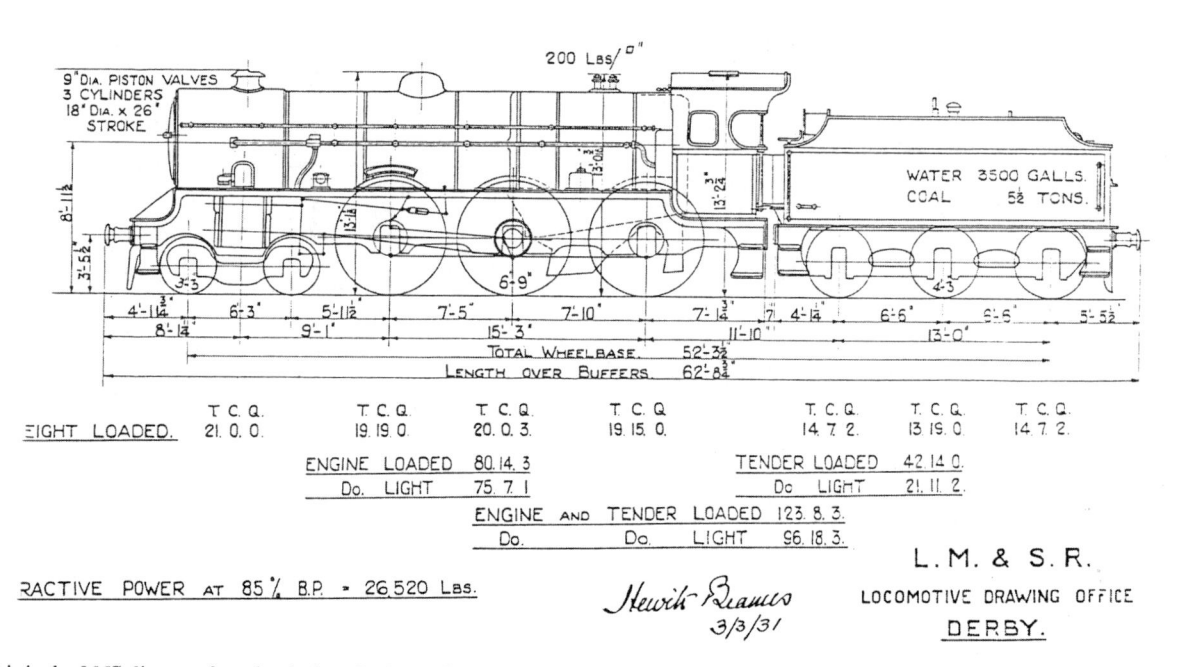

	T.C.Q	T.C.Q	T.C.Q	T.C.Q	T.C.Q	T.C.Q	T.C.Q
WEIGHT LOADED.	21. 0. 0	19.19. 0	20. 0. 3	19.15. 0	14. 7. 2	13.19. 0	14. 7. 2

ENGINE LOADED 80.14. 3   TENDER LOADED 42.14. 0
 Do.   LIGHT 75. 7. 1   Do.   LIGHT 21.11. 2
ENGINE AND TENDER LOADED 123. 8. 3
   Do.   Do.   LIGHT   96.18. 3

TRACTIVE POWER AT 85% B.P. = 26,520 LBS.

Hewitt Beames
3/3/31

L.M. & S.R.
LOCOMOTIVE DRAWING OFFICE
DERBY.

This is the LMS diagram for what is described as a Superheated Passenger Engine (Rebuilt Claughton) 5X and, as can be seen, the original was signed by Hewitt Beames.

This is the LMS engine diagram No. 173C for the Patriots in their parallel-boiler condition.

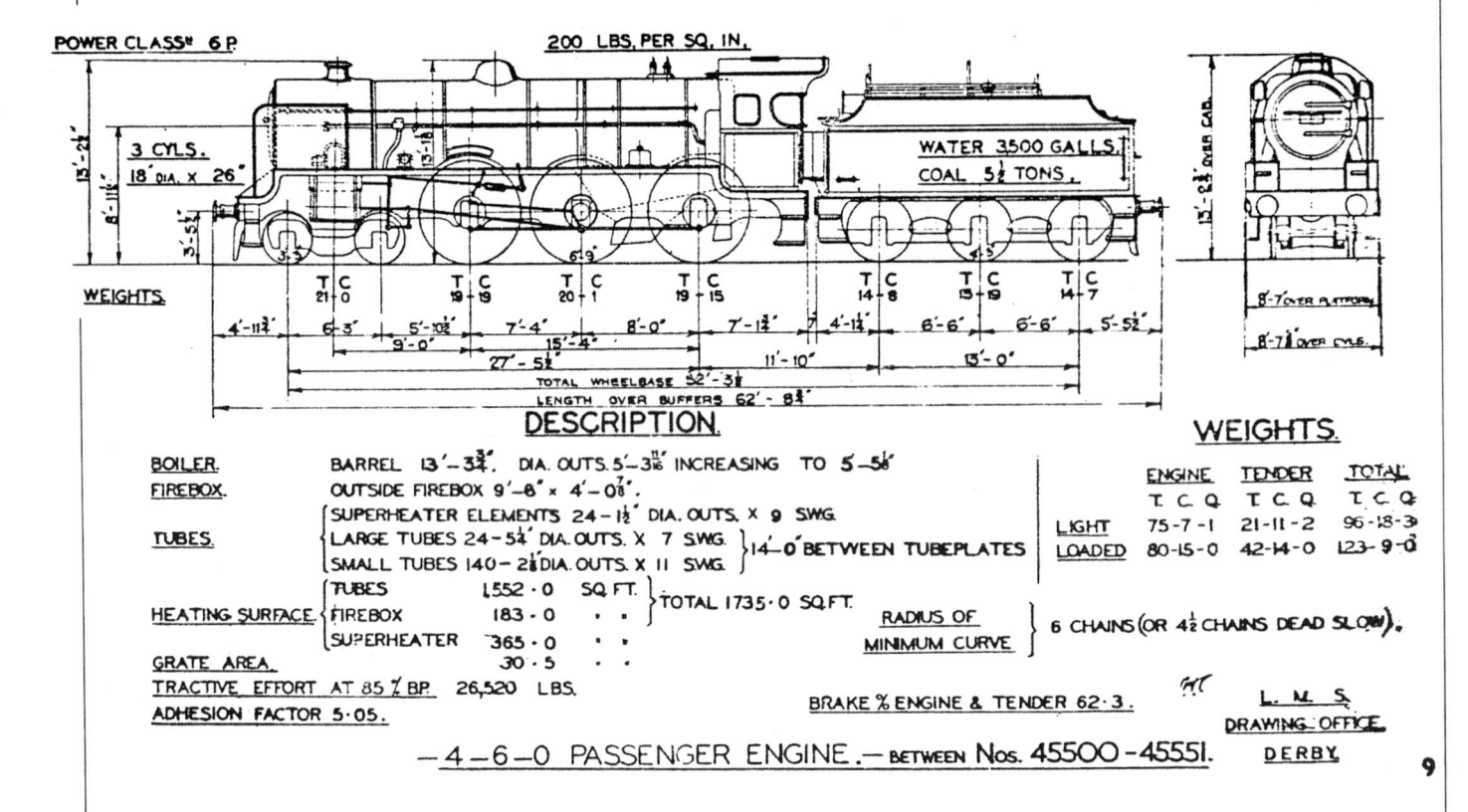

E.D.N? 173C

POWER CLASS" 6P 200 LBS. PER SQ. IN.

3 CYLS. 18" DIA. x 26"

WATER 3500 GALLS.
COAL 5½ TONS.

WEIGHTS

	T.C.	T.C.	T.C.	T.C.	T.C.	T.C.	T.C.
	21-0	19-19	20-1	19-15	14-8	15-19	14-7

4'-11¾" | 6'-3" | 5'-10½" | 7'-4" | 8'-0" | 7'-1¾" | 4'-1¼" | 6'-6" | 6'-6" | 5'-5½"
9'-0" | 15'-4"
27'-5½" | 11'-10" | 13'-0"
TOTAL WHEELBASE 52'-3¾"
LENGTH OVER BUFFERS 62'-8¾"

DESCRIPTION.

BOILER. BARREL 13'-3¾". DIA. OUTS. 5'-3 11/16" INCREASING TO 5'-5⅛"
FIREBOX. OUTSIDE FIREBOX 9'-8" x 4'-0⅞".
TUBES. { SUPERHEATER ELEMENTS 24 - 1½" DIA. OUTS. x 9 SWG.
LARGE TUBES 24 - 5¼" DIA. OUTS. x 7 SWG.
SMALL TUBES 140 - 2⅛" DIA. OUTS. x 11 SWG. } 14'-0" BETWEEN TUBEPLATES
HEATING SURFACE. { TUBES 1552·0 SQ.FT.
FIREBOX 183·0 " "
SUPERHEATER 365·0 " " } TOTAL 1735·0 SQ.FT.
GRATE AREA. 30·5 " "
TRACTIVE EFFORT AT 85% B.P. 26,520 LBS.
ADHESION FACTOR 5·05.

WEIGHTS.

	ENGINE	TENDER	TOTAL
	T.C.Q.	T.C.Q.	T.C.Q.
LIGHT	75-7-1	21-11-2	96-18-3
LOADED	80-15-0	42-14-0	123-9-0

RADIUS OF MINIMUM CURVE } 6 CHAINS (OR 4½ CHAINS DEAD SLOW).

BRAKE % ENGINE & TENDER 62·3.

L.M.S. DRAWING OFFICE DERBY.

— 4—6—0 PASSENGER ENGINE. — BETWEEN Nos. 45500 - 45551.

We conclude with this LMS engine diagram No. 272B for the Patriots in their taper-boiler condition.

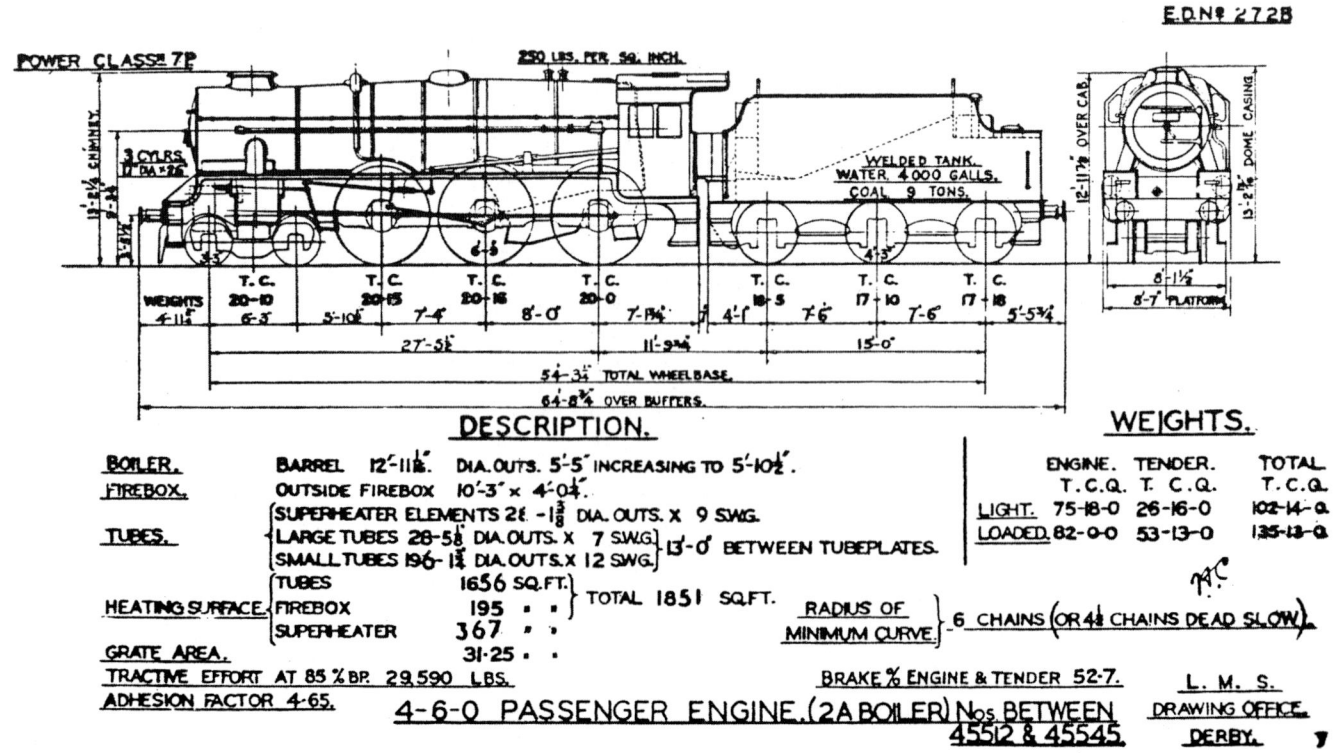

E.D.N? 272B

POWER CLASS" 7P   250 LBS. PER SQ. INCH.

3 CYLS. 17" DIA. x 26"

WELDED TANK.
WATER 4000 GALLS.
COAL 9 TONS.

WEIGHTS

T.C.	T.C.	T.C.	T.C.	T.C.	T.C.	T.C.
20-10	20-15	20-16	20-0	18-5	17-10	17-18

4'-11½" | 6'-3" | 5'-10½" | 7'-4" | 8'-0" | 7'-1¾" | 4'-1" | 7'-6" | 7'-6" | 5'-5¾"
27'-5½" | 11'-9¾" | 15'-0"
54'-3¾" TOTAL WHEELBASE
64'-8¾" OVER BUFFERS

DESCRIPTION.

BOILER. BARREL 12'-11½". DIA. OUTS. 5'-5" INCREASING TO 5'-10½".
FIREBOX. OUTSIDE FIREBOX 10'-3" x 4'-0¼".
TUBES. { SUPERHEATER ELEMENTS 28 - 1⅜" DIA. OUTS. x 9 SWG.
LARGE TUBES 28 - 5⅛" DIA. OUTS. x 7 SWG.
SMALL TUBES 196 - 1¾" DIA. OUTS. x 12 SWG. } 13'-0" BETWEEN TUBEPLATES.
HEATING SURFACE. { TUBES 1656 SQ.FT.
FIREBOX 195 " "
SUPERHEATER 367 " " } TOTAL 1851 SQ.FT.
GRATE AREA. 31·25 " "
TRACTIVE EFFORT AT 85% B.P. 29,590 LBS.
ADHESION FACTOR 4·65.

WEIGHTS.

	ENGINE.	TENDER.	TOTAL
	T.C.Q.	T.C.Q.	T.C.Q.
LIGHT.	75-18-0	26-16-0	102-14-0
LOADED.	82-0-0	53-13-0	135-13-0

RADIUS OF MINIMUM CURVE. } 6 CHAINS (OR 4½ CHAINS DEAD SLOW).

BRAKE % ENGINE & TENDER 52·7.

L.M.S. DRAWING OFFICE. DERBY.

4—6—0 PASSENGER ENGINE. (2A BOILER) Nos BETWEEN 45512 & 45545.